LEARNING SEARCH CONTROL KNOWLEDGE

**THE KLUWER INTERNATIONAL SERIES
IN ENGINEERING AND COMPUTER SCIENCE**

KNOWLEDGE REPRESENTATION, LEARNING
AND EXPERT SYSTEMS

Consulting Editor

Tom Mitchell

Carnegie Mellon University

Other books in the series:

Universal Subgoaling and Chunking of Goal Hierarchies. J. Laird,
P. Rosenbloom. A. Newell. ISBN 0-89838-213-0.

Machine Learning: A Guide to Current Research. T. Mitchell, J. Carbonell,
R. Michalski. ISBN 0-89838-214-9.

Machine Learning of Inductive Bias. P. Utgoff. ISBN 0-89838-223-8.

A Connectionist Machine for Genetic Hillclimbing. D.H. Ackley.
ISBN 0-89838-236-X.

Learning From Good and Bad Data. P.D. Laird. ISBN 0-89838-263-7.

Machine Learning of Robot Assembly Plans. A.M. Segre.
ISBN 0-89838-269-6.

Automating Knowledge Acquisition for Expert Systems. S. Marcus, Editor.
ISBN 0-89838-286-6.

LEARNING SEARCH CONTROL KNOWLEDGE
An Explanation-Based Approach

Steven Minton
Carnegie Mellon University

KLUWER ACADEMIC PUBLISHERS
Boston/Dordrecht/London

Distributors for the United States and Canada:
Kluwer Academic Publishers
101 Philip Drive
Assinippi Park
Norwell, Massachusetts 02061, USA

Distributors for the UK and Ireland:
Kluwer Academic Publishers
Falcon House, Queen Square
Lancaster LA1 1RN, UNITED KINGDOM

Distributors for all other countries:
Kluwer Academic Publishers Group
Distribution Centre
Post Office Box 322
3300 AH Dordrecht, THE NETHERLANDS

Library of Congress Cataloging-in-Publication Data

Minton, Steven.
  Learning search control knowledge : an explanation-based approach
/ by Steven Minton.
      p.   cm. — (The Kluwer international series in engineering and
computer science. Knowledge representation, learning, and expert
systems)
  Based on the author's thesis (Ph. D.)—Carnegie-Mellon University,
1988.
  Includes index.
  ISBN 0-89838-294-7
  1. Artificial intelligence.   2. Problem solving.   3. Machine
learning.   I. Title.   II. Series
Q335.M564 1988
006.3—dc19   88-23084
                                                                       CIP

To my family

Contents

Preface

The ability to learn from experience is a fundamental requirement for intelligence. One of the most basic characteristics of human intelligence is that people can learn from problem solving, so that they become more adept at solving problems in a given domain as they gain experience. This book investigates how computers may be programmed so that they too can learn from experience. Specifically, the aim is to take a very general, but inefficient, problem solving system and train it on a set of problems from a given domain, so that it can transform itself into a specialized, efficient problem solver for that domain.

Recently there has been considerable progress made on a knowledge-intensive learning approach, explanation-based learning (EBL), that brings us closer to this possibility. As demonstrated in this book, EBL can be used to analyze a problem solving episode in order to acquire *control knowledge*. Control knowledge guides the problem solver's search by indicating the best alternatives to pursue at each choice point. An EBL system can produce domain specific control knowledge by explaining *why* the choices made during a problem solving episode were, or were not, appropriate.

Unfortunately, acquiring control knowledge has a hidden cost that can often defeat its purpose. This is the cost of evaluating the control knowledge at each choice point during the search. To produce genuine efficiency improvement, an EBL system must generate control knowledge that is *effective* -- its benefits must outweigh its costs. Otherwise, the cumulative time cost of evaluating the learned control knowledge can severely reduce (or even outweigh) the savings incurred. I refer to this as the *utility* problem.

One answer to the utility problem is to search for "good" explanations -- explanations that can be profitably employed to control problem solving. Instead of simply adding control knowledge haphazardly, a learning system must be sensitive to the problem solver's computational architecture and the potential costs and benefits of adding knowledge. This book contains an analyis of the utility of EBL, and describes a method for searching for good explanations that has been implemented in the PRODIGY/EBL system. Given a problem solving trace, PRODIGY first selects what to explain, choosing from a set of strategies for optimizing performance. Then, after creating an initial explanation from the trace, PRODIGY searches for a representation of the resulting control knowledge that is efficient to match. Finally the system empirically tests the effectiveness of the control knowledge to determine whether it is actually worth keeping.

The research reported here includes a set of comprehensive experiments testing the performance of the PRODIGY/EBL system and its components in several domains. In addition, a formal description of EBL is presented, and a correctness proof for PRODIGY's generalization method is outlined.

The material in this book is largely taken from my dissertation. A number of people contributed to that effort, and they need to be acknowledged. First, I would particularly like to thank my advisor, Jaime Carbonell, and the members of my thesis committee, Allen Newell, Tom Mitchell, Jerry DeJong and Kurt VanLehn for their invaluable suggestions and support. I owe a great debt to the members of the PRODIGY group, especially Jaime Carbonell, Craig Knoblock and Dan Kuokka, who helped me in designing and implementing the PRODIGY problem solver, and to Oren Etzioni, Henrik Nordin, Yolanda Gil, who helped implement and debug the PRODIGY system and manual. Several people helped proofread my thesis and this book, including Bernadette Kowalski, David Steier, and the afore-mentioned Craig, Oren, and Dan.

I would also like to mention the helpful comments and suggestions I have received from many members of the AI community, especially Jack Mostow, Murray Campbell, Richard Keller, Smadar Kedar-Cabelli, David Steier, Pat Langley, Prasad Tadepalli, Sridhar Mahadevan, Paul Utgoff, Ranan Banerji, Saul Amarel, Winter Grosper, Tim Freeman, Paul O'Rorke, Ray Mooney, Milind Tambe and Jeff Schlimmer, to name just a few. Wendy Lehnert and Roger Schank deserve special thanks for getting me started in AI. And here's a grateful word for my sponsors, Bell Laboratories and the CMU Computer Science Department.

Finally, last but certainly not least, I want to thank my roommates, friends and family for making the times so good.

1. Introduction

1.1. Overview

This book investigates methods for learning to improve the efficiency of a general problem solver. Efficiency is a critical consideration for all problem solving systems. In practice, a general problem solving system[1] must be given enough information about the problem and how to solve it so that its search is restricted to a tractable space. Unfortunately, it is typically time-consuming and difficult for a human to provide such information.

For this reason, developing problem solvers that learn is of considerable interest. Ideally a problem solver would take a description of the actions possible in the world and learn methods for effectively solving problems from its own experience, much as a human would. Recently there has been considerable progress made on a knowledge-intensive learning approach, explanation-based learning (EBL), that appears to bring us closer to this possibility. EBL can produce *control knowledge* by analyzing the trace of a problem solving episode. Control knowledge guides the problem solver's search by indicating which direction to pursue at each choice point. An EBL system can produce domain specific control knowledge by explaining *why* the choices made during a problem solving episode were, or were not, appropriate.

Unfortunately, acquiring control knowledge has a hidden cost that can often defeat its purpose. This is the cost of evaluating the control knowledge at each choice point during the search. To produce genuine efficiency improvement, an EBL system must generate control knowledge that is *effective* -- its benefits must outweigh its costs. Otherwise, the cumulative time cost of evaluating the learned control knowledge can severely reduce (or even outweigh) the savings incurred. I refer to this as the *utility* problem.

The utility problem is related to the "tradeoff between search and knowledge"

---

[1]The term "general problem solver" is not precisely defined, but a general problem solver is at least a universal turing machine; that is, it can simulate any turing machine. Typically a general problem solver takes as its input a set of operators that describe a domain and a description of a problem in that domain. Its output is a sequence of operators that solve the problem.

that has been described in the AI literature [4, 22, 7]. Although appropriate domain knowledge can reduce the amount of search necessary to solve a problem, it is well known that one cannot add knowledge indiscriminately to an AI program and expect good performance. This point has been repeatedly demonstrated in the world of chess-playing programs, where currently the best programs are relatively dumb programs which perform search quickly and efficiently. Since it is difficult to add even hand-coded knowledge to a system, it is not surprising that learning programs face a formidable task when they automatically acquire new knowledge.

In chapter 2 of this book, I analyze the utility problem and argue that it is of general concern for EBL systems. With this motivation, I then introduce the PRODIGY problem solver and its EBL learning component. PRODIGY is a domain-independent problem solver that uses explicit control rules to guide its search. PRODIGY's EBL subsystem demonstrates that EBL can serve as a general method for producing control knowledge, and specifically addresses the utility problem. Three complementary capabilities are employed to produce effective control knowledge. First, PRODIGY can learn from a variety of phenomena, including solutions, failures and goal interactions. (Previous EBL problem solving systems were considerably more restricted.) Secondly, PRODIGY searches for a representation of the resulting control knowledge that can be evaluated efficiently. Finally, PRODIGY empirically tests the effectiveness of the control knowledge to determine whether it is worth saving.

In addition to the experimental aspect of this work -- the construction and evaluation of the PRODIGY/EBL architecture -- there is also a theoretical side. To provide a clear perspective of what EBL is, I introduce a well-defined model of EBL based on the notion of weakest preconditions. Following this, I describe a proof that PRODIGY's EBL method (actually, a simplified version of the method) is correct with respect to this model.

1.2. What is Explanation-Based Learning?

Learning from examples has long been a focus of machine learning research. In the 1970's researchers developed data-intensive, inductive learning methods which compared many examples of a concept to extract a general concept description [90, 54, 19]. In recent years many researchers have focused their attention on more powerful knowledge-intensive learning methods [57, 15, 47, 80, 23]. These "explanation-based methods", as they have come to be called, generalize from a single example of a concept by analyzing *why* the example is an instance of the concept. The explanation identifies the relevant features of the example.

1.2.1. The Terminology of Explanation-Based Learning

Several recent papers have contributed greatly to the emergence of a relatively standard terminology for describing explanation-based learning [15, 37, 57, 73]. Table 1-1 shows a high-level schema that I have adapted from Mitchell, Keller, and Kedar-Cabelli [57] specifying the input and output of EBL. As indicated by the schema, EBL begins with a high-level *target concept* and a *training example* for that concept. Using the *domain theory*, a set of axioms describing the domain, one can explain why the training example is an instance of the target concept. The explanation is essentially a proof that the training example satisfies the target concept. (The terminology of EBL can be cast into that of problem solving as well as that of theorem-proving, as pointed out by DeJong and Mooney [15]. I have chosen the latter terminology because it is widely standardized.)

By finding the weakest conditions under which the explanation holds, EBL will produce a *learned description* that is both a generalization of the training example and a specialization of the target concept. (In Chapter 11, a formal description of EBL is presented which discusses in detail what is meant by the terms "explanation" and "weakest conditions".) The learned description must satisfy the *operationality criterion*, a test which insures that the description will be an efficient recognizer for the target concept.

Given:

- **Target Concept: A concept to be learned.**

- **Training Example: An example of the target concept.**

- **Domain Theory: A set of rules and facts to be used in explaining why the training example is an instance of the target concept.**

- **Operationality Criterion: A predicate over descriptions, specifying the form in which the learned description must be expressed.**

Determine:

- **A description that is both a generalization of the training example and a specialization of the target concept, which satisfies the operationality criterion.**

Table 1-1: Specification of EBL (adapted from Mitchell *et al.* [57])

As an example (also adapted from [57]) consider the target concept (SAFE-TO-STACK x y), that is, object x can be safely placed on object y without object y collapsing. Let us suppose our training example is a demonstration that a particular book, "Principles of AI", can be safely placed upon a particular table, Coffee-Table-1. If our domain theory contains assertions such as those shown below, we can construct a proof that "Principles of AI" is safe to stack on Coffee-Table-1, because all books are lighter than tables. The resulting learned description would

therefore be (AND (IS-BOOK x) (IS-TABLE y)).
DOMAIN THEORY:

```
(IS-BOOK PRINCIPLES-OF-AI)
(SAFE-TO-STACK x y) if (OR (LIGHTER x y) (NOT-FRAGILE y))
(LESS-THAN w 5-LBS) if (AND (IS-BOOK x) (WEIGHT x w))
. . . . .
```

As indicated in the previous section, almost all EBL systems to date (including PRODIGY) assume that the domain theory is a complete and correct characterization of the domain. By "complete and correct", I mean that all positive instances, and only positive instances, of the target concept can be *proved* to be instances of the target concept using the theory. Thus, in these systems, the actual purpose of EBL is not to learn more about the target concept, but to re-express the target concept in a more operational manner. While the exact definition of operationality may vary depending on the learning system, efficiency for recognition is normally the implicit basis for any operationality criterion. (Otherwise, if efficiency were of no concern, the target concept could be used as is, since it is exactly defined by the domain theory.)

In fact, one can visualize a standard EBL program operating as follows. After being given a training example, EBL produces a learned description which is a generalization of the example. If the next training example is not covered by this description, another learned description is produced. If the third example is not covered by either of the two previous examples, another learned description is produced, and so on. Thus, the program incrementally re-expresses the target concept disjunctively, where each disjunct is one of the descriptions learned from an individual trial.

Supposedly the operationality criterion insures that each of the resulting disjuncts can be efficiently tested. However, this scheme completely ignores the cumulative cost of testing the disjuncts. So, even though each individual disjunct may be less expensive to test than the original target concept definition, testing the entire set of disjuncts may be considerably more expensive than testing the target concept definition. Furthermore, this simple model does not consider the relationship between the target concept and the problem solver whose performance is to be improved. Although the learned disjuncts may be efficient for recognizing the target concept, we have not specified how the learning process will be *used* to modify the problem solver. Obviously, if the problem solver's task is simply to recognize the target concept, then the disjuncts can simply replace the original target concept definition. However, in more sophisticated systems such as PRODIGY, which can learn from failures, goal-interactions, etc., the relationship between the problem solver and the target concept is more complex, and the effect of learning is dependent on how the system uses the learned disjuncts. Finally, as we will discuss in chapters 2 and 12, in practice the operationality criteria used in most EBL systems to date has been trivial and unrealistic, or even non-existent.

For these various reasons, if we specifically consider EBL systems that learn control knowledge (and almost all implemented EBL systems fall into this category), we find that learning may actually slow down the system. It may take longer to test the learned control knowledge than to run the original system without the control knowledge. More specifically, if we examine the learned control knowledge, we may find the following factors contributing to performance degradation:

- **Low Application Frequency:** A learned description may be useful when applied, but rarely applicable (i.e., overly specific). Thus the accumulated cost of repeatedly testing whether the description is applicable in the current state may outweigh the amortized benefit, even if the average cost of the test is low.

- **High Match Cost:** A learned description may be useful when applied, and may indeed be applied frequently, but the average cost of determining whether it is applicable may overwhelm any potential benefits. For example, the cost of matching the preconditions of a STRIPS-style macro-operator can be prohibitively expensive when the macro-operator represents a long chain of operators. If each individual operator in the system has approximately ten preconditions, then an operator chain of length ten may have up to one hundred preconditions. This can cause serious difficulties, as evidenced by the fact that the matching problem for precondition lists is NP-complete (as discussed in chapter 2).

- **Low Benefit:** A learned description may be of such marginal utility so as not to be worth the application overhead. For instance, consider a control rule in a robot navigation domain that searches through all possible paths to find one that has the fewest obstacles. This rule may not provide appreciable benefit if the robot can easily push obstacles out of the way.

This book can be viewed as an inquiry into the notion of an operationality criterion, since the operationality criterion is *supposed* to insure that the explanations satisfy the needs of the performance system. I consider what an operationality criterion should be for a practical problem solving system that learns control knowledge, and describe how to generate explanations that result in truly effective control knowledge.

1.3. EBL in the PRODIGY System

PRODIGY employs an EBL method called Explanation-Based Specialization (EBS) that is based on previous work by the author [47, 48] and other researchers [57, 15]. EBS takes a target concept description and specializes it to create the learned description. The specialization process proceeds by recursively expanding the target concept description using the substitutions defined by the domain axioms. The example is used to guide the selection of which axioms to use. The specialization process can be viewed as a proof process, since it is equivalent to expanding a proof that the example satisfies the target concept.

Three techniques are used in conjunction with PRODIGY's EBS method to make it more robust with respect to the utility problem:

1. **Multiple meta-level target concepts:** PRODIGY employs a variety of target concepts, so that it can not only explain why an operator succeeded, for example, but can also explain why an operator failed, or why two goals interfered, etc. (Almost all previous EBL systems are limited to learning from successful operator sequences.) After observing an example, PRODIGY can select from amongst its target concepts those that are most appropriate for learning from the example. Because of this, PRODIGY can learn powerful control rules that are well-tailored to a variety of problem solving systems. Moreover, PRODIGY's target concepts and theory are declaratively specified, so that additional target concepts can be included in the system.

2. **Compression Analysis:** The learned descriptions produced by EBL can be very expensive to match. Therefore, PRODIGY attempts to reduce their match cost by rewriting and simplifying them. This process, called *compression*, is equivalent to introducing simplification axioms into the original proof. Thus, it can be viewed as search within the space of alternative explanations in order produce one that is concise and easy to test.

3. **Utility Evaluation:** Even after the measures described above have been taken, PRODIGY is not guaranteed to produce learned descriptions that are necessarily effective as control rules. Therefore PRODIGY uses an explicit utility metric for evaluating the effectiveness of learned rules. The utility of a rule is determined by the cumulative time cost of matching the rule versus the cumulative savings in search time it produces. When a rule is learned from an example, the costs and benefits for that rule are estimated from the example and validated during subsequent problem solving. Only learned rules that have high utility are kept. In this way, the system can empirically evaluate the tradeoff between search and knowledge made by the learned rules.

To illustrate PRODIGY's EBL method let us consider an example from the blocksworld, a simple domain for demonstrating planning problems. (In subsequent chapters, more complex problem solving domains are considered.) Suppose that the problem is to achieve the goals (ON A B) and (ON B C) where blocks A and B are initially on the table (i.e. block A must be stacked on block B, which must be on block C). If the goal (ON A B) is achieved before (ON B C), then PRODIGY will have to undo the first goal in order to achieve the second. However, if the goals are achieved in the opposite order, then the problem can be solved directly. After observing the suboptimal plan which results when the goals are attacked in the wrong order, PRODIGY can learn a control rule that indicates that, in general, (ON y z) should be solved before (ON x y):

```
IF  (AND  (CURRENT-NODE node)
          (CANDIDATE-GOAL node (ON x y))
          (CANDIDATE-GOAL node (ON y z)))
    THEN (PREFER GOAL (ON y z) TO (ON x y))
```

This rule is learned as follows. First, PRODIGY observes that a goal interaction occurred in the example, and because GOAL-INTERFERENCE is one of its target concepts, it can map from the example to an explanation (a proof) that explains why the example is an instance of this general concept. Although the initial description produced by EBS contains literally hundreds of references (corresponding to the tests made by the problem solver while solving the problem) most of these can be simplified out using compression. Assuming that the problem solver is subsequently asked to stack other sets of blocks, PRODIGY's utility analysis will definitely judge this rule to be useful. Its match cost is low, and its benefit is high, since it improves search time (as well as improving the resulting plan as a side-effect). Furthermore, the rule is frequently applicable. (It is useful for building towers of arbitrary height, not just towers that are two blocks high, since PRODIGY's preference rules are transitive.) In fact, the control rule is as efficient as those typically produced by humans for this domain.

While PRODIGY does not always produce learned rules that are as good as hand-coded rules, the experimental results presented in chapter 10 are quite positive. They indicate that PRODIGY's performance is much better than would be expected from previous EBL methods for similar problem solvers.

1.4. Perspectives on the Learning Process

There are three perspectives for viewing the work presented in this book. The first and foremost is the *explanation-based perspective*, which has been the point of view adopted for most of this chapter. Within the EBL context, PRODIGY's distinguishing characteristic is that it searches for "good" explanations so that the rules it learns are powerful and inexpensive to evaluate, whereas other EBL systems do not discriminate between explanations. The search is a variation of generate and test. The initial explanations are incrementally generated by the EBS algorithm by explaining examples of PRODIGY's target concepts that arise during problem solving. The compression process then searches for an efficient representation for each of the explanations, and finally utility evaluation tests whether the learned descriptions are useful.

PRODIGY's learning method can also be viewed as a method for performance optimization. In other words, when PRODIGY learns to solve problems more efficiently for a given domain, we can view this as a form of incremental program optimization. (The traditional, but somewhat misleading, use of the term "program optimization" is intended here, as in "optimizing compilers". Traditionally, the purpose of program optimizers is to *improve* performance, but not necessarily to produce optimal performance.) We can view optimization strategies as falling into two categories. *Dynamic* optimization strategies modify a program based on its observed behavior, whereas *static* optimization strategies modify a program in isolation. For example, an optimizing compiler typically performs only static optimizations, such as constant folding and loop unrolling [1], which are based solely on the structure of the program. In contrast, PRODIGY performs its optimizations (the addition of search control rules) dynamically on the basis of the examples that are encountered. This *program optimization* perspective may at first appear to be only of academic interest, but in reality, PRODIGY's operators and inference rules are quite similar to PROLOG rules. In fact, Prieditis and Mostow [72] have experimented with EBL in a PROLOG environment, and the techniques described in this book may very well be applicable for dynamically optimizing PROLOG programs.

From a third perspective PRODIGY's learning can be viewed as a form of theory reformulation. The operators and inference for a given domain define a theory describing the domain. However, to borrow McCarthy's terminology [46], the theory may be epistemologically adequate, but still inadequate if one is concerned with solving problems in a reasonable time period with a particular problem solver. In other words, the theory may completely and correctly describe the domain, but it may not be useful for efficiently solving problems in the domain. To do so, it may be necessary to reformulate the theory. PRODIGY's learning process is equivalent to a simple form of reformulation which is limited to adding particular types of axioms (corresponding to the types of control knowledge that can be learned), rather than modifying pre-existing axioms. If one starts out with a perfect theory then there is no need for learning. Thus PRODIGY's learning, in effect, is an attempt to make the system's performance less dependent on the representation of the domain (the operators and inference rules).

This last perspective is important because it illustrates the difference between PRODIGY and other EBL systems, none of which consider the utility of the explanations they produce. These other systems may produce useful explanations, but then again they may not, depending on the way the domain is represented (as described in chapters 2 and 12). Of course, if one could count on having the domain represented the way one wanted, learning would not be necessary in the first place. Because in the real world one cannot count on being lucky, the learning system should be as robust as possible with respect to the domain encoding. To achieve robustness, PRODIGY introduces search into the learning process.

1.5. Scientific Contributions

The scientific contributions of this research include the following:

1. *Description and Analysis of the Utility Problem.* One of the primary contributions is to focus attention on the utility problem. Although it has

been documented in STRIPS-like systems by the author, and more recently in SOAR by Tambe and Newell [85] and in PROLEARN by Prieditis and Mostow [72], the problem has been largely ignored by the machine learning community. In this book, I argue that the utility problem is a general problem for EBL systems.

2. *New Extensions to Explanation-Based Learning:* To improve the utility of learning in PRODIGY three new extensions to EBL were devised and tested:

   a. **Meta-level target concepts** enable PRODIGY to learn from failures and goal-interactions, as well as success. In general, any phenomenon that can be observed during problem solving and explained can become the basis for learned control rules. This is possible because PRODIGY allows its target concepts and theory to be declaratively specified, and provides a general mechanism for mapping from a problem solving trace to an explanation.

   b. **Compression analysis** is a method for reducing the match cost of learned descriptions by rewriting and simplification. In practice, the compression is quite important for producing effective control knowledge. Because PRODIGY's explanations are machine-generated proofs, they tend to be verbose and redundant. The resulting learned descriptions frequently have hundreds of conditions, leaving ample opportunity for compression.

   c. **Utility evaluation** represents a realistic and practical improvement on the notion of operationality as employed in previous EBL systems. PRODIGY carries out an empirical cost/benefit evaluation of the rules that it learns.

3. *Presentation of a formal, logical specification of EBL:* Extending my previous work on EBL, I present a formal definition of EBL in terms of weakest premises. This enables a correctness proof for (a simplified version of) PRODIGY's EBS algorithm to be carried out.

Methodologically speaking, this research illustrates a two pronged approach -- there are both theoretical and experimental contributions. The experimental methodology is exemplified by the fully implemented PRODIGY system, and the sequence of experiments described in chapter 10. In order to test the system's overall performance, the experiments included running PRODIGY on a large corpus of randomly generated problems. The PRODIGY system (and manual [52]) is available to other researchers in the field for their inspection.

The experimental aspect of this research is complemented by more theoretical work illustrating the interplay between theory and practice. This is exemplified by the informal analysis of the general utility problem in chapter 2 and the formal definition of EBL (and correctness proof for PRODIGY's EBS method) in chapter 11.

1.6. A Reader's Guide

The following is a summary of the remaining chapters:

Chapter 2 contains a discussion and informal analysis of the utility problem, motivating the later chapters. Chapter 3 provides an overview of the PRODIGY problem solver. It is essential that the first four sections of chapter 3 be read in order to understand PRODIGY's learning component. The more detailed sections of this chapter may be skipped by the casual reader.

Chapters 4, 5 and 6 provide a vertical view of the learning process -- they describe each stage individually. Chapter 4 describes how PRODIGY examines a problem solving trace, selects relevant target concepts and examples and formulates an initial learned description using EBS. Chapter 5 describes the compression process, and chapter 6 describes utility evaluation. These chapters form the central core of the book.

Chapters 7, 8 and 9 provide a horizontal view of the learning process -- each describes how the entire process operates with respect to a given target concept. There are three main types of target concepts currently implemented, each of which constitutes a distinct learning strategy. (There are several individual target concepts per type, representing variations on a theme.) Thus, chapter 7 discusses learning from successful operator sequences, chapter 8 discusses learning from failures, and chapter 9 discusses learning form goal interactions. These chapters include in-depth examples which may be skimmed by the casual reader.

Chapter 10 provides a comprehensive analysis of the system's performance over several large sets of examples. Chapter 11 presents a formal description of explanation-based learning and outlines a proof of correctness for a simplified version of PRODIGY's EBS method. Chapter 12 contains a discussion of related work, and chapter 13 presents the conclusions.

The appendix contains a description of the task domains that PRODIGY was tested in. Details of the correctness proof for EBS, detailed results of the experiments testing the system's performance, and a listing of the architectural-level axioms that PRODIGY uses to formulate explanations can be found in the author's dissertation [53], available as a technical report from Carnegie-Mellon University.

2. Analyzing the Utility Problem

This research project was motivated largely by my observation that explanation-based learning is not guaranteed to improve problem solving performance. In this chapter, I discuss why this is so, and briefly review some theoretical and experimental results that bear on this issue.

2.1. Using EBL to Improve Performance

The most straightforward use for EBL is as a form of caching. An observed solution (or partial solution) can be generalized and stored so that similar problems (or subproblems) can be quickly solved in the future. Almost all EBL problem solving systems, including STRIPS [25], LEX2 [58], MORRIS [49] and the systems described by DeJong and Mooney [15], have relied on this strategy, or a minor variation of it.

In PRODIGY this strategy is called "learning from solutions", and it is only one of several optimization strategies available, such as learning from failures, and learning from goal interactions. These other optimization strategies can be considered extensions of the basic caching idea. In each case, the learning system is caching the result of a meta-level analysis of its own that differs from the problem solver's analysis. Therefore, although the learning system's analysis may be motivated by the problem solver's experience, the learned result is not a simple generalization of the solution.

In the next section, I analyze the utility of the straightforward caching method (i.e., learning from solutions). In later chapters we will see that the utility of the more sophisticated strategies can be treated similarly.

2.2. A Simple Model of EBL

Let us first consider a simple model of EBL for a forward-search problem solver or production system. As we will see, the model can be easily transformed into a backward search model, such as that employed by the PRODIGY problem solver, and it shares some important similarities with most EBL systems.

The problem solver's domain knowledge consists of a set of rules, each with a left-hand side and a right-hand side in the usual sense. The left-hand side is a conjunction of atomic formulas. The right-hand side indicates a single atomic formula that should be added to the set of working memory elements (WMEs) when the left-hand side is satisfied. Rules may have variables, but every variable on the right-hand side must also exist on the left-hand side. I will assume that there are no variables with the same names in different rules, to make the learning algorithm simpler. An illustrative set of rules is shown in table 2-1.

An initial state consists of a set of working memory elements. The objective is to produce a WME matching a given goal atomic formula. Whenever the system tests a rule, if the left-hand side of the rule is satisfied, then the system adds the right-hand side WME to working memory. If a rule is satisfied under multiple sets of bindings, then multiple WMEs are added, one for each set of bindings. However, if the rule has previously fired with the same set of bindings then the system does not bother to add a duplicate WME. (Note that WMEs are never deleted in this system.) We will assume that all rules are tested simultaneously, and that the system is run for as many cycles as is necessary to produce a goal WME (a WME element matching the goal formula).

Learning is very simple in this system. Let us say that the firing of a rule *contributes* to the production of a goal WME if the rule either directly adds the goal WME, or adds a WME that enables another rule to contribute to the goal WME. Thus, whenever the system produces a goal WME there will be a collection of rules that contributed to the goal. The contributing rules form a tree whose root is the last rule that fired, adding the goal. The learning algorithm then joins these rules into a single composite rule, which is added to the system. (The individual rules remain in the system.)

To be precise, let us suppose that the composite rule is formulated in the following manner. If one contributing rule fired before another contributing rule (i.e., on an earlier cycle), the first rule's conditions are ordered before those of the second rule. (Therefore the last conditions in the composite rule will be from the rule that directly contributed the goal WME.) Furthermore, all of the conditions in the individual contributing rules become conditions in the composite rule, except for any conditions matched by WMEs produced during the run. These are each replaced by an "equality" condition which insures that the composite rule preserves correctness.[2] Some examples will help to illustrate this.

In the first example in table 2-2, RULE1 fires, introducing a condition which

---

[2]No naming conflicts arise when combining distinct rules because, as mentioned earlier, all rules are assumed to have non-overlapping sets of variable names. Therefore the only case where naming conflicts arise is when the same rule occurs more than once in a collection of contributing rules. In this case, unique variable renamings must be employed for each use of the rule.

```
RULE1:                 RULE2:                 RULE3:
 (P1 a b)               (P1 e f)               (P8 h i j)
 (P2 a c)               (P5 e)                 (P9 h i)
 (P3 d)                 (P6 f)                 ---->
 (P4 a)                 (P7 e f g)             (P1 h i)
 ---->                  ---->
 (P6 a)                 (P4 f)
```

Table 2-1: Some Illustrative Rules

Example 1: RULE1 adds (P6 101) which matches (P6 *f*) in RULE2,
          enabling RULE2 to produce the goal (P4 101)

NEW-RULE-A:
```
(P1 a b)      ; first four conditions from RULE1
(P2 a c)
(P3 d)
(P4 a)
(P1 e f)      ; next four conditions from RULE2
(P5 e)
(EQUALS (f) (a)) ; 3rd condition of RULE2 replaced with
(P7 e f g)       ; condition specifying that f must equal a.
---->
(P4 f)
```


Example 2: RULE1 adds (P6 101) which matches (P6 *f*) in RULE2,
          and RULE3 adds (P1 108 101) which matches (P1 e *f*)
          in RULE2. RULE2 then produces the goal (P4 101).

NEW-RULE-B:
```
(P1 a b)   ; first four conditions from RULE1
(P2 a c)
(P3 d)
(P4 a)
(P8 h i j) ; next two conditions from RULE3
(P9 h i)
(EQUALS (e f) (h i)) ; last four conditions from RULE2, modified
(P5 e)               ; to insure that e and f equal h and i,
(EQUALS (f) (a))     ; and to insure that f and a are equal.
(P7 e f g)
---->
(P4 f)
```

Table 2-2: Some Composite Rules

matches RULE2, which in turn produces the goal. The learned rule, NEW-RULE-A, is the composition of the two rules, with (P6 *f*), the condition in RULE2 that was introduced by RULE1, replaced by the EQUALS condition that insures that *a* and *f* are equal. The second example illustrates a composition of three rules. Notice that the conditions in the learned rules are ordered in the same order are they are "encountered" during the match process. This will aid our analysis of the match cost of the learned rules.

Typically, the search carried out by production systems is described in terms of the rules that fire. The application of a rule corresponds to a branch in the search tree. However, because our learning system operates by composing rules, it is unrealistic to use rule applications as a primitive unit of computation. The reason is that the time spent matching the left-hand side of a rule typically varies with the size of the rule, and the learning process will produce large rules. Since an arbitrary (but finite) amount of computation may be performed in the matching phase (see section 2.5), it is more appropriate to consider this computation as part of the search.

A more reasonable model of search, one that includes the work done in the matcher, can be developed by considering the *tokens* produced internally as each rule is matched [27]. A token indicates what preconditions have matched, and under what bindings. For example, consider RULE1 from table 2-1, reproduced below:

```
RULE1:
(P1 a b)
(P2 a c)
(P3 d)
(P4 a)
--->
(P6 a)
```

Assume that the system matches conditions from left to right. Suppose there are two WMEs that match the first condition in RULE1, (P1 COW BROWN) and (P1 DOG BLACK). Then two tokens will be generated: (1 a=COW,b=BROWN) and (1 a=DOG,b=BLACK). The number 1 indicates that the tokens have matched the first condition. Then each of these tokens goes on to match the second condition, as shown in the match tree in figure 2-1. Let us suppose that there is no WME that matches (P2 COW c), and a single working memory element (P2 DOG ROVER) that matches (P2 DOG c). Thus a new token is generated, (2 a=DOG, b=BLACK, c=ROVER). At the third condition, let us suppose that there are two WME's that match (P3 d) and so two new tokens are generated. Finally, only one of these makes it past P4, where the last token is generated, causing the right-hand side to add (P6 DOG) to working memory.

The number of tokens generated during the match is equal to the number of branches in the "match tree", as can be seen in figure 2-1. We can use the number of tokens as a measure of the complexity of the match. Throughout the rest of the chapter, in considering the number of tokens generated I will assume that a top-to-bottom (or equivalently, left-to-right) match is used. I will also assume that the system is efficient and *never* generates the same token twice within a given rule. (This can be implemented via a Rete network [27].)

This metric enables us to compare the cost of matching a learned rule versus the cost of searching for a solution with the corresponding original rules. For example, consider the cost of matching NEW-RULE-A with the cost of matching RULE1 followed by RULE2 in Example 1, the same example in which NEW-RULE-A was

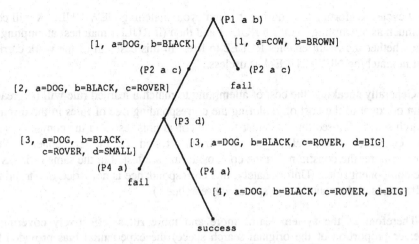

Figure 2-1: Tokens Generated By Matching RULE1

learned. For every token generated in RULE1, there is a corresponding token generated in NEW-RULE-A, since the first four conditions of NEW-RULE-A are equivalent to RULE1. Now consider the effect of the WME added by RULE1 on RULE2. There will be at least one new subtree of tokens attached at depth three of the match tree for RULE2, due to the addition of the WME by RULE1. (I.e., a new branch will emanate from every depth three node, because the WME matches the third condition of RULE2. These new branches will give rise to subtrees whose size depends on whether the fourth condition of RULE2 matches under the same bindings.) For each of the tokens generated in these new subtrees there are at least as many corresponding tokens generated by the last two conditions of NEW-RULE-A, since the same constraints are being tested. (Additionally, there may be tokens created in NEW-RULE-A at the fifth and sixth conditions that are not generated in RULE2. Later we will discuss this and other sources of potential inefficiency produced by the learning process.) The result is that for every token generated in RULE1, and for every token generated in RULE2 that is due to RULE1's activation, there is a corresponding token generated in NEW-RULE-A.

Although matching NEW-RULE-A requires as much or more work than matching the rules from which it is composed, it can still produce great savings overall. The reason is that the system can now produce the goal in one cycle rather than two, which eliminates all the work necessary to match the other productions during the second cycle. Thus the effect of composing rules is to focus the search so that lines that have previously been useful are examined first. In other words, learning composite rules provides *experiential bias*. This general observation about rule composition will be relevant at many points throughout this book.

Our example has illustrated a best-case scenario, where NEW-RULE-A eliminates almost an entire cycle of work. But the rule has a cost also. Consider a different example in which another rule, perhaps RULE3, produces the goal on the first cycle. Unfortunately, during the first cycle matching NEW-RULE-A will cost as much as attempting to match RULE1 and then (if RULE1 matches) attempting to see whether the result enables RULE2 to fire. In this case, all of the work carried out in matching NEW-RULE-A is useless.

Generally speaking, the cost of attempting to match a learned rule will be greater than or equal to the cost of exploring the corresponding tree of rules in the original search space. To see this, consider that the constraints tested in the composite rule are effectively identical to the constraints tested in the component rules. Furthermore, the constraints in the composite rule are tested in the same order as in the component rules. (Unfortunately, this correspondence is not strict, due to minor differences in the way the two spaces are searched.[3])

Therefore as the system learns more and more rules (effectively covering a greater proportion of the original search space) the experiential bias provided by learning tends to diminish. Consider the extreme case where all, or almost all, syntactically legal rule compositions (where a composition is a tree of rules that can be combined into a composite rule) have been learned over a long series of problem solving episodes. In this case, although producing the goal takes only a single cycle, the cost of matching all the learned rules will cost as least as much as searching the *entire* space of possibilities. In contrast, to produce the goal in the original search space normally only a portion of the search space need be explored. Thus, it may take considerably *more work* to find the goal than if the original set of rules had been used. (Here we are not even considering the fact that matching an individual learned rule can generate more tokens than matching the corresponding sequences of rules in the original space).

We can divide the set of syntactically legal rule compositions (i.e., trees of rules in the original space) into three distinct subclasses. First there are the *useful* compositions which at some point generate a goal WME and are therefore converted into composite rules. Then there are the *useless* compositions. These are compositions that generate tokens in the original search space, but never produce a goal WME. Thus they never become composite rules. Finally, there are the *unexplored* compositions; these are the compositions which never generate any tokens. They are syntactically legal, but the system never receives any input such that these compositions are "explored" during the search. Since the unexplored compositions are neither a factor in the original search space nor the learned search space, we can ignore them. Therefore the argument above leads us to the

---

[3]Matching the composite rule is typically more expensive, as described in the next section, because the tree structure of the original search space is partially lost in the composite rule. On the other hand, in some cases matching the composite rule may be less expensive, because if a condition early in the composite rule fails, the later conditions are not tested at all; in the original tree of rules, parallel branches are tested in parallel, so failure of a condition in one branch will not cut off search in another branch. The next section shows how to make an exact correspondence between the two search spaces.

conclusion that *the effectiveness of learning is highly dependent on the relative proportion of useful compositions to useless compositions.* The *lower* the proportion (the fewer useful compositions), the more likely that learning will produce significant savings. If there are only a few useful compositions compared to the number of useless compositions, then relatively few rules will be learned and there will be a large advantage to learning. The system will avoid having to explore all the useless compositions. On the other hand, in the extreme case where there are no useless compositions, all the compositions that the system explores will be converted into rules. In this case, learning will not improve performance (since there is no benefit) and will almost certainly degrade performance due to the inefficiencies it introduces (as discussed in the next section).

Before concluding this section, let me summarize more precisely the observations that my informal remarks have been based on. Suppose a token is generated in the original rule space. Consider the tree of rules that *contribute* to the generation of this token. (Here I have simply extended the definition of *contribute* given earlier to apply to any token, not just the goal token.) If the contributing tree of rules has been converted into a composite rule, then at least one corresponding token will be generated in the composite rule. Similarly, if a token is generated in a composite rule, there will be a corresponding token that will be generated by the original rules, if the system is allowed to run long enough. Finally, if every syntactically legal composite rule is formulated, there will be a one-to-very-many mapping from the tokens generated in the original rule space to the tokens generated by the composite rules.

2.3. Removing Inefficiencies

There are several obvious inefficiences in the learning scheme introduced in the last section. I will consider them briefly here, because the solutions are of general relevance to the EBL methods considered later.

One inefficiency that rule composition introduces is illustrated by NEW-RULE-B, the second example in table 2-2. This rule is created when RULE1 and RULE3 both fire, enabling RULE2 to fire. NEW-RULE-B is created from the constraints in RULE1, followed by the constraints in RULE3, followed by the relevant constraints in RULE2. Suppose that we have a state where seven WMEs would be produced by matching RULE1, and three WMEs would be produced by matching RULE2. Unfortunately, since NEW-RULE-B is matched from top-to-bottom a total of twenty-one tokens will make it past the sixth condition. In other words, seven tokens will make it past the first four conditions from RULE1 (corresponding to the seven WMEs produced by RULE1) and for each of these tokens, there will be three tokens generated when matching the two conditions from RULE3. The number of tokens that match the last condition from RULE1 are *multiplied* by the tokens generated by the conditions from RULE3. This occurs because the conditions from

RULE1 are independent of the conditions from RULE3 (assuming a top-to-bottom match of NEW-RULE-B). Because of this phenomenon, matching a composite rule may generate *more* tokens than the corresponding sequence of rules in the original search space.

One solution to this problem is to recapture the structure from the original search space in the composite rules. Figure 2-2 illustrates this solution in terms of a Rete network, such as that used in OPS5 [27]. The linear tree on the left represents a standard OPS5 top-to-bottom match of the composite rule NEW-RULE-B. Tokens flow down the tree. The modified tree on the right shows how to recapture the structure of the original search space. Here the conditions from each component rule are tested in a separate branch, and the branches are joined at the appropriate equality test. Thus, the conditions from RULE1 are tested in a separate branch from those in RULE3. This eliminates the multiplication of tokens that occurs when independent groups of constraints are tested.

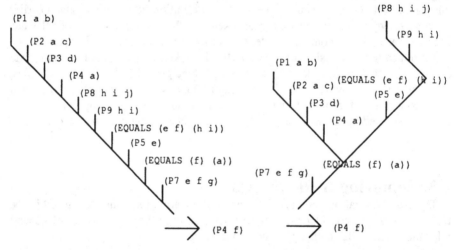

Figure 2-2: How Learning Can Introduce Inefficiencies

Interestingly, if this method is used to reconstruct the original structure of the search space within each composite rule, then the number of tokens generated in each composite rule will exactly equal the number of tokens generated by the corresponding tree of original rules[4]. (In the previous section, I said that *at least as many* tokens were typically generated in the composite rule.)

A second way to improve the efficiency of the learned rules is to remove the EQUALS constraints by performing variable substitutions. Thus NEW-RULE-A

---

[4]Presumably the same trick can be done within each of the original productions as well, so that the composite rules are no more efficient to match than the corresponding trees in the original search space.

would be transformed as shown below:

```
Original NEW-RULE-A:
(P1 a b)      ; first four conditions from RULE1
(P2 a c)
(P3 d)
(P4 a)
(P1 e f)      ; next four conditions from RULE2
(P5 e)
(EQUALS (f) (a))
(P7 e f g)
---->
(P4 f)


More efficient NEW-RULE-A:
(P1 a b)      ; first four conditions from RULE1
(P2 a c)
(P3 d)
(P4 a)
(P1 e a)      ; next three conditions from RULE2
(P5 e)
(P7 e a g)
---->
(P4 a)
```

The transformation, in effect, propagates the equality constraint forward in the precondition list, thus reducing the number of tokens that are generated. However, this does not change the observation made in the last section -- if a token is generated in the original rule space, and the contributing tree of rules has been converted into a composite rule, then a corresponding token will be generated in the composite rule. It merely reduces the inefficiency in the composite rule.

Another possibility is to re-order the conditions in the learned rules so that the conditions that generate tokens are closely followed by the conditions that test tokens. This well-known strategy (e.g., [85]) can be quite effective and may indeed enable the composite rule to be significantly more efficient than the original component rules. However, the re-ordering process is NP-complete, and it may require domain-specific knowledge about which conditions generate the most tokens and under what circumstances.

A fourth possibility is to use an indexing scheme or discrimination net so that duplicate work is avoided wherever possible. Note that many of the learned rules will have sequences of conditions in common with each other and with the original production rules. In fact, figure 2-3 illustrates one reason why the learning scheme tends to produce duplication of effort. In effect, the original search space is organized into a deep tree structure, and the learning scheme transforms that into a shallow tree structure, thereby introducing inefficiency. Indexing can help reclaim the original structure, and perhaps even create more sharing. Unfortunately indexing is a poorly understood area, and most current rule compilers (e.g., [27]) would not be able to recapture the original structure of the search space from our composite

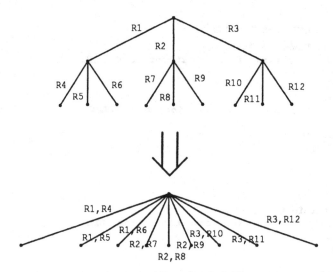

Figure 2-3: How Learning Can Introduce Inefficiencies

rules.[5]

All four of these techniques are essentially static methods for compiling or optimizing rule sets. Such techniques typically have various limitations, are generally not guaranteed to produce optimal behavior, and may conflict (for example the second technique outlined above tends to make indexing harder). Because of the difficulties inherent in designing domain-independent static optimization strategies, this investigation is primarily concerned with dynamic optimization strategies -- learning strategies -- whose power derives from exploiting both domain knowledge and experience.[6]

2.4. Extending the Simple Model

The learning model introduced in the previous section is a very simplistic model of EBL. However, it shares some important similarities with most EBL problem solving systems, and I claim that the issues that it raises are relevant to these other systems as well.

---

[5]Although current indexing schemes may be weak, this area may yet prove to be quite important. In fact, powerful rule indexing schemes may be easier to develop for specific learning schemes rather than for arbitrary rule sets.

[6]Static optimization techniques generally fall into two classes: intra-rule techniques (such as the first three techniques) that operate on a single rule, and inter-rule techniques (such as the last technique) that consider the rule set as a whole. Both intra-rule and inter-rule techniques are used by PRODIGY during the compression process described in chapter 5. However, they are applied as a secondary mechanism to improve the results of EBL, a dynamic optimization technique.

For example, let us consider the relationship between our simple model and the STRIPS MACROP system [25], an early, but influential, EBL problem solving system. (The STRIPS MACROP system and its relation to other early EBL systems is discussed in Chapter 12.) While our model is a forward search system, STRIPS is a means-ends analysis search system. Given a goal, STRIPS will consider applying only the rules that can produce that goal. If none of these rules are applicable, STRIPS will pick a rule, and subgoal on any of the rule's unmatched preconditions,[7] later backtracking if necessary. Once a sequence of operators is found that achieves the goal, STRIPS creates a composite operator.

We can easily convert our simple rule system so that it behaves similarly to STRIPS. Let us suppose that the rule system is modified to employ the same means-ends analysis control strategy as STRIPS. The matching process is used in two places. Given a goal, the set of relevant rules is determined by matching the goal against the atomic formulas added by the rules' right-hand sides. For each relevant rule, the appropriate bindings are then substituted into the rule's left-hand side which is matched against the current state. Notice that the first type of match -- the right-hand side match -- merely involves unifying two atomic formulas and is therefore of linear complexity [68]. On the other hand, the left-hand side match can be combinatorial, and corresponds exactly to the matching process described previously in this chapter. In fact, we can do away with the right-hand side match as a separate process in the following manner. Whenever a goal is encountered, instead of matching the right-hand side against the goal, we simply add an appropriate equality condition to the beginning of the rule's left-hand side, such that this condition is true iff the right-hand side match would succeed. Thus, given the goal (P6 101), for example, the left-hand side of RULE1 is modified as shown below:

```
ORIGINAL RULE1:                 MODIFIED RULE:
(P1 a b)                        (EQUALS (P6 P6) (a 101))
(P2 a c)                        (P1 a b)
(P3 d)                          (P2 a c)
(P4 a)                          (P3 d)
---->                           (P4 a)
(P6 a)                          ---->
                                (P6 a)
```

Matching the new left-hand side is identical in effect to carrying out the original right-hand side match followed by the original left-hand side match, and has the same complexity. We can now use the same token-based complexity metric developed earlier in this chapter for measuring the cost of search; as in our original model, we assume that the number of tokens generated during the match process is the dominant factor determining search time.

---

[7]For simplicity, I consider a simple form of STRIPS that matches preconditions. The original STRIPS employed a theorem prover to test preconditions.

Learning also proceeds similarly to that in our original model. Whenever a rule sequence is found that achieves a goal, a composite rule will be formed. However, let us assume that the conditions in the composite rule are ordered according to a "preorder embedding" of the contributing rules. In other words, suppose that component rule A achieved the kth precondition of rule B. Then the first k-1 preconditions of rule B are listed first, followed by the preconditions of rule A (and any other recursively embedded preconditions) and then the remaining preconditions (starting at condition k+1) of rule B. This ordering insures that during the match process the preconditions of the learned rule are matched in the same order as the preconditions of the corresponding rules in the original search space. Given this ordering convention, the observations described in the previous section will also hold for our STRIPS-like rule system.

Table 2-4 illustrates an example in which NEW-RULE-C is composed from RULE1 and RULE2. In the example (P4 101) is the goal. The system begins by testing the preconditions of RULE2 starting from the top, and (P6 101) is unmatched. Therefore the system subgoals on (P6 101), and attempts to match RULE1, after substituting 101 for a. The preconditions of RULE1 are satisfied, and the rule is applied. The system then goes on to finish matching the last condition of RULE2. Once RULE2 introduces the goal, the composite rule NEW-RULE-C is created from RULE1 and RULE2. The reader can verify that matching NEW-RULE-C tests the same conditions, in the same order, as in the original search space. Therefore, matching NEW-RULE-C will generate at least as many tokens as in the original search space.

The example is intended to illustrate that our model is equally useful for analyzing STRIPS-like systems. While I have only briefly outlined the relationship between the model and STRIPS-like systems, the key point is that matching the composite rule mimics the search carried out in the original search space.[8] Because the same constraints are tested in the same order, the number of tokens generated while matching the composite rule is greater than or equal to the number of tokens generated in carrying out the original search. Thus utility problems can arise when the learned rules cover a large proportion of the original space. Indeed, in previous research on the MORRIS project [49], I demonstrated empirically that such problems do arise in STRIPS-like systems in exactly the predicted manner. As in our model, the utility of MORRIS's macro-operators was observed to be highly dependent on the experiential bias that they encoded. Consequently, in situations where many macro-operators were learned, the average utility of the learned macro-operators was low or negative. And in fact, MORRIS often tended to produce many

---

[8]My analysis has ignored more sophisticated features such as delete lists, left-hand side quantifiers, negated preconditions, and so forth. In general, the inclusion of these features does not change the basic result of the analysis insofar as matching the composed rule must repeat the work done in the original search.

RULE1:	RULE2:	RULE3
(P1 *a b*)	(P1 *e f*)	(P8 *h i j*)
(P2 *a c*)	(P5 *e*)	(P9 *h i*)
(P3 *d*)	(P6 *f*)	---->
(P4 *a*)	(P7 *e f g*)	(P1 *h i*)
---->	---->	
(P6 *a*)	(P4 *f*)	

Table 2-3: Original Rules

```
Example: Goal is (P4 101). To match RULE2 system subgoals on
         condition (P6 101). Matching RULE1 achieves this
         subgoal, enabling RULE2 to be matched.
```

```
NEW-RULE-C:
(P1 e f)              ; first two conditions from RULE2
(P5 e)
(EQUALS (f) (a))     ; equality constraint
(P1 a b)              ; next four conditions from RULE1
(P2 a c)
(P3 d)
(P4 a)
(P7 e f g)           ; last condition from RULE2
---->
(P4 f)
```

Table 2-4: A Composite Rule

macro-operators -- in the STRIPS MACROP method used by MORRIS, all subsequences of a macro-operator are treated as macro-operators in their own right. This is a very liberal policy that populates the macro-operator space very quickly, saturating out the experiential bias. In addition, the negative impact of the learned macro-operators in MORRIS was partly attributed to duplication of effort among macro-operators, reminiscent of the duplication of effort arising from the inefficiencies in our simple rule system.

Although I have not analyzed other EBL programs in the same detail that I have analyzed STRIPS-like systems, it appears that our simple model is useful for analyzing most EBL, macro-operator, and chunking systems that employ variations of rule composition. The fundamental similarity between these techniques is discussed further in chapters 11 and 12.

2.5. Will the Utility Problem Go Away?

It is sometimes claimed that the utility problem will be "solved" by the development of highly parallel hardware and/or powerful indexing schemes. This opinion is based on the belief that either of these developments would make matching (and by extension, memory search) inexpensive. In this section I will attempt to show that the matching problem is a fundamental problem, computationally speaking, and will not go away. Thus, since matching can be expensive, the utility of learned rules will always be a question worth considering.

The basis of my argument rests on the fact that matching even a simple conjunctive set of preconditions is NP-complete [28, p. 233]. For more sophisticated languages the computational complexity of matching can be even higher (e.g., matching arbitrary first order sentences is PSPACE-complete). To see that matching conjunctive preconditions is NP-complete, consider that we can encode an arbitrary graph using conjunctive preconditions. For example, figure 2-4 shows a small directed graph and a set of preconditions that encode that graph. Obviously this encoding method can be extended to any graph. Thus we can reduce subgraph isomorphism to matching in the following manner. Given two graphs G and H, where H is a potential subgraph of G, first encode G as a set of working memory elements. Then encode H as a set of preconditions. To test whether H is isomorphic to a subgraph of G, simply test whether the preconditions match.

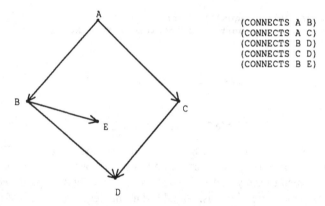

Figure 2-4: Encoding Graph Problems with Preconditions

In fact, one might argue that graph matching is a rather "artificial" problem that does not arise in "natural" domains, but this is dubious. For example, the original STRIPS domain, as well as the MORRIS domain, involved a set of rooms that were connected together and a robot that had to navigate between them, going to and fro, pushing blocks, etc. Thus the preconditions of the rules that were learned did indeed represent graph matching problems. (And in fact, many real-world problems can be reduced to graph matching problems.)

As an example illustrating the problems that can arise, consider the problem shown in figure 2-5 where MORRIS is given the problem of finding a path from RoomA to RoomF without repeating any intervening rooms. This particular problem can be easily solved relatively easily by depth-first search. The macro-operator that is learned indicates that a path between room-x1 and room-x6 exists if room-x1 is connected to room-x2 (with room-x2 not equal to room-x1), and room-x2 is connected to room-x3 and so on. This macro-operator expresses the "hamiltonian path" condition for six-node graphs. The general hamiltonian path problem for n-node graphs is another NP-complete graph matching problem.

Indeed, whenever MORRIS would attempt to match this macro-operator, the matcher would, in effect explore all non-cyclic paths of length six in the graph. This became quite expensive when more doors were opened between rooms, or more rooms were added. In fact, the system performed better without this macro, relying solely on simple depth-first search.[9] A similar slowdown was observed by the author when such problems were given to SOAR, another EBL-like problem solving system.

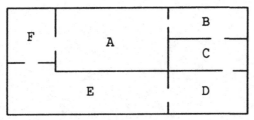

Figure 2-5: Example Room Configuration for Path Planning Problem

Because even the simple conjunctive matching problem is NP-complete, it is difficult to imagine that fast parallel hardware will "solve" the matching problem. It will certainly enable us to solve more difficult matching problems than we would be otherwise be able to, but eventually, given any fixed amount of hardware, there will be problems that are "too hard".

How about indexing and compilation schemes? In fact, for some subclasses of NP-complete problems, with enough space and pre-processing time, data-structures often can be designed that enable particular instances to be solved in polynomial time. For example, for the 6-node hamiltonian path problem, one can construct a (extremely large) table indicating for every 6-node graph, whether it contains a hamiltonian path. Then, given a particular graph, one can look up whether it contains a hamiltonian path. However, in practice, one does not typically have arbitrary space and pre-processing time available. Furthermore, assuming P does not equal NP, such pre-processing techniques must take more than polynomial time.

While fast hardware and good indexing schemes can be extremely useful, in general, they do not appear to be the solution to the utility problem. If a learning system can learn arbitrary formulas, then there will always be matching problems. Instead, the solution to the utility problem is to avoid learning overly expensive rules in the first place. The system should be sensitive to the costs and savings of the rules it learns relative to its computational architecture. An intelligent system must have an intelligent learning component -- one that learns good rules.

---

[9]Of course, macro-operator learning can perform quite poorly even when the problem is not NP-complete. For example, if the problem solver is asked to find *any* path from RoomA to RoomF, and a macro describing a path of length *n* is generated, matching this macro will generate all paths of length *n*.

3. Overview of the PRODIGY Problem Solver

PRODIGY's problem solver is the substrate on top of which the explanation-based learning system is built. The purpose of this chapter is to describe the problem solving architecture in enough detail so that the learning system and its effects can be properly understood. Special emphasis is given to those aspects of the problem solver that are particularly relevant to this thesis.

3.1. System Overview

The PRODIGY problem solver is intended to provide a testbed for research efforts in planning and learning. The entire PRODIGY system can be divided into four basic subsystems, as illustrated in figure 3-1:

- An advanced STRIPS-like [25] problem solver that provides a uniform control structure for searching with both inference rules and operators. The problem solver's search can be guided by domain-independent or domain-specific control rules.

- An explanation-based learning facility that can propose explanations about why a control decision was appropriate, and transform them into search control rules.

- A learning-by-experimentation module [8] for refining incompletely or incorrectly specified domain knowledge. Experimentation is triggered when plan execution monitoring detects a divergence between internal expectations and external expectations.

- A user-interface that can participate in an apprentice-like dialogue, enabling the user to evaluate and modify the system's behavior.

3.2. Using the Problem Solver

PRODIGY's problem solver is a general-purpose problem solver that employs a means-ends analysis search strategy. Although primarily oriented towards planning, the problem solver can also be employed as a theorem-prover or as a flexible reasoning engine for various expert system tasks. In order to solve problems in a particular domain, PRODIGY must first be given a specification of that domain, which consists of a set of operators and inferences rules for the domain. This section introduces a machine-shop scheduling domain to begin with.

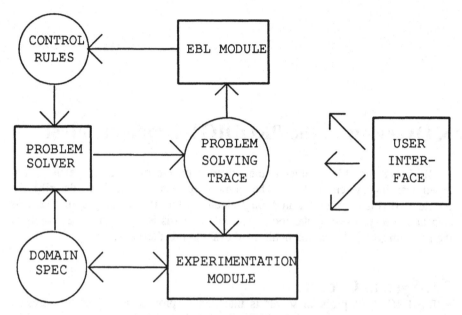

Figure 3-1:   System Overview

Other domains are introduced later to provide a varied set of examples.

Let us suppose that the shop contains a variety of machines, including a LATHE and a ROLLER (which are used to reshape objects), a POLISHER, and other simple machines. We assume that each machining operation takes one time unit. Given a set of objects to be drilled, polished, reshaped, etc., and a finite amount of time, the task is to schedule the objects on the machines so as to meet these requirements. (Note that we are considering a satisficing rather than an optimizing task.) The complete specification for this domain is given in Appendix I.

Each operator has a precondition expression that must be satisfied before the operator can be applied, and an effects-list that describes how the application of the operator changes the world. Precondition expressions are well-formed formulas in PDL, a form of predicate logic described in section 3.5 that serves as PRODIGY's description language. Negation, conjunction, disjunction, and existential quantification are allowed, as well as universal quantification over sets. (Constants are shown in upper case and variables are in italics.) The effects-list indicates atomic formulas that should be added or deleted from the current state when the operator is applied, reflecting the actions of the operator in the "world".

Let us take a close look at one of the operators given in the domain specification, the operator for scheduling the LATHE:

```
(LATHE  (obj  time  new-shape)
   (PRECONDS
      (AND  (IS-OBJECT  obj)
            (LAST-SCHEDULED  obj  prev-time)
            (LATER  time  prev-time)
            (IDLE  LATHE  time)))
   (EFFECTS
      ((DEL  (SHAPE  obj  old-shape))
       (DEL  (SURFACE-CONDITION  obj  old-condition))
       (ADD  (SURFACE-CONDITION  obj  ROUGH))
       (DEL  (PAINTED  obj  old-paint))
       (DEL  (LAST-SCHEDULED  obj  prev-time))
       (ADD  (SHAPE  obj  CYLINDRICAL)
       (ADD  (LAST-SCHEDULED  obj  time))
       (ADD  (SCHEDULED  obj  LATHE  time)))))
```

The LAST-SCHEDULED relation indicates the time period at which an object was last scheduled to be operated on. Thus, the first second and third preconditions of LATHE force the problem solver to schedule operations chronologically; once an object has been scheduled for a machine at time *t*, it cannot be scheduled for another operation at an earlier time period. (Initially, all objects are LAST-SCHEDULED at TIME-0.) This restriction has two purposes. First, it makes the problem solver's operation easier to understand. Secondly, it allows us to represent objects' properties in a straightforward manner; otherwise it would be necessary to explicitly represent the time at which each property was true. (Inefficiencies due to chronological scheduling can be largely compensated by control knowledge.) The last precondition of LATHE states that the LATHE must be idle -- there cannot be another object scheduled to be lathed during the same time period. The effects of the operator include scheduling the object on the LATHE, and updating the LAST-SCHEDULED relation. The effects-list also indicates that lathing changes the object's shape, and removes the paint and polish from its surface.

At any particular moment, the current state of the world is represented by a database containing a set of ground atomic formulas. There are two types of relations used in the system, primitive relations and defined relations. Primitive relations are directly observable or "closed-world". This means that the truth value of these relations can be immediately ascertained by a call to the state database. Primitive relations may be added to and deleted from the state database by operators. Thus, in our machine shop domain, the primitive relations include SCHEDULED and SHAPE. Primitive relations may also be *static*, such as (LATER TIME-5 TIME-2), in which case they are generally computed by the database rather than being explicitly maintained.

Defined relations, such as IDLE and CLAMPABLE, are inferred on demand using inference rules. The purpose of defined relations is to represent useful abstractions in the domain, allowing operator preconditions to be expressed more concisely. Inference rules only change the system's internal knowledge state, whereas operators change *both* the representation of the external world and the system's internal state. For example, the following inference rule defines the predicate IDLE by specifying that a machine is idle during a time period if no object is scheduled for that machine at that time period.

```
(IS-IDLE (machine time)
  (PRECONDS
    (NOT (EXISTS obj SUCH-THAT
                  (SCHEDULED obj machine time)))))
  (EFFECTS
    (ADD (IDLE machine time))))
```

Because inference rules are used in a manner similar to operators, PRODIGY can use a homogeneous control structure, enabling the search control rules to guide the application of operators and inference rules alike.

3.3. An Example Problem
Once the domain has been specified, problems are presented to the problem solver by describing an initial state and a goal expression to be satisfied. The goal expression for our example problem is:

```
(AND (SHAPE OBJECT-A CYLINDRICAL)
     (SURFACE-CONDITION OBJECT-A POLISHED))
```

This expression is satisfied if there is an object named OBJECT-A that is polished and has a cylindrical shape.

	TIME-1	TIME-2	TIME-3	TIME-4....				TIME-20
LATHE	OBJECT-B							
ROLLER	OBJECT-C							
POLISHER		OBJECT-B						

Figure 3-2: Initial State

The initial state for our example is illustrated in figure 3-2. In the initial state OBJECT-B and OBJECT-C have already been scheduled, while OBJECT-A has yet to be scheduled. Let us suppose that the schedule consists of 20 time-slots, and that OBJECT-A is initially unpolished, oblong-shaped, and is cool. The search tree for this example is shown in figure 3-3.

The left side of each node shows the goal stack and the pending operators at that point. The right side shows a subset of the state that is relevant to our discussion. For example, at node three, the current goal is to clamp the object. This is a precondition of the POLISH operator, which is being considered to achieve the higher goal of being polished. The predicates like CYLINDRICAL and HOT in the figure are shorthand for the actual formulas, such as (SHAPE OBJECT-A CYLINDRICAL) and (TEMPERATURE OBJECT-A HOT).

If an expression does not match in the current state, the unmatched conditions become subgoals. The system selects a subgoal to work on first, then selects a relevant operator (or inference rule), matches the preconditions against the database, and subgoals further if the match does not succeed. Any of these choices can be mediated by control rules, as described in section 3.4.

In our example, the first top-level goal (SHAPE OBJECT-A CYLINDRICAL) is not true in the initial state. To achieve this goal PRODIGY considers the operators LATHE and ROLL, since these operators add effects which unify with this goal. At this point PRODIGY arbitrarily decides to try ROLL first; there are no control rules which indicate otherwise. In order to satisfy the preconditions of ROLL, PRODIGY must infer that OBJECT-A is available and the machine is idle at the desired time. Assume that previously acquired control knowledge indicates a preference for the earliest possible time slot, time-2. After rolling the object at time-2, PRODIGY attempts to polish the object, but the preconditions of POLISH specify that the object must either be rectangular, or clamped to the polisher. Unfortunately, clamping fails, because rolling the object has raised its temperature so that it is too hot to clamp without deforming object or clamp. Since there is no way to make the object rectangular, the attempt to apply POLISH fails.

Backtracking, PRODIGY then tries rolling the object at time-3, and then time-4, and so on, until the end of the schedule is reached at time-20. Each of these attempts fails to produce a solution, because the object remains HOT (or cools down insufficiently, if the domain specification was a bit more realistic). As we will see, when learning is interleaved with problem solving, PRODIGY can reason about the failures and therefore backtrack more intelligently. In any event, the problem-solver finally succeeds when it eventually backs up and tries LATHING rather than ROLLING.

3.4. Control Rules

As PRODIGY attempts to solve a problem, it must make decisions about which operator to use and which subgoal to pursue. These decisions can be influenced by control rules for the following purposes:

1. *To increase the efficiency of the problem solver's search.* Control rules guide the problem solver down the correct path so that solutions are found faster.

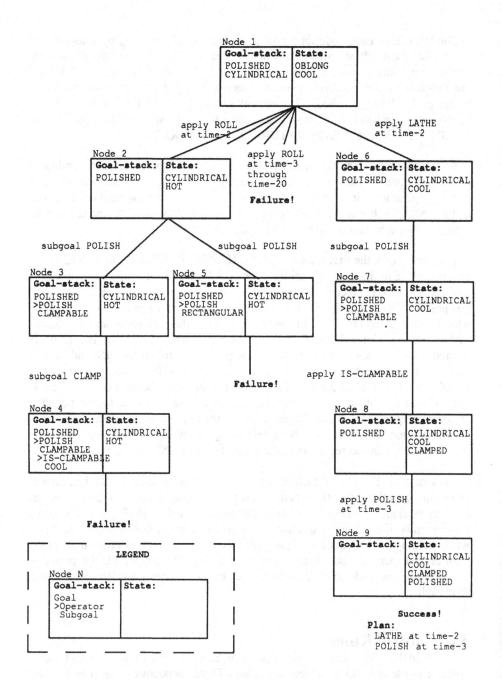

Figure 3-3: Search Tree for Scheduling Example

2. *To improve the quality of the solutions that are found.* There is usually more than one solution to a problem, but only the first one that is found will be returned. By directing the problem solver's attention along a particular path, control rules can express preferences for solutions that are qualitatively better (e.g., more reliable, less costly to execute, etc.).

3. *To direct the problem solver along paths that it would not explore otherwise.* As with most planners, for efficiency PRODIGY normally explores only a portion of the complete search space. This is accomplished through the use of default control rules. For example, PRODIGY will not normally explore all permutations of conjunctive sets of subgoals. However, when these default heuristics prove too restrictive, they can be selectively overridden by additional rules.

PRODIGY's reliance on explicit control rules, which can be learned for specific domains, distinguishes it from most domain independent problem solvers. Instead of using a least-commitment search strategy, for example, PRODIGY expects that any important decisions will be guided by the presence of appropriate control knowledge. If no control rules are relevant to a decision, then PRODIGY makes a quick, arbitrary choice. If in fact the wrong choice was made, and costly backtracking is necessary, an attempt will be made to learn the control knowledge that must be missing. The rationale for PRODIGY's *casual commitment* strategy is that control rules are expected to guide any decision with significant ramifications. Thus Prodigy's "cleverness" derives from learned or hand-coded control rules without incurring the overhead of weak domain-independent search strategies. For this reason, our emphasis is on a simple problem solving architecture which can produce sophisticated behavior when given the appropriate knowledge.

There are four types of decisions that PRODIGY makes during problem solving. First it must decide what node in the search tree to expand next; a depth-first expansion of the search tree is the default. Each node consists of a set of goals and a state describing the world. After a node has been picked, one of the node's goals must be selected, and then an operator relevant to this goal must be chosen. Finally, a set of bindings for the parameters of that operator must be decided upon.

Control rules can be employed to guide these four decisions. Each control rule has a left-hand side testing its applicability and a right-hand side indicating whether to SELECT, REJECT, or PREFER a particular candidate. For example, the control rule depicted in table 3-1 is a preference rule used in deciding which of the candidate operators at a node to attempt first. In this case the rules state that if ROLL and LATHE are candidate operators at the current node, ROLL should be preferred over LATHE.

To make a control decision, given a default set of candidates (nodes, goals, operators, or bindings, depending on the decision), PRODIGY first applies the applicable selection rules to select a subset of the candidates. (If no selection rules

```
IF  (AND  (CURRENT-NODE  node)
          (CURRENT-GOAL  node  (SHAPE  obj  shape))
          (CANDIDATE-OPERATOR  node  ROLL)
          (CANDIDATE-OPERATOR  node  LATHE))
THEN  (PREFER OPERATOR ROLL TO LATHE))
```

Table 3-1: An Operator Preference Rule

are applicable, all the candidates are included.) Next rejection rules further filter this set, and finally preference rules are used to order the remaining alternatives. The preferences among the remaining alternatives can be viewed as a directed graph. Cycles in the preference graph are ignored. (I.e., if A is preferred over B and B is preferred over A, then PRODIGY actually considers neither to be preferred over the other.) The most preferred candidate is a candidate over which no other candidate is preferred, after taking into account the rule for cycles. If backtracking is necessary, the next most preferred is attempted, and so on, until all candidates are exhausted.

Notice that the left-hand-side of the control rule is written in PDL, the same language as the preconditions for operators and inference rules, though different predicates are used. Meta-level predicates such as CURRENT-NODE and CANDIDATE-NODE are used in control-rules, whereas the predicates used in operators and inference rules are domain-level predicates, such as SHAPE and IDLE. A stock set of meta-level predicates is provided with PRODIGY.

```
IF  (AND  (CURRENT-NODE  node)
          (CURRENT-GOAL  node  (SHAPE  obj  shape))
          (CANDIDATE-OPERATOR  node  ROLL)
          (ADJUNCT-GOAL  node  (POLISHED  obj)))
THEN  (REJECT OPERATOR ROLL)
```

Table 3-2: An Operator Rejection Rule

Another example control rule is shown in table 3-2. This operator rejection rule states that if the current goal at a node is to reshape an object and the object must subsequently be polished, then we should reject the ROLL operator. Notice the use of the meta-level predicate ADJUNCT-GOAL; if a goal is an ADJUNCT-GOAL at a node, then it will be achieved after the current goal. (The adjunct goals at a node include the candidate goals that were not chosen to be the current goal.)

The example problem from the previous section illustrates why this rule is appropriate: polishing OBJECT-A after rolling it turned out to be impossible. Had the system previously learned this rule, the problem would have been solved directly, without the costly backtracking at Node1. In chapter 8, I will return to this example and show how this rule is learned by PRODIGY.

3.5. PRODIGY's Description Language (PDL)

There are several types of rules used in the PRODIGY system: operators, inference rules, search control rules and proof-schemas (which are used in the EBL system). However, all of the rules are essentially IF-THEN rules, and PRODIGY uses a single description language, PDL, to represent their left-hand sides. PDL is a form of predicate logic, and allows existential and universal quantification, conjunction, disjunction and negation. The next few sections describe the syntax and semantics of PDL, and how the language is actually used within the system.

3.5.1. Syntax

The syntactically legal expressions in PDL can be specified as follows:

- Every atomic formula is a legal expression.

- If $F_1, F_2...F_n$ are expressions, then so is their conjunction:

  (AND F_1, F_2 ... F_n)

  and their disjunction:

  (OR F_1, F_2 ... F_n)

- If F is an expression then so is its negation:

  (NOT F)

- If F is an expression, G is an atomic formula and (v_1 v_2...) is a list of variables then the following is a legal expression:

  (EXISTS (v_1 v_2...) SUCH-THAT G
      F)

  as well as:

  (FORALL (v_1 v_2...) SUCH-THAT G
      F)

3.6. Semantics

The following defines what it means for a PDL expression to match a state:

- An atomic formula matches iff there is a ground relation in the state that unifies with the formula.

- A conjunctive expression matches iff all of its conjuncts match the state.

- A disjunctive expression matches iff one or more of its disjuncts match the state.

- The negation of an expression matches iff the expression does not match the state.

- An existentially quantified expression consists of a list of variables, a generator expression and a subexpression. Such an expression matches iff there exists an assignment of values to each of the variables, such that both the generator expression and the subexpression match.

```
Example:
(EXISTS (obj time) SUCH-THAT (SCHEDULED obj POLISHER time)
    (AND (TEMPERATURE obj COOL)
        (SHAPE obj CYLINDRICAL)))
```

This expression matches iff there is an object scheduled to be POLISHED that is cool and cylindrical.

- A universally quantified expression consists of a list of variables, a generator expression and a subexpression. A universally quantified expression matches iff for all variable assignments such that the generator expression matches the state, the subexpression also matches the state.

```
Example:
(FORALL (obj time) SUCH-THAT (SCHEDULED obj POLISHER time)
    (AND (TEMPERATURE obj COOL)
        (SHAPE obj CYLINDRICAL)))
```

This expression matches iff all objects scheduled to be POLISHED are cool and cylindrical.

Normally, one defined the semantics of a language by describing what it means for an expression to be *true*. Here I have instead defined the semantics of PDL in terms of the primitive notion of *match*. The purpose is to avoid confusion between the internal state of the problem solver and the external state of the world. An expression can be *true* in the external world, but fail to *match* the internal state because the problem solver has not yet inferred the requisite knowledge. Thus, the semantics given above make it clear that we are always referring to the internal state of the problem solver when we use PDL as a description language.

3.6.1. The Role of Generators in PDL

In order to understand PDL, it is necessary to appreciate the role of generators in quantified expressions. Let us consider how PRODIGY actually determines whether an expression matches a state. PRODIGY matches an expression from top-to-bottom (or equivalently, left-to-right). Thus, when matching a quantified expression, PRODIGY first matches the generator, finding all possible sets of bindings (variable assignments) under which the generator is true. Then, for each set of bindings, PRODIGY tests whether the subexpression is true. If the quantifier is existential, PRODIGY must insure that at least one set of bindings satisfies the subexpression. If the quantifier is universal, the system must check that *all of the bindings* satisfy the subexpression.

The matching process can be regarded as a search, as described in the previous chapter. However, since PRODIGY's language is more complex than the simple conjunctive language described in the previous chapter, the "match tree" is an AND/OR tree, rather than a simple OR-TREE. To illustrate this, consider the expression shown below. The generators G1 and G2 generate values for x and y, respectively. (Notice that the values of y are dependent on the values for x.) All true relations with the predicates G1, G2, P and Q are also shown.

```
(EXISTS (x) SUCH-THAT (G1 x)
        (AND (P x)
             (FORALL (y) SUCH-THAT (G2 x y)
                 (Q y)))
```

Values for G1:
(G1 A)
(G1 B)
(G1 E)

Values for P:
(P A)
(P B)
(P C)

Values for G2:
(G2 A J)
(G2 A K)
(G2 A L)
(G2 B J)
(G2 D J)
(G2 D K)
(G2 E J)
(G2 E L)

Values for Q:
(Q G)
(Q H)
(Q I)
(Q J)
(Q K)
(Q M)
(Q N)

Figure 3-4 shows the AND/OR tree that is explored by the matcher. The paths emanating from the top-level node correspond to the values for x generated by G1. The top-level node is an OR-node, since x is existentially quantified. The children of the top-level node all test the conjunction (AND (P x)(FORALL....). They are AND-nodes, since both conjuncts must be true for the conjunction to be true. The diagram also indicates that the universally quantified expression (FORALL (y)..) creates an AND-node; the expression succeeds only if all the paths generated by G2 succeed.

In general OR-nodes correspond to existentially quantified expressions and disjunctions, while AND-nodes correspond to universally quantified statements and conjunctions. All leaf nodes correspond to atomic formulas. Negations simply reverse the result of the subtree of which they are the root.

If the match succeeds, the matcher returns all the sets of variable bindings under which the expression matches. This is a potential source of inefficiency, because in some applications it is sufficient to return only a single set of bindings. However, since the matcher does not know whether a given set of bindings will lead to a solution (even though the operator may be immediately applicable), it must return all bindings so that the problem solver can consider the full set of alternatives.

The matcher also returns a list of subgoals for each failed path in the tree. At the end of each failed path in the explored tree there will be an atomic formula that was determined to be false. This formula becomes a subgoal for the path. In addition

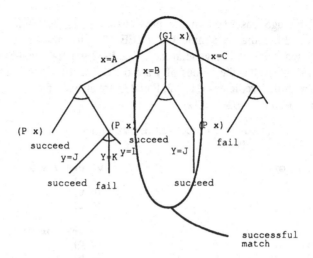

Figure 3-4: An AND/OR Match Tree

PRODIGY does a quick check for any other false formulas that would have shown up further down the path and these also become subgoals. Only fully instantiated formulas are considered; PRODIGY does not take the time to expand any more generators along the failed path, as this would be prohibitively expensive.

3.6.2. Extensions to PDL

There are two minor, but quite useful, extensions to the basic PDL language that enable complex expressions to be concisely formulated. The first extension allows existential quantification to be specified implicitly. Specifically, any existentially quantified expression that is not within the scope of a negation can be abbreviated as a conjunction. Thus the expression below, in which (P x) is the generator and (Q x) is the test, can be abbreviated as follows:

```
(EXISTS (x) SUCH-THAT (P x)
        (Q x))
goes to:
(AND (P x) (Q x))
```

Thus, the existential quantification of x is implicit.[10]

The second extension to the language is to add another form of quantifier, in addition to EXISTS and FORALL. The new quantifier, LET, is the same as EXISTS, except that the generator expression must always generate a single value. Thus, the following statement, which is true if OBJECT1 is hotter than 300 degrees,

---

[10]The scope of an implicitly quantified variable is *inside* the scope of an enclosing universally quantified statement iff all occurrences of that variable are physically within the statement. Generally the use of existential shorthand is avoided in such cases to avoid confusion.

can be rewritten as follows:

```
(EXISTS (tmp) SUCH-THAT (TEMPERATURE OBJECT1 x)
               (HOTTER x 300-DEGREES))
```

       goes to:

```
(LET (x) SUCH-THAT (TEMPERATURE OBJECT1 x)
          (HOTTER x 300-DEGREES))
```

This transformation is legal because every object has a unique temperature. The LET construct is used primarily for the benefit of the EBL module. It facilitates the simplification process that occurs after explanations have been formulated.

3.7. The Problem Solver's Control Structure in Detail

Previous sections in this chapter provided an overview of the problem solver's control structure. In this section, I describe the control structure in more detail.

A problem consists of an initial state and a goal expression. To solve a problem PRODIGY must find a sequence of operators and inference rules that produces a state satisfying the goal expression. (Henceforth in this chapter I use the term "operator" to refer to both inference rules and operators, since they are quite similar in form. In the rare case where it is necessary to distinguish the two, I will be explicit.) The search tree starts out as a single node. A node is defined by a state and a set of goals. The goals at the *top-level* (or root) node arise from matching the goal-expression given in the problem statement against the initial state. Note that *goals* are always literals -- atomic formulas or negated atomic formulas. (The term *goal expression* is reserved for an arbitrary expression that gives rise to goals in the matching process.)

As described previously, the tree is expanded by repeating a decision cycle that involves choosing a node, choosing a goal at that node, choosing an operator, and then choosing bindings for the operator. At this point, if the operator's preconditions are satisfied then the operator can be applied, generating a new node with a new state and fewer goals. Otherwise, PRODIGY subgoals on the preconditions, generating a new node with the same state and additional subgoals. (The goals are kept in a stack, as detailed in the following subsections.) Thus, in either case, a new node is created. The search terminates after creating a node with an empty set of goals (i.e., a node whose state satisfies the top-level goal expression).

As described earlier, each choice in the decision cycle is mediated by control rules. Initially there is a default set of candidates at a choice point. The control rules can indicate that a candidate should be selected, rejected, or preferred over another candidate.

3.7.1. Choosing a Node

When choosing a node, the default set of candidates are all the nodes in the search tree that have not yet been exhausted. (A node is completely exhausted when PRODIGY has explored all alternatives for achieving the goals at the node, and thus created all possible children for that node). If no control rules are applicable, PRODIGY chooses the last node that has been created. Thus depth-first search is the default strategy for exploring the search space.

3.7.2. Choosing a Goal

Once a node has been chosen, the next step is to determine a goal to work on. As was described earlier, each node comes with a default set of candidate goals. These are the unsatisfied atomic formulas found by the matcher as it attempted to match the preconditions of the operator at the parent node. (The root node of the search tree has no parent, and thus the candidate goals of the root node are determined by matching the top-level goal expression.)

3.7.3. Choosing an Operator

After choosing a current goal, a current operator must be chosen. The default set of candidates consists of all operators that are *relevant* to the goal. An operator is relevant to a goal if it has an effect that can produce the goal. We note that a goal is a literal, that is, either an atomic formula, or a negated atomic formula. If the goal is a positive literal (i.e., not negated), then the operator must have an added-effect that unifies with the goal in order to be relevant. If the goal is a negative literal (i.e., negated), the operator must have a deleted-effect that unifies with the goal.

An operator may have more than one effect that unifies with the goal. Unifying an effect with the goal produces a partial set of candidate bindings for the operator. The next step is to expand this set of bindings into a complete set of bindings.

3.7.4. Choosing a Set of Bindings for the Operator

Once a relevant operator has been chosen, a set of bindings for the operator must be chosen. The process of choosing the bindings for an operator is referred to as "instantiation". The bindings indicate values for the variables that are existentially quantified in the operator's preconditions. As indicated above, matching the operator's effects against the current goal generates alternative sets of partial bindings. For each set of partial bindings, PRODIGY calls the matcher and attempts to match the operator's preconditions. The matching process generates further candidate bindings for the operator, as well as subgoals necessary to achieve the preconditions under those bindings. For efficiency, the matcher examines the preconditions from top-to-bottom as previously described in section 3.6.1, rather than carrying out a complete partial match. Thus, as soon as the matcher discovers that a certain set of bindings requires subgoaling, it does not continue trying to extend those bindings into a complete set. (This is one reason why PRODIGY is not *complete* in the logical sense; because of this heuristic, there may be solutions to problems that PRODIGY cannot find.) Once all the candidate sets of bindings have been determined, PRODIGY will, in the absence of explicit preference rules, prefer those sets of bindings that do not require subgoaling.

```
(STACK (ob underob)
    (PRECONDS (AND (OBJECT ob)
                   (HOLDING ob)
                   (OBJECT underob)
                   (CLEAR underob)))
    (EFFECTS ((DEL (HOLDING ob))
              (DEL (CLEAR underob))
              (ADD (ARMEMPTY))
              (ADD (CLEAR ob))
              (ADD (ON ob underob))))))
```

Table 3-3: Blocksworld STACK operator

To clarify this, let us consider an example. The STACK operator, shown in table 3-3, is taken from the well known "blocksworld" domain. The initial state for our example problem is shown in figure 3-5. BLOCKA is being held, and BLOCKB is on BLOCKC. Let us assume that the goal is: (ARMEMPTY).

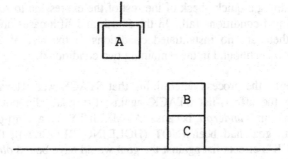

Figure 3-5: Initial State

STACK is relevant to the goal, since STACK adds the formula (ARMEMPTY). After determining that STACK is relevant, PRODIGY will attempt to match its preconditions. Matching the preconditions of STACK first generates an *ob* to be stacked, and then an *underob* than it will be stacked on. Specifically, the preconditions (OBJECT *ob*) and (OBJECT *underob*) generate the bindings for *ob* and *underob* respectively. The following five sets of bindings and their associated subgoals result from the matching process:

BINDINGS	SUBGOALS
1. ((*ob* BLOCKA) (*underob* BLOCKA)	(CLEAR BLOCKA)
2. ((*ob* BLOCKA) (*underob* BLOCKB)	none
3. ((*ob* BLOCKA) (*underob* BLOCKC)	(CLEAR BLOCKC)
4. ((*ob* BLOCKB))	(HOLDING BLOCKB)
5. ((*ob* BLOCKC))	(HOLDING BLOCKC)

The second set of bindings produces no subgoals, and therefore the operator can be immediately applied with this set of bindings. (In fact, the default strategy for choosing among candidate bindings is to prefer those that enable the operator to be immediately applied. However, just because the operator can be applied with this set of bindings does not guarantee that a global solution will be found. For example, if the goal expression had been (AND (ARMEMPTY) (CLEAR BLOCKB)), it would be necessary to use different bindings, even though (ARMEMPTY) can be immediately achieved by stacking BLOCKA on BLOCKB).

The fourth and fifth sets of bindings illustrate how the top-to-bottom operation of the matcher influences the binding process. After binding *ob* to BLOCKB, as in the fourth set of bindings, the matcher immediately fails on the condition (HOLDING BLOCKB), so no bindings are produced for *underob*. The same thing occurs in the fifth set of bindings, when the condition (HOLDING BLOCKC) fails. In general, the matcher stops exploring a path in the match tree as soon as a condition fails, and it returns that condition as a subgoal. Additional subgoals for that path are determined by doing a quick check of the rest of the expression to see whether any already instantiated conditions fail. In the fourth and fifth cases above, when the matcher fails there are no instantiated conditions in the rest of the expression (because *underob* is unbound in the remaining two conditions).

In this example, the process determining that STACK was relevant to the goal (.i.e., matching the effects-list STACK against the goal) did not generate any bindings for *ob* and *underob* because ARMEMPTY is a zero-place relation. However, if the goal had been (NOT (HOLDING BLOCKA)), the process of matching STACK's effects-list against the goal would have bound *ob* to BLOCKA. In this case, matching the preconditions would have generated only the first three alternatives shown above.

3.7.5. Creating a New Node

After a set of bindings for the current operator has been chosen, PRODIGY will create a new node, a child of the current node. This process of creating the child node varies slightly depending on whether the instantiated operator is applicable, or subgoaling is necessary. In the latter case, the following events take place:

1. The subgoals necessary to achieve the instantiated preconditions become the candidate goals for the child node.

2. The goal-stack for the child node is created by taking the parent node's goal-stack, and pushing the new goal that was selected (at the parent node) onto the stack.

3. The state of the child node is set equal to the state of the parent node.

4. PRODIGY checks to make sure that there is no goal cycle. A goal cycle occurs if one of the candidate goals for the child is subsumed (i.e., matched) by a goal on the goal stack. A goal cycle signals an infinite regress, and therefore if a goal cycle is detected, the child node is terminated and declared a failure.

If the instantiated operator that was chosen at the parent node can be applied (i.e., its preconditions match the current state) then the following events take place:

1. The candidate goals for the child node are determined by rematching the preconditions of the operator that generated the parent node. (I discuss this in more detail below.)

2. The goal-stack for the child node is created by popping the parent node's goal-stack.

3. The state of the child node is created by taking the parent node's state, and applying the instantiated operator.

4. PRODIGY checks to make sure that there is no state cycle. A state cycle occurs if the new state is equivalent to a state higher up in the tree (i.e., at one of the node's ancestors). A state cycle indicates that no progress has been made, and therefore if a state cycle is detected the child node is terminated and declared a failure.

As indicated above, after applying an operator the candidate goals for the child node are determined by rematching the preconditions (or the top-level goal-expression) that created the goals at the parent node. This is illustrated in the search tree (figure 3-3) for the scheduling example described earlier in this chapter. After the inference rule IS-CLAMPABLE is applied, the goal at Node8 is generated by popping the goal stack, and in effect, resetting the conditions that existed at Node6 without going through the usual decision cycle. In other words, PRODIGY does not bother to redo the work that was done at Node6 in selecting the goal (SURFACE-CONDITION OBJECT-A POLISHED), the operator POLISH, and the bindings for POLISH, since these decisions are still valid at Node8. Node8 is referred to as a *clone* of Node6, since the context at Node6 is identical to that at Node8 (except that the state has changed). In fact, PRODIGY's user-interface displays the search tree in a manner that emphasizes the relationship between clones by folding the tree into an AND/OR tree. A detailed description of the structure of PRODIGY's search tree is given in the PRODIGY manual [52].

3.8. Domains

In this book, the examples are taken from four domains: the blocksworld domain, the machine shop scheduling domain described earlier in this chapter, an extension of the simple robot planning domain used by STRIPS [25], and a complex "3-D gridworld" robot planning domain. Their specifications are given in the appendix.

The blocksworld domain consists of four operators, UNSTACK, STACK, PICKUP and PUTDOWN. For PRODIGY and similar domain-independent problem solvers [65], solving problems in this domain without control knowledge is surprisingly difficult, in part because the problem space is highly exponential. Of course, other specifications for the domain can be created in which the problem space does not have an exponential structure. In fact, small changes in the specification of any domain can have significant repercussions on the problem solver's performance. In the blocksworld, for example, one can add the condition (NOT (EQUAL ob underob)) to the STACK operator (shown in both table 3-3 and appendix I.3), so that the problem solver will never consider stacking a block on itself (which it has a tendency to do). This is actually an obtuse way of encoding control knowledge in the domain specification; is was no way an object could be stacked on itself anyway since (HOLDING ob) and (CLEAR ob) can never be simultaneously true. With the additional precondition in the STACK operator, when a subgoal such as (ON BLOCKA BLOCKA) arises PRODIGY will immediately realize that it cannot be achieved. In contrast, with the original specification the problem solver might spend a long time exploring all ways to achieve (HOLDING ob) and (CLEAR ob) before concluding that the goal is unachievable. By learning control knowledge PRODIGY can overcome such difficulties.

The machine shop scheduling domain is a version of the many-object, many-machine scheduling problem. Although the domain specification has been simplified so that objects have only a small number of properties, the domain illustrates the range of problems that PRODIGY can handle. Furthermore, this domain has the desirable characteristic of being non-spatial. The other three domains are primarily spatial, and thus to humans appear quite simple.

The extended STRIPS domain includes the operators from the original STRIPS domain for moving a robot through rooms and pushing boxes. The domain has been augmented with operators for picking up objects and locking and unlocking doors, which makes the problems somewhat more challenging.

The 3-D gridworld domain is by far the most complex of the three domains and is primarily used for demonstration purposes. In this domain, the world is represented by a finite 3-D grid containing a robot and a set of objects with fixed orientations. The robot can pick up, move and climb onto objects. Almost all problems within this domain (which typically involve moving the robot and/or objects into particular locations) are completely intractable without control knowledge. Writing control knowledge for this domain is challenging; a human programmer, after a month of full-time work, produced an incomplete set of control rules which only enabled a small subset of problems in the domain to be solved. Typically, if the problem solver diverges from the solution path it becomes completely lost. In fact, the problem solver was once accidently run for several hours on a gridworld problem, and when the user returned, 27,000 nodes had been generated, the Lisp system had eaten up an enormous amount of space, and the problem solver was no nearer the solution.

3.9. Advanced Features

The PRODIGY system includes a variety of additional capabilities that enhance it's flexibility and useability. Since most of these are only of tangential importance in so far as this book is concerned, I mention them only briefly.

3.9.1. Complex Descriptions

The scheduling domain has been somewhat simplified in order to enhance the readability of the examples. For example, the shape of an object is represented by a simple atom, such as CYLINDRICAL. Thus, for example, one indicates that object PART1 is cylindrical as follows: (SHAPE PART1 CYLINDRICAL). However, it is perfectly legal to have relations over complex data-structures as well as over atoms. Thus a more realistic description of the shape of PART1 might be: (SHAPE PART1 [CYLINDRICAL [LENGTH 3] [WIDTH 5]]). In this case, the shape is represented by a complex data-structure, [CYLINDRICAL [LENGTH 3] [WIDTH 5]] rather than a simple atom. Given this representation of a shape, to break out a field such as the width one would use a static relation such as "IS-WIDTH", which would be implemented by a function in PRODIGY. Thus, for example, one would test whether the width of an object is less that 7 as follows:

```
(AND (SHAPE obj shpe)
     (IS-WIDTH wdth shpe)
     (LESS-THAN wdth 7))
```

Other, more complex, PRODIGY domains (such as the gridworld domain described in appendix I) freely make use of this capability.

3.9.2. Negated Goals and Goals with Variables

To achieve an expression, PRODIGY first attempts to match the expression in the current state. As described earlier, this process can give rise to new goals (subgoals) if the expression does not match. As stated earlier, goals are arbitrary literals. Thus the matching process may give rise to goals that are negated, and they may have variables. For example, legal goals in the scheduling domain include:

```
(ON x BLOCKA)
(NOT (ON BLOCKA BLOCKB))
(NOT (ONTABLE x))
```

The first goal is true in any state where there is a block on BLOCKA. The second goal is true in any state where BLOCKA is not ON BLOCKB. The third goal is true in any state where no block is on the table.

3.9.3. Reason Maintenance

The PRODIGY system includes a simple reason maintenance system that keeps track of the justifications for any inferences that are made [20, 24]. Whenever an inference rule is applied, PRODIGY not only adds the inferred formula to the state, but also records the primitive (i.e., closed-world) relations that enabled the rule to fire. These primitive relations are referred to as the justifications for the inference.

In contrast, when an operator (as opposed to an inference rule) is applied, PRODIGY creates a new state by transferring all of the primitive relations in the old state to the new state, after adding and deleting the relations indicated by the operator's effects. The reason maintenance subsystem then examines each inferred relation in the old state in order to determine whether it can be transferred to the new state. If the justifications for the inferred relation are true in the new state, then the inferred relation is also true in the new state. However, if any of its justifications have been deleted by the operator, the inferred relation cannot be transferred over. (It may or may not be true in the new state, there is no way of knowing.)

3.9.4. Negated Effects in Inference Rules

As described earlier, operators may add and delete assertions while inference rules may only add assertions. Suppose we want PRODIGY to produce a state in which (NOT (P A)) is true. If P is a primitive (i.e., closed-world) predicate, then PRODIGY can use an operator which deletes P. However, if P is a defined predicate (added by inference rules) then no operator can explicitly delete P. In some systems, one method for inferring negated expressions is to show that no rule sequence can produce the expression. This method, commonly referred to as "negation by failure" is well-known, but it cannot be used in this case because it would presume that if something cannot be inferred, it is false. As an alternative, PRODIGY allows the user to write inference rules that explicitly add negative literals. For example, the inference rule shown below might be used in the scheduling world to infer that a machine is not idle.

```
(INFER-NOT-IDLE mach time)
    (PRECONDITIONS (SCHEDULED obj mach time))
    (EFFECTS ((ADD (NOT (IDLE mach time))))))
```

3.9.5. Meta-Predicates

PRODIGY has a standard set of meta-predicates that can be used in the left-hand side of control rules. These include predicates, such as CURRENT-NODE and CURRENT-GOAL, that describe the choices PRODIGY has made in the current decision cycle, as well as other similar predicates that are used to describe the current status of the problem solver. The following are the commonly used meta-predicates that are referred to in the examples in this book:

(CURRENT-NODE *node*)
(CURRENT-GOAL *node goal*)
(CURRENT-OP *node op*)
(CURRENT-BINDINGS *node bindings*) *node*

These are used to test whether a candidate has been chosen in the current decision phase.

(CANDIDATE-NODE *node*)
(CANDIDATE-GOAL *node goal*)
(CANDIDATE-OP *node op*)
(CANDIDATE-BINDINGS *node bindings*)

These test whether a value is among the current candidate set of candidates at a decision point.

(KNOWN *node expression*)

This tests if an expression is known at a node. The matcher is called to match the *expression* at the *node*.

(ADJUNCT-GOAL *node goal*)

An adjunct goal at a node is a goal that was a candidate at some higher level node but not chosen. (Thus the adjunct goal will be achieved after the chosen goal.)

(ON-GOAL-STACK *node goal*)

Tests whether a goal is on the goal stack at a node.

(IS-TOP-LEVEL-GOAL *node goal*)

Tests whether *goal* is a top-level-goal (an unsatisfied goal from the original goal expression in the problem statement).

(IS-EQUAL *x y*)
(NOT-EQUAL *x y*)

Tests for equality and inequality.

The system includes other meta-predicates, including some that the learning system does not currently take advantage of but that may be useful for users writing their own control rules. These include PROVABLE and ACHIEVABLE, which test whether an arbitrary expression is true or achievable (respectively) in the current state. Both of these predicates operate by invoking PRODIGY recursively.

In addition, the user can write his own meta-predicates in Lisp, although this may interfere with the learning mechanism. Therefore, I assume that the user does not make use of this capability.

3.9.6. Conditional Effects

The effects-list of an operator can specify that an effect occurs only under certain circumstances when the operator is applied. A conditional ADD is specified as shown below, and DELETEs are handled analogously:

```
(OPERATOR-NAME
    (PRECONDITIONS ...)
    (EFFECTS ....
        (IF expression (ADD formula))
        ....)
```

A conditional ADD specifies the formula should only be added (to the current state) if the expression is true when the operator is applied. If there are multiple ways to bind the variables in the expression, then multiple formulas will be added. An example of an operator with conditional effects is shown below:

```
(BLOW-UP (bomb)
    (PRECONDITIONS ((TRIGGERED bomb))
    (EFFECTS ((ADD (DESTROYED bomb)
                  (IF (AND (IS-OBJECT x)
                           (NEAR x bomb))
                      (ADD (DESTROYED x))))))
```

When the operator BLOW-UP is applied, the bomb is destroyed, as well as *all* objects that are near the bomb.

3.9.7. Interleaving Goals

One of the drawbacks of the original STRIPS architecture is that the problem solver solves only one goal at a time, to the exclusion of other goals. For example, let us suppose that STRIPS was given the task of delivering packages A and B to Pittsburgh. Package A is initially in San Francisco, and Package B is initially in Los Angeles. The relevant operators are "take-plane", "deliver-package" etc. STRIPS would never consider flying to San Francisco, then to Los Angeles and then to Pittsburgh. Instead, because it only works on one goal at a time, it would only consider flying to San Francisco, delivering package A in Pittsburgh, then flying to Los Angeles, and delivering Package B in Pittsburgh.

In general, because STRIPS is limited to solving one goal at a time, it will miss certain solutions to problems. In fact, there will be some problems it will not be able to solve at all. (Sussman's anomaly [83] falls into this category). Thus this limitation is one source of *incompleteness* in STRIPS. Control rules can overcome this limitation in PRODIGY. For example, by selecting goals that are not normally candidate goals, PRODIGY can effectively interleave goals. To return to our package delivering task, after electing to fly to San Francisco, but before considering how to return to Pittsburgh, a control rule can divert attention to the goal of delivering the Los Angeles package. By interleaving goals, PRODIGY can operate similarly to non-linear planners. Much of the cost of non-linear planning can be avoided if the requisite control rules are domain-specific. However, this capability has just begun to be investigated within the PRODIGY system, and as it is not directly considered in this book, I will forego further discussion of this topic.

3.9.8. User-Interface

One of the goals of the PRODIGY project is to improve the interface between the domain expert and the machine so that the domain expert can understand the problem solving process, provide advice, and correct and/or refine the domain specification. In contrast to several earlier learning apprentice systems [56, 66] PRODIGY is not intended to be a passive apprentice that merely "watches over the expert's shoulder". Instead, the expert can interact with the system when necessary so that learning may also occur in a more directed manner. Although the goal of the system is to minimize the burden on the expert, one should not be misled into believing that a passive learning system necessarily achieves this goal best. Generally the expert is interested in bringing the system up to speed as quickly and painlessly as possible. Exploiting the master-apprentice relationship to the fullest extent enables the learning process to be more focused, and of course subsumes passive observation if the expert does not provide any direct interaction.

In practice, having a good user-interface is crucial to taking full advantage of the master-apprentice relationship. To increase the communication bandwidth between the program and a teacher, the user-interface includes the following features:

- An optional graphics module that shows a picture of the changing state of the world as PRODIGY solves a problem.

- A package for printing a trace of the system as it is running.

- An interactive analysis facility that enables the teacher to view the search tree, ask questions about control decisions, and offer advice. The analysis facility can be invoked either during a problem solving episode by interrupting the problem solver, or after a solution is returned.

- An interface to the learning sub-system that enables the expert, if he so desires, to specify what aspect of the search tree the learning should focus on. Similarly the learning system can ask the expert what to explore when there are too many possibilities.

- The capability for the expert to refine domain or control knowledge as the result of observing a problem solving run.

In the machine-shop example described earlier, the expert (i.e., the teacher) could have observed the system's behavior by watching the graphics facility, watching the trace of the run, or invoking the analysis facility. If the analysis facility was invoked during the run, he could have advised PRODIGY to try LATHING as opposed to ROLLING. Finally, he could have advised the learning system to analyze why ROLLING failed. In this case, the example is so simple that, as shown in chapter 10, the learning system is perfectly capable of analyzing this problem completely (in a reasonable time period) without the expert's help. However, the results reported in chapter 10 also indicate that learning proceeds more quickly if the system is first presented with small examples that focus its attention on isolated control problems. The user-interface is designed so that the expert will have a better grasp of the state of the problem solver's knowledge, and thus enable him to provide appropriate tutoring.

4. Specialization

We now turn our attention to the actual mechanics of explanation-based learning in PRODIGY. This chapter and the following two will describe the learning process in terms of its components: specialization, compression, and utility evaluation.

Explanation-based learning can be viewed as a method for specializing a target concept description in order to produce a more efficient or operational description. The specialization process is carried out by explaining why a particular example satisfies the target concept description. In PRODIGY, a module called the OBSERVER is responsible for specializing the target concept. It is the OBSERVER's task to scan the problem solving trace for examples of PRODIGY's target concepts. When it finds an example of a target concept, the OBSERVER invokes an algorithm called EBS to explain why the example satisfies the target concept definition. By keeping track of the premises of the explanation, the OBSERVER can construct a specialized description of the target concept. The other two modules of the EBL subsystem, the COMPRESSOR and the MONITOR, are then responsible for simplifying the learned description (in order to reduce its match cost) and evaluating the utility of the learned description. Figure 4-1 shows a schematic view of the EBL subsystem and its relationship to the problem solver.

The following sections describe how target concepts are specified and how the OBSERVER selects examples of target concepts. In addition, the EBS algorithm is described in detail and illustrated by an example.

4.1. Target Concepts

Currently, for each of the four search control decisions that PRODIGY can make (i.e., choosing a node, goal, operator, or bindings, as described in the previous chapter), there are four target concepts: SUCCESS, FAILURE, SOLE-ALTERNATIVE, and GOAL-INTERFERENCE. (Thus there are sixteen individual

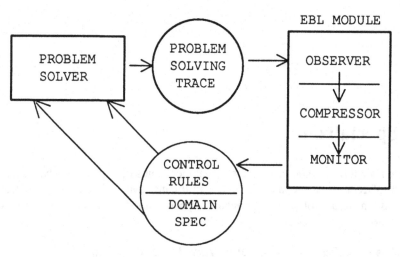

Figure 4-1: Schematic of the PRODIGY/EBL System

target concepts available.[11]) In general, a control choice is said to *succeed* if it leads to a solution. Similarly, a choice *fails* if there is no solution to be found along that path. A choice is a *sole alternative* if all other alternatives fail. Finally, a choice results in *goal-interference* if either a previously achieved goal is undone, or a previously satisfied precondition of a subsequent action in the plan is undone. The table below indicates the type of control rule that the system learns from each target concept type.

Target Concept Type	Control Rule Type
Succeeds	preference rule
Fails	rejection rule
Sole-alternative	selection rule
Goal-interference	preference rule

Individual target concepts are described to the system using a declarative *target concept specification*. For example, the target concept specification for OPERATOR-FAILS is shown in table 4-1. The specification includes a template for building the resulting control rules, the name of a recognizer-function for identifying examples of the concept in the search tree, and other relevant information.

Each of the system's target concepts corresponds to a strategy for optimizing problem solving performance. The initial set of target concepts is not intended to be

---

[11]Not all of these are actually used in the implementation. As described in chapter 8, NODE-IS-SOLE-ALTERNATIVE is not a useful target concept. NODE-SUCCEEDS and NODE-CAUSES-GOAL-INTERFERENCE are only used for intermediate results, since the current version of PRODIGY does not correctly handle node preference rules. Finally BINDINGS-IS-SOLE-ALTERNATIVE is not implemented due to the complexity of writing the requisite theory.

complete in any sense. It simply represents one particular set of learning strategies. The set of target concepts is extensible, so that additional target concepts can be included in the system as they are needed. For example, in certain planning domains it may be worthwhile to learn about advantageous goal interactions that can occur when goals are interleaved. The addition of this target concept would complement the present strategy of learning to avoid disadvantageous goal interactions.

```
Target Concept: (OPERATOR-FAILS op goal node)
Example Recognizer: (PICK-OUT-OP-FAILURES node)
Example Selection Heuristics: (.......)
Rule Construction Template:
    IF (AND (CURRENT-NODE node)
            (CURRENT-GOAL node goal)
            (CANDIDATE-OPERATOR op node)
            (OPERATOR-FAILS op goal node))
    THEN (REJECT OPERATOR op)
```

Table 4-1: Target Concept Specification for OPERATOR-FAILS

4.2. Scanning the Search Tree for Examples

Explanation-based learning can be employed after the problem solver has terminated, or it may be interleaved with problem solving. In either case, it is the OBSERVER's task to examine the explored search tree and select instances of the target concept to serve as training examples. Once the OBSERVER has selected an example, it employs the EBS algorithm to specialize the target concept definition in accordance with the example. As the specialization proceeds, the COMPRESSOR is called to simplify the explanation, and when this process is completed the newly learned description is cast as a search control rule by the MONITOR. The OBSERVER then selects another target concept and training example, and the process repeats until a fixed time limit is exceeded, or the search tree has been fully analyzed.

The OBSERVER normally selects training examples by carrying out a bottom-up, or *postorder* traversal of the search tree: children are analyzed before parents, from left to right in the search tree. Bottom-up processing is used because the analysis of a node is frequently dependent on the analysis of nodes below it, and due to limited time, PRODIGY may not have the opportunity to examine the entire tree (which may consist of thousands of nodes). Because the learning process begins at the leaves of the tree and works upwards, improvement on subsequent runs will occur even if the learning process must be terminated (due to time constraints) before the entire tree can be examined.

To recognize instances of target concepts in the search tree, PRODIGY employs a set of functions called *example-recognizers*. Each target concept is associated with an example-recognizer, which takes a node in the search tree and identifies any instances of the target concept that occurred at the node. The name of the example-recognizer is indicated in the target concept specification.

After recognizing a potential training example, PRODIGY then uses *training example selection heuristics* to eliminate uninteresting examples. For example, a selection heuristic may indicate that an example of OPERATOR-SUCCEEDS is interesting only if the problem solver had first tried another operator that failed at that node (such as at Node1 in the scheduling example shown in figure 3-3 of the previous chapter.) In essence, these heuristics, which are domain independent but target concept specific, pre-select the examples based on the expected utility of the rules that they would produce. Each target concept specification lists the relevant training example selection heuristics. The heuristics are procedurally encoded.

The normal method of examining the search tree can be altered by an expert when the system is running as a learning apprentice (see chapter 3, section 3.9.8). The expert can request that the learning system focus its attention on a particular section of the tree, or even specify that the system focus on a particular target concept or training example.

4.3. Constructing an Explanation: The EBS Method

PRODIGY creates search control rules by explaining why a target concept definition is satisfied by a training example. In order to construct explanations, it is necessary to have a theory describing the architecture of the problem solver, as well as a theory that describes the task domain (such as our machine-shop world). Therefore, PRODIGY contains a set of hand-coded *architecture-level* axioms that serve as its theory of the problem solver, and a set of *domain-level* axioms that are automatically derived from the domain specification. Together, these sets of axioms are referred to as *proof schemas*. Each proof schema is a conditional (whose left-hand side is written in PDL) that describes when a concept (i.e., an atomic formula) is true.[12] Table 4-2 shows several proof schemas used for specializing OPERATOR-SUCCEEDS.

The domain-level proof schemas define concepts in terms of the effects and preconditions of the operators, inference rules, and control rules in the domain.[13] The architectural-level schemas define concepts in terms of the more primitive domain-level schemas. For example, the schemas for OPERATOR-SUCCEEDS state that an operator *op* succeeds in solving goal *g* at node *n* if the operator directly

---

[12]For correctness of the learning algorithm, the concept described by each schema must be represented by an atomic formula with no constants, and each variable in the formula must occur at most once. This does not limit expressiveness, since any relevant restrictions can be included in the "if" part of the schema. A correctness proof is outlined in chapter 11.

[13]The set of domain-level schemas grows as new control rules are added to the domain.

ARCHITECTURE-LEVEL SCHEMAS:

Schema-S1: An operator succeeds if it directly solves the goal.
```
(OPERATOR-SUCCEEDS op goal node)
if (AND (MATCHES-EFFECT goal op)
        (APPLICABLE op node))
```

Schema-S2: An operator succeeds if it succeeds after a precursor operator is applied.
```
(OPERATOR-SUCCEEDS op goal node)
if (AND (APPLICABLE pre-op node)))
        (OPERATOR-SUCCEEDS op goal child-node)
        (CHILD-NODE-AFTER-APPLYING-OP child-node pre-op node)))
```

DOMAIN-LEVEL SCHEMAS:

Schema-D1: POLISH is applicable if its preconditions are satisfied
```
(APPLICABLE op node)
if (AND (MATCHES-OP op (POLISH obj time)
        (KNOWN node (AND (IS-OBJECT obj)
                         (OR (SHAPE obj RECTANGULAR)
                             (CLAMPABLE obj POLISHER))
                         (LAST-SCHEDULED obj prev-time)
                         (LATER time prev-time)
                         (IDLE POLISHER time)))
```

Schema-D2: IS-CLAMPABLE is applicable if its preconditions are satisfied.
```
(APPLICABLE op node)
if (AND (MATCHES-OP op (CLAMP obj time mach))
        (KNOWN node (AND (HAS-CLAMP mach)
                         (TEMPERATURE obj COLD)))
```

Schema-D3: An effect of the operator POLISH is that the object is polished.
```
(MATCHES-EFFECT goal op)
if (AND (MATCHES-OP op (POLISH obj time))
        (MATCHES goal (SURFACE-CONDITION obj POLISHED)))
```

Table 4-2: Illustrative Proof Schemas for Specializing OPERATOR-SUCCEEDS

solves the goal (i.e., the operator has an effect which unifies with the goal), or applying another operator results in a node at which the operator succeeds in solving the goal.

PRODIGY does not create an explicit explanation structure. Instead, the system recursively expands the weakest preconditions of an (implicit) explanation, using a method we refer to as *Explanation-based Specialization* (EBS).A target concept is specialized by retrieving a proof schema that describes the concept, and recursively specializing the formulas in the schema. The recursion terminates upon encountering primitive concepts -- concepts that are not described by any proof schemas. For efficiency, the specialization process is interleaved with simplification, which is described in the next chapter.

When there is more than one schema that describes a concept (i.e. the concept is disjunctively defined) as is the case with OPERATOR-SUCCEEDS, the system selects a proof schema that is consistent with the training example. (In other words, a schema that describes why the training example is a valid instance of the concept). To find the appropriate schema we allow each concept to be associated with a *discriminator* function which examines the search tree and selects a schema corresponding to the example. Thus, there is no search involved in the EBS algorithm; the construction of the initial explanation can be viewed as a purely knowledge-based process.

The actual EBS algorithm is described in table 4-3. The algorithm initially starts with a formula representing some target concept. Specialization is accomplished as follows. If the formula is a conjunction or existential, its subformulas are recursively specialized and simplified by EBS. If the formula is atomic, and not primitive, then EBS retrieves a proof schema consistent with the training example (as described above), and recursively processes the schema. If the formula is a negation, EBS simply returns the formula unchanged. (Recursively specializing the internal formula would generalize the formula as a whole, leading to an incorrect, overgeneral result.) The case for a universally quantified formula is slightly more complicated because the generator produces multiple training examples for the body of the formula. Therefore, for each of the training examples produced by the generator, PRODIGY recursively calls EBS on the body of the formula. The result is that the body of the formula is replaced by the disjunction of the specializations.

After the EBS process terminates, we are left with a learned description that is a specialization of the target concept. The EBS process has created the learned description by recursively expanding a proof tree -- the "explanation". The learned description represents the weakest conditions under which the explanation holds (as discussed further in chapter 11). At this point, a search control rule can be constructed by filling in the *rule construction template* given in the target concept specification. This is a simply a matter of replacing the target concept in the template with the learned description.

4.3.1. EBS and Bias

In inductive learning, the notion of *bias* refers to the (often implicit) preference used by the learning program to select a particular candidate generalization when there is a set of generalizations that are consistent with all the observed instances [59, 87]. The term is equally relevant when discussing explanation-based learning, since a range of generalizations are possible given a single instance and a target concept definition. The bias in an explanation-based system shows up when the system selects a particular level of generality to express an explanation. The most general explanation would be identical to the target concept definition. The

Procedure **EBS** specializes a formula with respect to an example:

- If the formula is an existential formula,(EXISTS (x_1...) SUCH-THAT generator body), then return:

  (EXISTS (x_1...) SUCH-THAT (EBS generator generator-example)
    (EBS body body-example))

- If the formula is a universal formula, (FORALL (x_1...) SUCH-THAT generator body), then there will be a set of examples for the body of the expression, one for each set of bindings that satisfies the generator expression. For each of these sub-examples, specialize the body of the expression. Replace the body of the expression with the disjunction of these specializations. Return the result:

  (FORALL (x_1...) SUCH-THAT generator
    (OR (EBS body body-example$_1$)
        (EBS body body-example$_2$) ...))

- If the formula is a conjunctive formula, (AND F1 F2...), then specialize each conjunct accordingly, and return the result:

  (AND (EBS F1 F1-example) (EBS F2 F2-example)....)

- If the formula is a disjunctive formula, (OR F1 F2...), then specialize the first disjunct that succeeded, e.g. F2, and return the result: (EBS F2 F2-example)

- If the formula is a negative formula, (NOT F), then return the formula unchanged: (NOT F)

- If the formula is atomic and primitive, (P...), then return the formula unchanged: (P ...)

- If the formula is atomic and not primitive, (P...)

  1. Call the discriminator function associated with the predicate P to retrieve a schema consistent with the training example. The schema will be a conditional of the form: (P x_1 x_2...) if Schema-Body

  2. Replace the variables x_1, x_2... with the corresponding values in the formula.

  3. Uniquely rename all other variables in Schema-Body.

  Return the result: (EBS Schema-Body Schema-Body-example)

Table 4-3: The EBS Method

most specific would explain the example, and only the example. EBL systems generally produce an explanation that lies somewhere between these extremes, in an attempt to maximize generality and efficiency.

The generality of the explanations produced by EBS is primarily determined by the proof schemas. In particular, the bias depends on which concepts are primitive and which concepts are disjunctively defined (i.e. described by more than one proof schema). For example, one can increase the specificity of the explanations by taking a primitive concept and defining it in terms of several lower level schemas. Thus, when an explanation is produced, this concept will be specialized by one of the newly introduced schemas. The disjunction effectively partitions the concept into more specific concepts. Because the bias of resulting explanations is determined by the choice of proof schemas, we can view the EBS process as a knowledge-based learning method.

4.4. EBS: An Example

Let us return to our scheduling example from chapter 3 to illustrate how the OBSERVER operates. The rightmost path of the search tree depicted in figure 3-3 shows the operators and inference rules that succeeded in producing a solution.

The following example shows how PRODIGY would explain why applying the POLISH operator at Node8 was appropriate. The explanation can then be extended to explain why the operators preceding POLISH were useful. The target concept and training example are given below.

```
Target concept:
  (OPERATOR-SUCCEEDS op goal node),
Training example:
  (OPERATOR-SUCCEEDS POLISH (SURFACE-CONDITION OBJECT-A POLISHED) NODE8)
```

To explain why the POLISH operator was successful, PRODIGY will specialize the concept OPERATOR-SUCCEEDS. In this case, since POLISH directly solved the goal, the system begins by retrieving Schema-S1 in table 4-2, the schema consistent with the training example. The system then recursively specializes the subconcepts APPLICABLE, and MATCHES-EFFECT as shown below. The specializations performed at each step are indicated by underlining.

```
Target concept: (OPERATOR-SUCCEEDS op goal node)

Specialize (OPERATOR-SUCCEEDS op goal node) using Schema-S1:

 (AND (MATCHES-EFFECT goal op)
      (APPLICABLE op node))

Specialize (MATCHES-EFFECT goal op) using Schema-D3:

   (AND (AND (MATCHES-OP op (POLISH obj-x time-x))
             (MATCHES goal (SURFACE-CONDITION obj-x POLISHED)))
        (APPLICABLE op node))

Specialize (APPLICABLE op node) using Schema-D1:

   (AND (AND (MATCHES-OP op (POLISH obj-x time-x))
             (MATCHES goal (SURFACE-CONDITION obj-x POLISHED))
        (AND (MATCHES-OP op (POLISH obj-y time-y))
             (KNOWN node (AND (IS-OBJECT obj-y)
                               (OR (SHAPE obj-y RECTANGULAR)]
                                   (CLAMPABLE obj-y POLISHER))
                              (LAST-SCHEDULED obj-y time-z)
                              (LATER time-y time-z)
                              (IDLE POLISHER time-y))))
```

The key points during this process are the specializations of APPLICABLE and MATCHES-EFFECT, both of which are disjunctive concepts. The appropriate specializations are determined by discriminator functions which retrieve the schemas consistent with the training example.

After some trivial simplifications performed by the system the specialized concept is re-expressed as follows:

```
(OPERATOR-SUCCEEDS op goal node)
if (AND (IS-EQUAL op POLISH)
        (MATCHES goal (POLISHED obj))
        (KNOWN node (AND (IS-OBJECT obj-y)
                          (OR (SHAPE obj RECTANGULAR)
                              (CLAMPABLE obj POLISHER))
                         (LAST-SCHEDULED obj time-z)
                         (LATER time-x time-z)
                         (IDLE POLISHER time-x))))
```

This expression simply states that an operator succeeds in solving a goal at a node if the operator is POLISH, the goal is to have an object's surface condition polished, and the preconditions of POLISH are known to be satisfied at the node. (An expression is KNOWN at a node if it matches the state at that node.)

Let us continue with our example and demonstrate how this result serves as a lemma explaining why inferring that OBJECT-A is CLAMPABLE at Node7 enabled the subsequent application of POLISH.

```
Target concept:
  (OPERATOR-SUCCEEDS op goal node),
Training example:
  (OPERATOR-SUCCEEDS POLISH (SURFACE-CONDITION OBJECT-A POLISHED) NODE7)
```

As is evident from the search tree, applying IS-CLAMPABLE at node7 was necessary to achieve the CLAMPABLE precondition of POLISHED.[14] Therefore, when the system specializes OPERATOR-SUCCEEDS, Schema-S2 (the recursive proof-schema for OPERATOR-SUCCEEDS) is retrieved:

```
(AND (APPLICABLE pre-op node)
     (OPERATOR-SUCCEEDS op goal child-node)
     (CHILD-NODE-AFTER-APPLYING-OP child-node pre-op node)))
```

First, APPLICABLE is specialized by a domain-level schema specifying that the preconditions of IS-CLAMPABLE must be known at *node*. Next, OPERATOR-SUCCEEDS is specialized by replacing it with our lemma after making appropriate variable substitutions. (Lemmas are essentially cached results which are used whenever the system has previously specialized a target concept with an identical training instance.) Finally, specializing CHILD-NODE-AFTER-APPLYING-OP identifies the effects that were added by IS-CLAMPABLE, enabling the simplifier to eliminate the constraints on *node*. (This last specialization accomplishes the "backpropagation" of constraints that has been a familiar aspect of earlier EBL work [86].) The resulting expression states that POLISH will eventually succeed when the preconditions of the sequence <IS-CLAMPABLE, POLISH> are satisfied:

```
(OPERATOR-SUCCEEDS op goal node)
if (AND (IS-EQUAL op POLISH)
        (KNOWN node (AND (IS-OBJECT obj-y)
                         (TEMPERATURE obj-y COOL)
                         (HAS-CLAMP POLISHER)
                         (LAST-SCHEDULED obj time-z)
                         (LATER time-x time-z)
                         (IDLE POLISHER time-x)))))]
        (MATCHES goal (POLISHED obj)))
```

This result can in turn be used to explain that LATHE is appropriate when the sequence <LATHE, IS-CLAMPABLE, POLISH> is applicable and the goal is to polish an object and make it cylindrical. However, having illustrated the EBS process, we will go no further. It is sufficient to point out that these results can be trivially transformed into operator-preference control rules.

---

[14]Although IS-CLAMPABLE is an inference rule, as we have previously indicated, PRODIGY's control structure does not distinguish between inference rules and operators, and therefore the success of IS-CLAMPABLE is treated as an instance of OPERATOR-SUCCEEDS.

4.5. Utility Issues

As I have previously emphasized, the rules produced by EBS are not *guaranteed* to produce performance improvement. For example, the results from Node7 and Node8 shown above have negative utility because there are no operators other than POLISH that will be considered when the goal is to polish an object, and therefore no control knowledge is necessary. (Thus, as will be described in chapter 7, the training example selection heuristics for OPERATOR-SUCCEEDS will indicate that the examples at Node7 and Node8 are not worth learning from.) However, the higher level result indicating that LATHE is appropriate when the goal is to produce a polished, cylindrical object (and the operator sequence <LATHE, IS-CLAMPABLE, POLISH> is applicable) is more useful, since it will enable the system to avoid first trying ROLL.

Previous EBL research projects have largely ignored the utility issue even though they use similar learning mechanisms. (In fact, the example in the previous section was chosen partly because it mirrors the USEFUL-OP example described by Mitchell, Keller and Kedar-Cabelli [57].) This investigation pays particular attention to this issue, though I defer an in-depth discussion of the utility of PRODIGY's target concepts, and the learning strategies they represent, until chapters 7, 8 and 9 where the strategies are individually discussed.

4.6. Summary

It is the responsibility of the OBSERVER to select training examples for the system's target concepts from a problem solving trace. The OBSERVER invokes the EBS algorithm to explain why each training example satisfied its target concept, in order to produce a specialized description of the target concept. The input to the OBSERVER consists of the following:

- A problem solving trace.

- A set of target concept specifications, each of which includes a template for constructing a search control rule, training example selection heuristics (procedurally encoded), and the name of a training example recognizer function.

- A set of architectural-level proof schemas (axioms) that are hand-coded for each target concept. These must be accompanied by a set of discriminator functions for mapping from the problem solving trace to an appropriate proof.

- A set of domain-level proof schemas. These schemas are directly extracted by the system from the operators, inference rules and control rules for the domain. An appropriate set of discriminator functions is built into the system.

The output of the OBSERVER is a set of descriptions which are simultaneously generalizations of the training examples provided by the trace, and specializations of the system's target concepts.

5. Compression

The utility of a search control rule in PRODIGY is highly dependent on its *match cost*, the time cost of matching its left-hand side. Whenever PRODIGY checks to see whether a control rule is applicable, this time cost is incurred. In order to reduce the match cost of the rules that it learns, PRODIGY uses a process called *compression*. Given a description, the compression module (the COMPRESSOR) attempts to find a semantically equivalent description that is less expensive to match. The process is similar to the rather vague notion of "simplification". However compression, unlike simplification, is specifically intended to reduce a description's match cost. In practice, compression also tends to make descriptions more concise and thus easier to read, but this is considered a fortuitous side effect.

The compression process is interleaved with the EBS specialization process. Thus, we can view PRODIGY as operationalizing a target concept using two types of transformations, specialization and compression. Alternately, in EBL terms, we can say that the compressor searches for a "good" representation of the initial explanation -- one whose premises are efficient to match. In any case, as we will see, compression is important for producing useful control rules.

5.1. How Compression is Used

Compression comes in two distinct forms. *Intra-description* compression simplifies a single description and *inter-description* compression combines descriptions that have been learned from multiple examples.

Let us first consider an example of intra-description compression. Suppose PRODIGY is given a problem in the blocksworld, and (ON BLOCKA BLOCKA) arises as a subgoal (as can happen given the standard formalization shown in Appendix I). The following learned description, which states that (ON *x* *x*) is unachievable, can be simplified as shown below. In doing so the compressor employs some simple equivalence preserving transformations and a domain-specific axiom stating that a block is either on the table, on another block, or being held.

```
(FAILS node)
if (AND (CURRENT-GOAL node goal)
        (MATCHES goal (ON x y))
        (OR (AND (KNOWN (ONTABLE y))
                 (EQUAL x y))
            (AND (KNOWN (HOLDING y))
                 (EQUAL x y))
            (AND (KNOWN (ON y z))
                 (EQUAL x y)))))
reduces to:

(FAILS node)
if (CURRENT-GOAL node (ON x x))
```

The second description is equivalent to the first description, and considerably more efficient to match.

In addition to simplifying individual descriptions, the COMPRESSOR can also combine results from multiple examples to reduce total match cost. Specifically, inter-description compression is used to combine descriptions of the same target concept. For example, let us suppose that PRODIGY has learned the two descriptions shown below which state that HOLDING a block is achievable if the block is on the table or on another block. These results can be combined into a single rule stating that the goal of HOLDING a block is always achievable, as shown below:

```
(SUCCEEDS node)
if (AND (CURRENT-GOAL node goal)
        (MATCHES goal (HOLDING x))
        (KNOWN node (IS-BLOCK x))
        (KNOWN node (ON-TABLE x)))

(SUCCEEDS node)
if (AND (CURRENT-GOAL node goal)
        (MATCHES goal (HOLDING z))
        (KNOWN node (IS-BLOCK y))
        (KNOWN node (IS-BLOCK z))
        (KNOWN node (ON z y)))

reduce to:

(SUCCEEDS goal node)
if (CURRENT-GOAL node (HOLDING x))
```

In general, inter-description compression tends to be successful at reducing match cost only when the descriptions share common terms; simply joining two descriptions with an "OR" does not reduce match cost. If the combined description does not reduce match cost appreciably, then it will not be kept.[15]

5.2. Implementing Compression

Compression is carried out in three phases. In the first phase, partial evaluation is used. In the second phase, simple domain-independent logical transformations are applied. Finally, the third phase employs a restricted theorem prover to take advantage of domain-specific simplification axioms.

Each of these three phases is successively more time consuming. To maximize the efficiency of the learning process, intra-description compression is carried out as follows. In the first phase, partial evaluation is interleaved with the EBS process after each specialization step. This is useful because partial evaluation is very cheap and it often speeds up the EBS process, since reducing a disjunct to TRUE (or conjunct to FALSE) means that the remainder of the expression need not be specialized. The second phase of compression, which involves applying simple logical transformations, is only carried out for node-level results generated during the EBS process. Finally, the theorem prover is used only once per rule, after the EBS process has returned the learned description. This scheme attempts to strike a balance; compression is applied as soon as possible, thereby improving the space and time costs of EBS, but the more time-intensive compression processes are applied conservatively.

Inter-description compression is invoked only after a rule has been formulated. At that point, the system attempts to combine the rule with previously learned rules. However, the system selects only those previously learned rules that refer to the same goals and operators (otherwise, inter-description compression will certainly fail to achieve any meaningful results). After joining two or more rules disjunctively, the second and third compression phases are re-applied. The first phase is considered unnecessary since each rule has individually undergone partial evaluation, and in practice, repeating this phase tends not to improve the result.

The following subsections describe each of the three phases in detail.

5.2.1. Partial Evaluation

Partial evaluation is a well-known program manipulation technique whose uses include optimizing programs, open-coding functions, and generating compilers from interpreters. As described by Kahn [32], a partial evaluator is an interpreter that,

---

[15]Doing so would introduce many rules with disjunctions. This would not necessarily by bad by itself, but it would have a cascading effect. Once a reject rule or select rule is learned, a corresponding domain level proof schema is added to the system for explaining failures that occur when the control rule fires. Thus the left-hand sides of learned rules tend to become embedded in control rules that are learned later.

with only partial information about a program's (or subprogram's) inputs, produces a specialized version of the program which exploits the partial information. For example, a simple partial evaluator for Lisp can partially evaluate the form (**append x y**) to (**cons f y**) when x is known to be (**list f**). In a sense, a partial evaluator operates by propagating constraints through a program, and evaluating low-level functions whenever the constraints on their inputs are strong enough to determine their results.

PRODIGY uses partial evaluation to "optimize" logical descriptions, as opposed to programs, but the distinction is immaterial. Descriptions and programs can be viewed as one and the same, as illustrated by PROLOG. In PRODIGY, the EBS algorithm can be viewed as a recursive-descent interpreter which expands the target concept using the proof schemas. Propagating the constraints which are encountered during the expansion (i.e., specialization) process allows many of the primitive formulas to be directly evaluated. For example, consider the following target concept and schemas:

```
Target Concept:  (P xy)

Schema-1:
  (P x y)
  if (AND (Q x)
          (IS-CAR z x)
          (NOT-EQUAL z ON-TABLE)
          (IS-CDR w x)
          (IS-CAR v w)
          (IS-EQUAL y v))


Schema-2:
  (Q u)
  if (MATCHES u (ON a b))
```

The predicates IS-CAR and IS-CDR are equivalent to the lisp functions **car** and **cdr**. For example, IS-CAR is true if its first argument is the car of its second argument. Thus (IS-CAR 9 (9 4 5)) is true because 9 is the car of the list (9 4 5). After specializing the target concept (P x y), without using partial evaluation, we have the following result:

```
(P x y)
if (AND (MATCHES x (ON a b))
        (IS-CAR z x)
        (NOT-EQUAL z ON-TABLE)
        (IS-CDR w x)
        (IS-CAR v w)
        (IS-EQUAL y v))
```

At this point, because the value of x is partially specified by the MATCHES condition, the value of z can be determined to be the constant ON, and thus the condition (NOT-EQUAL z ON-TABLE) evaluates to TRUE. Similarly, the variables *w* and *v* can be determined to be equal to the list (*a b*) and the variable *a*, respectively, and thus the result simplifies to:

```
(P x y)
if (MATCHES x (ON y b))
```

In general, PRODIGY can propagate three types of constraints. The system can keep track of the fact that two values may be equal, that a list may match another list or that a node may be described by a description. In order to take advantage of this information, static predicates can be declared "evaluable", in which case, if a particular subset of their input values are known, their output values can be automatically calculated. This is possible because, as described in chapter 3, static predicates, such as IS-CAR, can be directly implemented by functions in the PRODIGY system.

Partial evaluation is carried out as the EBS algorithm expands the explanation, after each specialization step. To show a realistic example of how partial evaluation operates in PRODIGY, let us consider the architectural-level schemas shown in table 5-1, which describe when two atomic formulas match. These schemas are used to calculate the bindings under which a goal matches a formula in an operator's add-list. For example, (ON *x y*), a member of STACK's add-list (see Appendix I for the definition of STACK) matches with the goal (ON BLOCKA BLOCKB) under bindings ((*x* BLOCKA) (*y* BLOCKB)), i.e., *x* is bound to BLOCKA and *y* is bound to BLOCKB.

```
Schema-A1:
(ATOMIC-MATCH bindings lit1 lit2)
if (AND (IS-NULL lit1)
        (IS-NULL lit2)
        (IS-NULL bindings)))


Schema-A2:
(ATOMIC-MATCH bindings lit1 lit2)
if (AND (NOT (IS-NULL lit1))
        (LET (arg1) SUCH-THAT (IS-CAR arg1 lit1)
        (LET (arg2) SUCH-THAT (IS-CAR arg2 lit2)
        (LET (rest1) SUCH-THAT (IS-CDR rest1 lit1)
        (LET (rest2) SUCH-THAT (IS-CDR rest2 lit2)
        (LET (sub-bindings) SUCH-THAT
                (ATOMIC-MATCH sub-bindings rest1 rest2)
          (OR (AND (IS-CONSTANT arg1)
                   (IS-EQUAL arg1 arg2)
                   (IS-EQUAL bindings sub-bindings))
              (AND (IS-VARIABLE arg1)
              (LET (pair) SUCH-THAT
                      (MAKE-BINDINGS-PAIR pair arg1 arg2)
                   (IS-CONSISTENT-BINDINGS
                           bindings pair sub-bindings))))))))))
```

Table 5-1: Architectural-level Schemas Defining ATOMIC-MATCH

As specified previously, the predicates IS-CAR and IS-CDR are equivalent to the lisp functions **car** and **cdr**. Similarly, IS-NULL tests whether a list is null, IS-CONSTANT and IS-VARIABLE test whether a value is a constant or a variable, and IS-EQUAL tests whether two constants are equal, The meaning of the remaining predicates will become clear as we proceed through the example. The use of the LET quantifier is not strictly necessary (as explained in section 3.6.2), but improves the schema's readability.

Normally, by the time ATOMIC-MATCH is specialized, *lit1* has already been set equal to a member of the addlist of an operator by a domain-level axiom. So let us assume that lit1 is equal to (ON *x y*). Similarly, the goal has normally been specialized to an atomic formula, such as (ON v1 v2). (Note that while lit1 is constrained to be the actual formula in STACK's add-list, the constraints on the goal are more general than the actual goal (ON BLOCKA BLOCKB). Thus, the target concept (ATOMIC-MATCH *bindings lit1 lit2*), can be represented as shown below, because lit1 and lit2 have been constrained in the earlier part of the explanation:

```
Target-concept:
    (ATOMIC-MATCH bindings (ON x y) (ON v1 v2))
Example:
    (ATOMIC-MATCH bindings (ON x y) (ON BLOCKA BLOCKB))
```

After the EBS process terminates, we will be left with the result:

```
(ATOMIC-MATCH bindings (ON x y) (ON v1 v2))
if (MATCHES bindings ((x v1) (y v2)))
```

Let us step through the explanation process to see how this happens. First, a discrimination function determines that Schema-A2 is the schema consistent with the example, as opposed to Schema-A1. Immediately, (NOT (IS-NULL *lit1*)) is evaluable, and evaluates to TRUE. Similarly, the CARs and CDRs can be evaluated, with the result that *arg1* is set equal to ON, *arg2* to ON, *rest1* to (*x y*) and *rest2* to (*v1 v2*). Then the sub-concept (ATOMIC-MATCH *bindings* (*x y*) (*v1 v2*)) is recursively specialized, which results in *sub-bindings* being set to ((*x v1*)(*y v2*)). Finally, the first disjunct in the disjunction evaluates to our final result, and the second disjunct evaluates to FALSE, because the value of *arg1* is a constant, ON, as opposed to a variable.

For completeness, the full sequence of recursive specializations and their results are shown below:

```
Target-concept: (ATOMIC-MATCH bindings (ON x y) (ON v1 v2))
Example:(ATOMIC-MATCH bindings (ON x y) (ON BLOCKA BLOCKB))
Specialized by: Schema-A2
Recursive specialization:
   Target-concept: (ATOMIC-MATCH bindings (x y) (v1 v2))
   Example:(ATOMIC-MATCH bindings (x y) (BLOCKA BLOCKB))
   Specialized by: Schema-A2
   Recursive specialization:
      Target-concept: (ATOMIC-MATCH bindings (y) (v2))
      Example:(ATOMIC-MATCH bindings (y) (BLOCKB))
      Specialized by: Schema-A2
      Recursive specialization:
         Target-concept: (ATOMIC-MATCH bindings nil nil)
         Example:(ATOMIC-MATCH bindings nil nil)
         Specialized by: Schema-A1
         Result: (MATCHES bindings nil)
      Result: (MATCHES bindings ((y) (v2)))
   Result: (MATCHES bindings ((x v1) (y v2)))
Result: (MATCHES bindings ((x v1) (y v2)))
```

The recursive calls to ATOMIC-MATCH proceed in a similar Lisp-like manner. For example, stepping through the first recursive call, (ATOMIC-MATCH *bindings* (*x y*) (*v1 v2*)), we find that Schema-A2 is again the appropriate schema, and again, IS-NULL, IS-CAR, and IS-CDR are all evaluable. However this time *arg1* is bound to *x*, a variable, rather than a constant. Thus, after the specialization of ATOMIC-MATCH, the first disjunct evaluates to FALSE. In the second disjunct, MAKE-BINDINGS-PAIR is evaluable; it takes *arg1*, which is bound to *x*, and *arg2*, which is bound to *v1*, and creates the list (*x v1*) which represents a bindings pair. Now IS-CONSISTENT-BINDINGS is also evaluable. It takes the new pair of bindings (*x v1*), conses them to the front of the *sub-bindings*, (*y v2*), and then returns the result: (MATCHES *bindings* ((*x v1*)(*y v2*))).

The recursion terminates with the subcall: (ATOMIC-MATCH *bindings* NIL NIL). Using Schema-A1, this simply evaluates to (MATCHES *bindings* NIL), in the obvious manner.

Specializations similar to this example occur over and over during the explanation process. For example, in the process of explaining why a goal failed, PRODIGY must describe why every formula in every operator's effect-list did, or did not match the goal. Partial evaluation makes this process practical, because it provides an extremely fast way of simplifying an explanation.

5.2.2. Taking Advantage of Logical Equivalences

In the second phase of compression PRODIGY employs a set of built-in domain independent transformations that exploit logical equivalences. Some representative transformations that PRODIGY uses are detailed below:

• Redundant subexpression elimination: Redundant subexpressions in conjunctive and disjunctive expressions can be collapsed. For example (AND A B A) can be represented as (AND A B).

- AND/OR collapsing: Expressions such as (AND A B (AND C D)) can be reduced to (AND A B C D). The analogous operation can be done with disjunctive expressions.

- TRUE/FALSE elimination: Expressions such as (AND A B TRUE) can be represented as (AND A B). Similarly (AND A B FALSE) can be simplified to FALSE. The analogous operations are relevant for disjunctive expressions.

- EQUAL propagation: Expressions of the form:

      (AND (IS-EQUAL x 4)(P x)(Q x y))

  can be represented as:

      (AND (P 4)(Q 4 y))

  if the scope of x does not extend outside the conjunction.

- Generator pruning: Expressions such as:

      (FORALL (x y) SUCH-THAT (AND (P x)(Q y))
              (W x))

  can be simplified to:

      (FORALL (x) SUCH-THAT (P x)
              (W x))

  This transformation eliminates unnecessary generators.

- Expression raising: Common subexpressions in conjunctive and disjunctive expressions can be raised. For example, the expression:

      (AND (OR (P x) (Q x))
           (OR (P y) (R y)))

  can be represented as follows, assuming that the scope of x and y do not extend outside the conjunction:

      (AND (P x)
           (OR (Q x)(R x)))

- Unquantified subexpression raising: Subexpressions which are within the scope of a quantifier, but independent of the quantified variable can be raised. For example, the expression:

      (FORALL (x) SUCH-THAT (P x)
          (OR (Q x)
              (R y)))

  can be expressed as:

      (OR (R y)
          (FORALL (x) SUCH-THAT (P x)
              (Q x)))

5.2.3. Conjunct Reordering

In addition to the purely domain-independent transformations, such as those described above, PRODIGY employs additional transformations that can take advantage of specific types of domain information. The most interesting of these is conjunct reordering, which attempts to order the conditions in conjunctive expressions. Three heuristics for reordering conjuncts are employed. First, when there is a choice of generators for a variable, a generator which generates only a single value for the variable should be preferred. Secondly, the distance (i.e., number of intervening conditions) between generators and the tests which depend on them should be minimized. Thirdly, all conjuncts which are not atomic formulas or negated atomic formulas (e.g. universally quantified formulas and disjunctions) should be located at the rear of the expression where they are less likely to be frequently tested.

To order conjuncts according to the first criterion, PRODIGY must determine if a generator can generate multiple values or not. Therefore, for each meta-predicate in the system, PRODIGY is given a list indicating which combination of values will generate single values. For example, the formula (CURRENT-GOAL *node goal*) will only generate a single value for the variable *goal* if *node* is bound. For domain-level predicates, the same information can be garnered from the simplification axioms that the user provides to the system (for use by the theorem-prover, as described in the next section). When the simplification axioms are loaded, PRODIGY specifically scans them for axioms of the form shown below, and the information is saved for conjunct reordering.

    (IS-EQUAL y z) if (AND (P x y) (P x z))

This particular axiom indicates that the second argument to **P** will only generate a single value when the first argument is bound. If the user does not provide any such axioms, PRODIGY will assume that all domain-level predicates can generate multiple values. In an earlier version of the system, to aid reordering PRODIGY employed statistics describing how many values a predicate could generate. However, although promising, this capability was not included in the current system because of the difficulty in determining the requisite information.

After selecting and determining an order for the generators according to the first heuristic, PRODIGY then moves their tests up as far as possible in the expression. Thus, the tests follow the generators as closely as possible. Finally, following the third heuristic, all conjuncts that have internal structure (universal formulas and disjunctions) are moved to the rear of the expression.

5.2.4. Domain-Specific Transformations

In the third phase of the compression process, PRODIGY employs a simple theorem prover to take advantage of domain-specific simplification axioms. For example, in the blocksworld, the theorem prover can use the following axioms to make the simplifications shown below. The first axiom states that only one block can be held at a time, and the second states that a block is either being held, on the table, or on another block. The simplified rule states that putting a block on the table can always be achieved. (Note that the compression process preserves the meaning of a description, and therefore the rule states the same thing before and after compression. The meaning is simply more obvious after compression.)

```
Axioms:
1. (IS-EQUAL x y)
   if (AND (HOLDING x)
           (HOLDING y))

2. (FORALL (x) SUCH-THAT (TRUE)
      (OR (HOLDING x)
          (ON-TABLE x)
          (EXISTS (y) SUCH-THAT (ON y x))))


Initial Rule:
(SUCCEEDS g n)
if (MATCHES g (ON-TABLE x)
   (KNOWN n (AND (OR (AND (HOLDING x)
                          (HOLDING y))
                (ON-TABLE x)
                (ON x z))

Compressed Rule:
(SUCCEEDS g n)
if (MATCHES g (ON-TABLE x))
```

Simplification axioms state facts that are true in all initial states and that are preserved by operator applications. Unfortunately, such axioms cannot easily be inferred from the operators and inference rules themselves, and therefore must be supplied by the user. They can be included as part of the initial domain specification or interactively provided by the user during the learning process. One practical difficulty is that there is no obvious way for the user to know when he has supplied a "complete" set of axioms. Thus, interactively adding simplification axioms as they are needed (by looking at the learned rules) seems to be a reasonable way of extending the domain specification. This is consistent with the apprenticeship idea that permeates the PRODIGY project, but it would be preferable if the user did not have to give the system the exact axioms in a "learning by being told" mode. (In general, I have ignored the problems involved in providing the system with a correct and complete domain specification.)

PRODIGY's theorem prover is based on the fundamental deduction principle, described by Brown [5]:

> "Almost all steps in an automatic deduction should take place by a method of replacement of P expressions by equivalent simpler Q expressions involving as few redundant subexpressions as possible, and the smaller the P expressions, the better. (A few steps may involve generalization of the theorem, but these are deliberate steps taken with due consideration -- not the mindless application of basic

generalizing inference rules)."

Brown's theorem prover uses rules of the form **P=Q if C**. The theorem prover will replace an expression P by the expression Q if it can prove that expression C holds. Brown gives an example of one such rule for positive number theory:

```
(ADD1 (SUB1 N)) = N
if (> N 0)
```

The condition (> N 0) is necessary because (SUB1 0) is undefined -- negative numbers are disallowed in positive number theory.

PRODIGY's theorem prover uses rules that are similar in spirit to Brown's. The rules are of the form (P iff Q) if (PC & MC). An important difference is that Brown's rules have a single condition, C, that is tested before P is replaced by Q, whereas PRODIGY's rules has two conditions, MC and PC. MC is a "match condition" that PRODIGY must match in the expression to be simplified, and PC is a "prove condition" that PRODIGY must prove from the expression to simplified. (If MC is the atom TRUE, then PRODIGY's scheme is essentially the same as Brown's.) Thus, given a description containing a subexpression P, PRODIGY's theorem prover will backchain; it will first attempt to match MC, and if successful, recursively attempt to prove PC. For example, consider a simplification axiom encoded in PRODIGY's scheme:

```
[(INROOM obj2 rm) iff (TRUE)]
if [(INROOM obj1 rm) & (NEXT-TO obj1 obj2)]
```

This rule states that if *obj1* is in some room, and *obj1* is next to *obj2*, then *obj2* is also in the room. The rule can only be applied if PRODIGY can determine that (INROOM *obj1* rm) and (NEXT-TO *obj1* obj2) both hold. However, the truth of the match condition, (NEXT-TO *obj1* obj2), must be determined without recursively invoking the theorem prover. For example, the rule is useful for performing the reduction shown below. (Assume that (INROOM *w* ROOM4) can be proved from (IS-WINDOW *w* ROOM4).)

```
(AND (IS-WINDOW w ROOM4)    reduces to:  (AND (IS-WINDOW w ROOM4)
     (NEXT-TO w x)                            (NEXT-TO w x)
     (INROOM x ROOM4)                         (HAVE-KEYS ROOM4))
     (HAVE-KEYS ROOM4))
```

The use of two conditions, MC and PC, as opposed to a single condition as in Brown's scheme, provides the user with even more control over the theorem-proving process. However, the idea is consistent with Brown's scheme, for Brown argues that the recursive proof process must be relatively cheap for practical theorem provers.[16]

---

[16]Note that Brown's SYMEVAL system addresses many issues that we have completely ignored here. PRODIGY's theorem prover is specifically designed as a simplifier for PDL expressions.

It is the reliance on theorem proving in this third stage of compression that makes compression a potentially unbounded search. However, it also provides a very general framework for viewing the compression process. In the next section we will explore the costs of compression in more detail.

5.3. The Cost of Compression

Compression is a potentially costly process, however, the cost applies only in the learning phase. There is no cost to the performance system since compression should always produce better control rules (as discussed in the next section). For the purposes of this dissertation, I assume that improving the efficiency of the performance system is the primary concern, and therefore time spent learning is not a major issue. However, it is worthwhile considering this issue briefly, since theoretically the compression process could be quite time consuming.

In the early stages of this research project, I considered using the theorem prover to do the entire compression process. However, this soon proved to be untenable due to the expense involved. Simply put, theorem proving tends to be difficult to control. As it turned out, much of the compression process could be handled by special purpose processes that could take advantage of partial evaluation (phase one) and simple domain-independent logical equivalences (phase two). The overhead of general theorem proving turned out to be needed only to exploit the infrequent simplifications that these more efficient mechanisms could not handle. In the current learning scheme, the first two phases of compression are interleaved with the EBS process, and consequently are applied quite frequently, while the theorem-proving phase (the third phase) is used only after the EBS process has terminated.

Of course, theoretically speaking, the theorem proving process used in phase three can still be unbounded even after phase one and two have been completed. Thus, in addition to the use of constraining PC and MC conditions (described in the last section), the theorem prover is normally given a depth bound beyond which it will not recur, and a time bound. The theorem prover incrementally simplifies the learned description until it either runs out of rules to apply, or exceeds the fixed time bound.

Another suggested scheme for implementing compression (suggested by Allen Newell) was to use PRODIGY itself as a theorem prover to implement the compression process. Presumably, appropriate control rules could guide the theorem proving process, eliminating the control problems that arise with a general theorem prover. Furthermore, this would allow us to study the effect of learning on compression process itself. This scheme, although elegant, was rejected due to the overhead of using PRODIGY for low-level work. Simply put, Lisp runs significantly faster than PRODIGY. The emphasis in this dissertation is not on the generality of the PRODIGY problem solving architecture (flexible though it is) but on translating problem solving experience into effective control rules.

In practice, I have found that the current compression process runs reasonably quickly. Typically, the time spent learning is within the same order of magnitude as the time spent problem solving, although this can vary greatly depending on how many training example/target concept pairs are selected by the observer (as documented in [53]). Admittedly, the third phase of compression will tend to become more costly as the number of simplification axioms grows. However, the cost can be limited by the use of the time bound, in effect trading effectiveness for time.

5.4. The Benefits of Compression

An underlying assumption of this work, alluded to in the previous section, is that compression will always produce better control rules. To see why this is a reasonable assumption let us examine the effects of each of the compression phases:

1. Phase One: PRODIGY's partial evaluation is guaranteed to produce more easily evaluated descriptions. If the evaluations performed by compression were not carried out, they would have to be carried out each time the rule was tested. Thus, compression takes care of the work at "compile time" rather than "run time".

2. Phase Two: The domain-independent transformations carried out in phase two have been carefully designed to decrease match cost. For example, redundant subexpression elimination reduces the number of tests that have to be made during the match process. (It should be obvious that the other transformations listed in section 5.2.2 also tend to decrease match cost). However, these transformations are *not* guaranteed to produce better rules, because as a side-effect they may perform re-orderings that increase the match cost. Even so, detrimental re-orderings have only infrequently been observed, and their impact is generally reduced by the deliberate knowledge-based ordering transformations that PRODIGY applies.

3. Phase Three: The simplifications carried out by the theorem prover are also not guaranteed to produce better rules. However, this is largely under the control of the user who writes the simplification axioms for each domain. As described in section 5.2.4, the format of the deduction rules allows the user to control the theorem proving process so that the simplifications are generally productive.

In practice, as shown in chapter 10, the compression process produces dramatic improvements in the descriptions generated by EBS. However, it is difficult to provide an exact measure of how well the compression process performs (within the range of possible implementations). It is worth noting that, in a theoretical sense, there is no "optimal" compressor (that is guaranteed to halt) because the compression problem is undecidable. To see this, consider that the most easily evaluated expressions are TRUE and FALSE. Therefore an optimal compressor would be able to classify descriptions as either true, false, or satisfiable. Since first order logic is undecidable, this is impossible.

Intuitively, intra-description compression is *most likely* to be useful when the premises of the explanation can be succinctly characterized. For example, an explanation of why a subtree failed can often be succinctly expressed when there is a single underlying reason for the failures at the leaf nodes. If the failures at the leaf nodes cannot be described in terms of some underlying commonality, then there is typically less opportunity for compression.

Inter-description compression, on the other hand, is *most likely* to be useful when the explanations being combined describe complementary cases. For example, in the STRIPS domain, if PRODIGY discovers in one case that it is possible to travel between two connecting rooms when the door is open, and in another case that it is possible to travel between them when the door is closed (by opening the door), then it can deduce that it is always possible to travel between them.

An actual, system-generated example illustrating the utility of the compression process is shown in table 5-2. The first expression was produced by the EBS process (*after* partial evaluation). The second expression is the compressed result.

5.5. Summary

It is the COMPRESSOR's responsibility to take descriptions produced by the EBS process and simplify them in order to reduce their match cost. The compression process consists of three phases: partial evaluation, the application of domain-independent logical transformations, and the application of domain-specific simplification axioms by a theorem prover. For intra-description compression, the input to the COMPRESSOR[17] consists of the following:

- A description produced by EBS.

- A set of domain-specific simplification axioms.

- A time-bound and a depth-bound for the theorem-prover.

The output is an equivalent description of lower match cost. For inter-description compression, the input also includes all of the descriptions produced earlier by EBS from the same target concept. The output is a new description of lower match cost that is equivalent to the disjunction of two or more of the input descriptions.

---

[17]As described previously, the COMPRESSOR also employs a set of functions to carry out partial evaluation of static predicates, and a set of domain-independent transformations to exploit logical equivalences. However, for all intents and purposes, these are built into the system, and so they are not considered as input to the compressor.

```
(NODE-RESULTS-IN-GOAL-INTERFERENCE node)
if (AND (IS-EQUAL v2 (HOLDING v3))
        (CURRENT-GOAL node (HOLDING v3))
        (IS-EQUAL v6 UNSTACK)
        (AND (AND (IS-EQUAL node v10)
                  (IS-EQUAL (HOLDING v3) v9)
                  (IS-EQUAL UNSTACK v8)
                  (AND (IS-EQUAL v9 (HOLDING v7))
                       (IS-EQUAL UNSTACK v8)
                       (KNOWN v10 (NOT (ON-TABLE v7)))))
             T
             (FORALL (v88) (KNOWN node (OBJECT v88))
                (OR (AND (IS-EQUAL node v58)
                         (IS-EQUAL (HOLDING v3) v57)
                         (IS-EQUAL UNSTACK v56)
                         (IS-EQUAL (v3 v88) v55)
                         (AND (IS-EQUAL v57 (HOLDING v54))
                              (IS-EQUAL v56 UNSTACK)
                              (IS-EQUAL (v54 v53) v55)
                              (KNOWN v58 (NOT (ON v54 v53)))))
                    (AND (IS-EQUAL node v52)
                         (IS-EQUAL (HOLDING v3) v51)
                         (IS-EQUAL UNSTACK v50)
                         (IS-EQUAL (v3 v88) v49)
                         (AND (IS-EQUAL v51 (HOLDING v48))
                              (IS-EQUAL v50 UNSTACK)
                              (IS-EQUAL (v48 v47) v49)
                              (KNOWN v52(NOT (ON v48 v47)))))
                    (AND (IS-EQUAL node v46)
                         (IS-EQUAL (HOLDING v3) v45)
                         (IS-EQUAL UNSTACK v44)
                         (IS-EQUAL (v3 v88) v43)
                         (AND (IS-EQUAL v45 (HOLDING v42))
                              (IS-EQUAL v44 UNSTACK)
                              (IS-EQUAL (v42 v41) v43)
                              (KNOWN v46 (NOT (ON v42 v41)))))
                    (AND (NOT (KNOWN node (CLEAR v3)))
                         (AND  (IS-EQUAL CLEAR CLEAR)
                               (IS-EQUAL v3 v202)
                               (WAS-DELETED node (CLEAR v202))
                         (IS-EQUAL v203 v201)))))))))))


(NODE-RESULTS-IN-GOAL-INTERFERENCE node)
IF   (AND (CURRENT-GOAL node (HOLDING v7))
          (KNOWN node (NOT (ON-TABLE v7)))
          (WAS-DELETED node (CLEAR v7))))
```

Table 5-2: Example Illustrating the Effect of Compression

6. Utility Evaluation

After an explanation has been constructed and a new control rule formulated, its utility must be evaluated. The task of utility evaluation is the responsibility of a module called the MONITOR. Given a new control rule, the MONITOR first estimates the rule's utility, and if the rule appears promising adds it to the list of active control rules in the system. The utility estimate is then validated empirically by the MONITOR during subsequent problem solving, and the rule is deactivated if its utility is determined to be negative.

This chapter discusses the process of utility evaluation in detail. We first describe the cost/benefit formula that defines utility, and then discuss the processes of utility estimation and validation.

6.1. Defining Utility

The utility of a search control rule refers to usefulness of the rule for improving the problem solver's performance. Performance is measured only in terms of search time, excluding other factors such as the quality of the solutions that are found. Thus, the utility of a rule with respect to a series of problems can be defined solely in terms of the effect that the rule has on the system's problem solving efficiency:

Formula 6-1:

> Utility = Average-search-time-without-rule - Average-search-time-with-rule

Thus, to measure the utility of a rule over a set of problems one can run the system without the rule in question, and then run the system with the rule, and measure the total difference in time. If we assume that the problem solver is being tested over some suitably random set of problems in the domain, we can refer to the expected utility of a rule on an "average" problem independent of any particular sequence of problems.

This definition captures the essence of utility, but does not provide much insight into the factors that influence utility. If we assume that the primary cost of having the rule in the system is due to the match time expended in repeatedly matching the rule, and the primary savings results because fewer nodes need be explored, then we can refine our formula as shown below.

Formula 6-2:

$$\text{Utility} = (\text{AvrSavings} \times \text{ApplicFreq}) - \text{AvrMatchCost}$$

where
AvrMatchCost = the average time cost of matching the rule.
AvrSavings = the average time savings when the rule is applicable.
ApplicFreq = the probability that rule is applicable when it is tested.

For example, if a rule costs an average of 100 milliseconds to match, saves an average of 100,000 milliseconds when applicable, and is applicable 1 out of 100 times it is matched, then it has an average utility of 900 milliseconds. That is, the rule can be expected to decrease overall search time by an average of 900 milliseconds per match attempt.

To calculate the average savings one must know both the average number of nodes saved by employing the rule, and the average time necessary to explore these nodes. Note that the average time for exploring a node should not include the time matching the control rule in question. Furthermore note that the average number of nodes saved may actually be negative, since preference rules can be wrong, in which case they may lead the problem solver astray. The average match time calculation must include the time spent by the matcher regardless of whether the match was successful or not. (On individual trials the match time may vary dramatically depending on how far the match progresses.)

6.2. Measuring Utility

While both of the cost/benefit formulas given in the previous section provides a precise definition of utility, in practice it is difficult to use either of them directly. Employing the first formula is impractical because it requires running the system over a representative set of problems twice for each potential rule. This would be a formidable task, especially since the EBL learning component may produce several potential rules per problem (sometimes as many as twenty or thirty in the experiments described in chapter 10). Directly employing the second formula is also problematic, since it is overly expensive to measure the savings for each rule; this would require exploring all the alternatives pruned during the search by the rule.[18]

There is another problem, in addition to the difficulty in measuring utility. Ideally we would like to learn a set of rules and test those rules on subsequent trials, while simultaneously employing the learning mechanism to produce more rules during these subsequent trials. However, often the learned rules are truly hideous, in that their match cost *far* outweighs their benefits. Unfortunately, the inclusion of such

---

[18]An additional complication is that the average time saved per node may vary depending on the number of control rules in the system.

poor rules may adversely effect subsequent rules that are learned. Specifically, when learning from a failure or a goal interaction, the explanation typically employs schemas describing the preconditions of any selection and rejection rules that fired during the problem solving episode. (For each selection and rejection rule, there exists a corresponding domain-level proof schema describing its left-hand side). Thus, as new control rules are learned, their left-hand sides often have embedded in them the left-hand sides of rules learned earlier. Therefore, if there are many poor rules in the system then newly learned rules are likely to be of low (or negative) utility, in effect creating a chain reaction.

To overcome these two difficulties, PRODIGY employs a two-stage method for utility evaluation. First the system employs an initial estimate of the match cost and savings for each newly learned control rule, and only if the rule appears useful is it included in the active set of control rules. This greatly reduces the likelihood of a chain reaction of poor rules. Secondly, during subsequent problem solving, the actual match cost and match frequency of the rules are directly measured. However, the system does not measure the actual savings derived from each rule, but instead, relies on the savings estimate produced during the first phase.

6.2.1. Estimating Utility

The initial utility estimate is carried out by examining the training example that produced the rule. PRODIGY examines the cost and savings that the learned rule would have produced had it been present prior to encountering the example. Obviously, the rule would have been applicable, because the rule was learned from the example.

From the training example, an estimate of the rule's match cost can be determined empirically, simply by measuring the time cost of matching the rule. The estimate is liberal, since the match cost tends to be higher when the rule is applicable.

The savings estimate is determined by measuring the time spent exploring the portion of the tree that would have been eliminated by the control rule. Notice that regardless of whether the rule is a selection, rejection, or preference rule, if it improves search performance it does so by discarding or deferring candidates (at a decision point) that would otherwise be explored before the successful path was found. For selection and rejection rules, it is a simple matter to identify the part of the tree that would have been pruned by the rule, and the time that was spent exploring it. It is assumed that no acceptable solution path lies within the pruned section of the tree. (This assumption is appropriate given the current set of target concepts in PRODIGY, since selection and rejection rules are only learned from analyzing failures.) For preference rules the situation is slightly more complex. The subtree that would have been deferred because of the preference rule may in fact contain solutions. In estimating the savings, PRODIGY first examines the deferred subtree to see whether any alternative solutions were generated within it. (Although PRODIGY normally halts when it finds a single solution, the search tree may have been expanded further during the learning phase in order to verify goal interactions, as described in chapter 9.) If a solution was generated, then PRODIGY considers the savings to be the difference in solution time between the deferred subtree, and the preferred subtree. This captures the fact that preferring a shorter solution over a longer solution (that may involve goal interactions, for example), generally saves problem solving time. If no solution was found within the subtree in question, then PRODIGY simply considers the savings to be the cost of exploring the deferred subtree.

The drawback of this scheme is that there is no way of estimating the application frequency of the learned rule. However, by simply comparing the match cost estimate against the savings estimate PRODIGY can filter out rules that are highly unlikely to be useful, since their cost would presumably outweigh their savings even if they were *always* applicable. In practice, this has turned out to be a surprisingly effective method for trimming the initial set of rules that is produced.

The initial utility estimate is thus based on a single empirical measurement of the rule's cost and benefit. In an earlier version of the implementation, the match cost of control rules was estimated analytically, using a model of the matcher and an estimate of the number of tokens generated by each condition. (This information was also used for condition reordering by the compressor). This was determined to be less effective and more complex than the simple empirical test that is now done. In general, analytical estimation seems to be superior only where there is a strong source of knowledge about the match frequency of predicates (and combinations of predicates). In the domains I examined, it seemed to be too great a burden on the user to require him to provide the necessary knowledge for each domain. In general, it is unlikely that either empirical or analytic methods will be strictly preferable -- it depends on the knowledge that is available.

6.2.2. Empirical Utility Validation

After the control rules that pass the utility estimation test are added to the problem solving system, their actual cost is then measured during subsequent problem solving. However, for the reasons previously described, PRODIGY does not directly determine their actual savings, as this would be impractical. Thus, instead of validating the savings estimate, PRODIGY simply uses it as is.

To carry out the utility calculation, PRODIGY keeps a running total of the accumulated match cost for each rule. Similarly, a running total for the accumulated savings is maintained by adding the estimated savings to the total savings every time the rule is applicable. If the accumulated savings is greater than the accumulated match cost, then the rule's utility is positive. (This corresponds to multiplying formula 6-2 by the number of trials. It is more efficient than directly employing the formula since it is not necessary to keep re-calculating the average match cost and application frequency.)

Using the savings estimate rather than the actual savings may cause problems if the estimate is too high, in which case the rule will appear to have a higher utility than it actually does. If the estimate is too low and the rule is discarded, at least there is the possibility that it will be relearned during a subsequent problem solving episode.

If the utility of a rule becomes negative, it is discarded, and added to the list of "inactive" control rules. This list could presumably be used to prevent negative utility rules from being relearned and discarded over and over again, but this capability has not been implemented.

A potential problem with this scheme is that normally, even a good rule's utility will be negative until it is applicable for the first time, due to its match cost. To prevent rules from being immediately discarded, each rule is initially credited with the costs and savings that it would have produced given the example from which it was learned (i.e. its initial utility estimate).

6.3. Interactions between Rules

Discarding rules of negative utility will always improve performance, assuming that the sequence of trial problems is a representative sample, and that the savings estimate accurately reflects its real value. However, I should mention that simply discarding rules is not necessarily the *best* strategy for improving performance. The problem is that ordering interactions between rules are ignored. For example, suppose that the system has two operator rejection rules, RULE-S and RULE-G, such that 99% of the time that RULE-S fires, RULE-G will also fire, rejecting the same operator. Let us also assume that RULE-G is a very general rule that is often applicable when RULE-S is not.[19] Unfortunately, if RULE-S is always considered before RULE-G, then whenever RULE-S fires, RULE-G will not have an opportunity to fire (because the operator has already been rejected). Thus, when RULE-S is ordered before RULE-G in PRODIGY's list of rules, they may both appear to be of moderate utility, but if the order is reversed, a more accurate picture will emerge, since RULE-G will receive a much higher rating than RULE-S. The point of this example is simply to show that rule ordering influences utility. Although the strategy of discarding rules with negative utility will always improve performance, it may result in a "local maximum". To find the best combination of rules, PRODIGY would have to use the much more expensive strategy of reordering all potentially interacting rules before deciding which rules to discard.

---

[19]If RULE-G is strictly more general than RULE-S, RULE-S will presumably be eliminated by inter-description compression.

6.4. The Costs and Benefits of Utility Analysis

Due to the fact that PRODIGY estimates the savings of rules, rather than actually measuring their savings over a series of examples, utility analysis has low overhead. Although measuring the match cost requires maintaining statistics for each rule, the necessary measurements and calculations can be done quickly and in constant time (per match attempt). Experimentally, the overhead of utility validation has been observed to be less than 1% of the problem solver's runtime for sequences of problems described in chapter 10. The benefit of utility evaluation is that after a learned rule has been added to the system, we can be sure that it is having a positive effect (assuming that the estimation and validation measurements are correct).

Chapter 10 describes experimental data showing the utility of utility evaluation. As predicted, the results indicate that the system's performance can degrade radically without utility evaluation.

6.5. Summary

The MONITOR module carries out utility evaluation after learned rules have been compressed. This is a two-phase process. First each rule is given a utility estimate based on its cost and benefit relative to the problem from which it was learned. If the estimate is positive, the rule is kept. Then empirical match-cost measurements are carried out during subsequent problem solving to determine if the rule's cumulative match cost outweighs its cumulative savings (which are estimated). The input to the MONITOR consists of the following:

- A set of candidate control rules.

- A sequence of problems.

The output is the subset of the rules that are determined to be of positive utility.

7. Learning from Success

We now turn our attention to the target concepts that PRODIGY currently employs, and the corresponding explanations that are produced. Each of the four types of target concepts can be viewed a distinct learning strategy. This chapter discusses how PRODIGY learns from solutions using the SUCCEEDS target concepts. The following chapter describes how the system learns from failures and sole-alternatives (where all other alternatives fail). Finally, chapter 9 describes how PRODIGY learns from goal-interferences.

Most of the previous work on explanation-based learning has focused on learning by observing solutions to problems. In the following sections, I describe how PRODIGY extends this approach in order to learn preference rules. As it turns out, learning from solutions is not only PRODIGY's simplest learning strategy, it also tends to be its weakest strategy. After describing how the strategy is implemented, I discuss its limitations, and attempt to characterize the types of situations for which it is best suited.

7.1. Methods for Learning from Success

For many problems solvers, including PRODIGY, a solution consists of a sequence of operators that convert the initial state into a goal state. There have been a number of approaches proposed for learning from successful operator sequences. One of the best known methods is the STRIPS MACROPS technique [25], an early form of EBL. After solving a problem, STRIPS would take the resulting operator sequence and generalize it. The generalized operator sequence was then stored as a "macrop". During subsequent problem solving, subsequences of the macrop could be re-used in order to improve problem solving efficiency.

A variation of the STRIPS macro-operator approach was adopted in several others systems, including the LEX2 system (only partially implemented) described by Mitchell et. al [58]. LEX2 would analyze a successful operator sequence in order to learn the generalized conditions under which the sequence was applicable. However, unlike STRIPS, LEX2 only applied the *first* operator in the sequence when the preconditions of the sequence were matched. This would appear to be less efficient then the STRIPS approach, which applies the entire operator sequence when its preconditions are applicable. However, the single-operator approach used by LEX2 was complemented by a second phase in the learning process; LEX2 combined the learned preconditions of all the useful sequences that began with the same operator. The purpose was to produce a single description which efficiently described when the operator was appropriate. In the LEX2 system, inductive learning was used to combine these multiple sets of preconditions. As we will see, PRODIGY uses a similar "single-operator" approach when learning from success, except that compression is used to combine the preconditions of sequences that begin with the same operator. If the system can discover efficient descriptions indicating when to select each operator, then single-operator learning can be very effective. In contrast, because the macro-operator approach relies on maintaining all useful sequences of operators, a macro-operator system may often be faced with a combinatorically unmanageable situation (unless useful sequences are very sparse in the search space).

Another potential advantage of single-operator learning over macro-operator learning is that the performance system still plans one operator at a time. This enables the system to take shorter paths through the state space when they arise serendipitously, rather than being rigidly locked into pre-established sequences of operators. This rigidity problem was readily apparent in the MORRIS macro-operator learning system [49]. For example, in an experiment in the STRIPS robot problem solving domain, MORRIS observed a solution in which the robot moved from one room to the next by going to the door, opening it, and moving through the doorway. After generalizing this operator sequence the system would exhibit the following behavior: If asked to move the robot into an adjoining room, the system would have the robot open a closed door rather than choosing a door that was already open (if one existed), due to the influence of the macro-operator. Furthermore, if there was only a single door, and it was open, the problem solver would first have the robot close the door so that the macro-operator would apply. Thus macro-operator learning emphasizes the efficiency of search, but by narrowing the search, it effectively puts blinders on the problem solver. Consequently although macro-operator learning may be more efficient in some cases, single operator learning may be better with regard to maintaining the flexibility of the problem solver. And, as was pointed out in the previous paragraph, the efficiency problems in single operator learning can be overcome if one can concisely describe when each operator is appropriate.

While there has been little work comparing the relative advantages and disadvantages of macro-operator learning and single operator learning, Porter and Kibler [70] have considered some of these issues in their work with "loosely packaged" macro-operators.

7.2. How PRODIGY Learns from Success

After PRODIGY finds the solution to a problem, the solution sequence is analyzed in order to produce preference rules. Given a particular solution sequence (or subsequence), EBS can explain why the sequence was applicable. This process isolates the preconditions for the sequence, which become the left-hand side for the resulting preference rule.

There are four target concepts for learning from success that can be employed to drive the EBS process:

1. (NODE-SUCCEEDS *node*): A node succeeds if there exists a sequence of operators that solve the goals at that node.

2. (GOAL-SUCCEEDS *node goal*): A goal at a node succeeds if there exists a sequence of operators that solve the goal at the node.

3. (OPERATOR-SUCCEEDS *node goal op*): An operator succeeds in solving a goal at a node if the operator is relevant to the goal, and there exists a sequence of operators with the operator as the last member of the sequence, such that after applying this sequence, the goal is solved.

4. (BINDINGS-SUCCEED *node goal op bindings*): A set of bindings succeeds in solving a goal at a node if there exists an operator that succeeds in solving the goal at the node with those bindings.

All four of these target concepts are defined in terms of the success of an operator. The top-level proof schemas used to explain OPERATOR-SUCCEEDS are listed below. (Lower-level schemas are described in [53].) These schemas state that an operator *op* succeeds in solving goal *g* at node *n* if either: the operator directly solves the goal (i.e., the operator has an effect which unifies with the goal), applying another operator results in a node at which the operator succeeds in solving the goal, or subgoaling results in a node at which the operator succeeds.

```
Schema-S1: An operator succeeds if it directly solves
the goal.
(OPERATOR-SUCCEEDS op goal node)
if (AND (MATCHES-EFFECT goal op)
        (APPLICABLE op node))

Schema-S2: An operator succeeds if it succeeds after
a precursor operator is applied.
(OPERATOR-SUCCEEDS op goal node)
if (AND (APPLICABLE pre-op node)))
        (OPERATOR-SUCCEEDS op goal childnode)
        (CHILD-NODE-AFTER-APPLYING-OP childnode pre-op node)))

Schema-S3: For an operator to succeed, subgoaling may
be necessary.
(OPERATOR-SUCCEEDS op goal node)
if (AND (CHILD-NODE-AFTER-SUBGOALING childnode pre-op node)
        (OPERATOR-SUCCEEDS op goal childnode)))
```

7.3. Heuristics for Selecting Examples of Success

PRODIGY uses several heuristics to determine which examples of SUCCESS should be analyzed. As mentioned in chapter 4, example selection heuristics are necessary because there are typically many examples of PRODIGY's target-concepts in a given search tree, most of which would produce useless rules. When possible, it is more efficient to filter out these examples before producing the control rules, rather than relying on utility evaluation to eventually discard the majority of the rules. (However, utility evaluation is still necessary as a second pass filter, since it may be impossible to know whether an example will definitely produce an effective control rule.) PRODIGY's heuristics for selecting examples of SUCCESS are described below:

1. Highest-success heuristic: Let us suppose that an operator is selected to solve a subgoal at node K, and after subgoaling the operator is eventually applied at node K+N. Then, according to the definition of SUCCESS (given in the previous section), the operator has succeeded at each of the N nodes starting at node K and ending at node K+N. Actually, however, the primary example of interest is the first example at node K. This is the point at which the operator was chosen from among the set of candidate operators relevant to the goal. Explaining this example requires N recursions through the definition of operator succeeds, but all of the N intermediate examples can be thrown out once they have been used to explain the higher-level success. If there are J operators used in a solution, then this heuristic filters the set of examples from order J^2 to J.

2. Others-have-failed heuristic: It is only useful to learn from a candidate's success if other candidates have been previously tried, and have failed. In other words, if the first candidate to be tried immediately led to as solution, there is no need to learn any control knowledge (at least as evidenced from that example). This situation may arise, for instance, when there is only a single operator relevant to a subgoal, or when existing control knowledge is sufficient to determine the appropriate candidate.

3. Previously-learned-from-success heuristic: In some cases PRODIGY may have previously learned a preference rule indicating that a candidate will succeed, but conflicting preferences prevent this candidate from being tried first. In this case PRODIGY will not attempt to learn an additional rule, since it will only duplicate the recommendation of the previously learned rule. (PRODIGY does not use a voting scheme. When a set of preferences conflict, all are ignored.)

4. Global-success heuristic: Although an operator may succeed in solving a subgoal, it may not be on the eventual solution path because subsequent subgoals may be unsolvable. In general, we say that a candidate may succeed locally but not globally. Only candidates that succeed *and* lead to a global solution, rather than a local solution, are

considered interesting examples of SUCCESS. This is a conservative heuristic; it is effective at filtering out candidates that succeed locally, but produce unsolvable goal interferences.

7.4. Examples of Learning from Success

This section will illustrate some prototypical cases in which learning from success produces performance improvement.

7.4.1. Scheduling Domain Example

Let us first consider an example from the machine-shop scheduling domain. The goal is to produce a schedule for bolting two parts together, PART1 and PART2, that do not yet have have the holes necessary for the bolt. The BOLT and DRILL-PRESS operators, shown in table 7-1 for the reader's convenience, are taken from the domain specification given in appendix I. To simplify this example, we will assume that the PUNCH operator does not exist; therefore, DRILL-PRESS is the only available operator for drilling holes.

The BOLT operator takes two parts and bolts them together, creating a third composite object. The two component parts cease to exist as individual entities after they have been bolted together. The preconditions of BOLT specify that the two objects must have holes in an appropriate orientation[20]. Typically the orientation is supplied by the goal statement. For example, the goal statement for our example problem is given in table 7-2 along with the relevant information from the initial state. For expository purposes we have simplified the goal statement so that the orientation is just represented by an atom, such as ORIENTATION1; in reality it would be a data-structure indicating the faces of the objects to be joined, the hole angle, and other spatial information, all of which is irrelevant to our example.

The DRILL-PRESS operator includes several similar preconditions. The only important one, as far as our example is concerned, is that there must be a bit available that is the same size as the hole to be drilled.

Solving the problem is relatively straightforward. Backward-chaining from the goal, PRODIGY chooses the first relevant operator, BOLT. However, there are several alternative sets of bindings that are considered. In particular, there are a

---

[20]As described in chapter 3, in representing these operators some simplifying assumptions have been made. For example, the BOLT operator takes an orientation which specifies the position and angle for the bolt relative to the parts, and does a simple CAN-BE-BOLTED test. This static predicate is implemented by a lisp function, but for more realistic learning we would not want to have such a black box.

```
(BOLT (obj1 obj2 new-obj time bolt)
   (PRECONDS
       (AND
          (IS-OBJECT obj1)
          (IS-OBJECT obj2)
          (CAN-BE-BOLTED obj1 obj2 orientation)
          (IS-BOLT bolt)
          (IS-WIDTH width bolt)
          (HAS-HOLE obj1 width orientation)
          (HAS-HOLE obj2 width orientation)
          (LAST-SCHEDULED obj1 prev-time1)
          (LAST-SCHEDULED obj2 prev-time2)
          (LATER time prev-time1)
          (LATER time prev-time2)
          (IDLE BOLTING-MACHINE time)
          (COMPOSITE-OBJECT new-obj orientation obj1 obj2)))
      (EFFECTS
        ((DEL (LAST-SCHEDULED obj1 prev-time1))
         (DEL (LAST-SCHEDULED obj2 prev-time2))
         (ADD (LAST-SCHEDULED new-obj time))
         (ADD (IS-OBJECT new-obj))
         (DEL (IS-OBJECT obj1))
         (DEL (IS-OBJECT obj2))
         (ADD (JOINED obj1 obj2 orientation))
         (ADD (SCHEDULED new-obj BOLTING-MACHINE time)))))

(DRILL-PRESS (obj time hole-width)
   (PRECONDS
      (AND
         (IS-OBJECT obj)
         (IS-DRILLABLE obj orientation)
         (NOT (SURFACE-CONDITION obj POLISHED))
         (LAST-SCHEDULED obj prev-time)
         (LATER time prev-time)
         (IDLE DRILL-PRESS time)
         (HAVE-BIT hole-width)))
     (EFFECTS
        ((ADD (HAS-HOLE obj hole-width orientation))
         (DEL (LAST-SCHEDULED obj prev-time))
         (ADD (LAST-SCHEDULED obj time))
         (ADD (SCHEDULED obj DRILL-PRESS time)))))
```

Table 7-1: The BOLT and DRILL Operators

number of different bolts available, with various widths. Only one of those widths
will work, since there is only one drill bit available. However, this constraint is not
yet apparent to the system. After picking one of the wrong bolts, PRODIGY tries
drilling PART1. In checking the preconditions for DRILL, the system first tests
whether PART1 is drillable and unpolished. Only then does it discover that the
HAVE-BIT constraint is unsatisfied (and unachievable). Backtracking, it then
selects another bolt, and tries drilling once again. Eventually, once the correct bolt
is selected, the problem solver schedules the two DRILL operations and to carries
out the necessary inferences (e.g., inferring that the machines are IDLE) in a
straightforward manner.

```
Goal: (JOINED PART1 PART2 ORIENTATION1)

Initial-state description:
     (AND (HAVE-BIT .2)
          (IS-BOLT B1)
          (IS-WIDTH .2 B1)
          (IS-BOLT B2)
          (IS-WIDTH .3 B2)
          (IS-BOLT B3)
          (IS-WIDTH .3 B3)
          (IS-BOLT B4)
          (IS-WIDTH .4 B4)
          (IS-BOLT B5)
          (IS-WIDTH .4 B5)
          (TEMPERATURE PART1 COLD)
          (TEMPERATURE PART2 COLD)
          (IS-OBJECT PART1)
          (IS-OBJECT PART2)
          (LAST-SCHEDULED PART1 0)
          (LAST-SCHEDULED PART2 0)
          .....)
```

Table 7-2:   Goal Statement and Initial State

After solving the problem, PRODIGY can learn from the success of the various operators that were employed. The most useful of the resulting learned descriptions is the one shown in table 7-3. (The description indicates conditions under which the bindings for BOLT lead to success.) In fact, the resulting rule "solves" exactly the difficulty that PRODIGY had in this example -- choosing the bindings for BOLT. The rule indicates a preference for the bindings which will enable the operator sequence <DRILL..DRILL..BOLT> to succeed.

Let us consider whether this rule will be useful. The rule appears daunting because of the number of preconditions. In fact, the conditions come directly from the operators that PRODIGY tested during the actual search.[21] If the preconditions of the control rule are listed in the same order as they were encountered during the search, then the cost of matching the control rule will be approximately the same as the cost of exploring, or verifying, the solution sequence. This illustrates of the tradeoff between search and matching described in chapter 2.

In fact, the preconditions of the control rule are *not* listed in the same order as they are encountered during the search. This is one of the benefits of compression. For example, the bit width constraint is tested directly after the bolt is generated in the rule. Thus, the cost of matching of the rule is less than the cost of verifying the

---

[21]Some of the operators' preconditions, such the HAS-HOLE precondition of BOLT, are not present in the control rule because they are added by the preceding drilling operations. There are also additional conditions in the control rule that are not present in the individual operators' preconditions, such as (NOT-EQUAL v8 v9), which are necessary to insure that the preconditions and effects of the individual operators unify with each other in the proper manner.

solution sequence. This is especially important since the benefits of this rule are obviously *less* than the benefits of exploring the solution sequence -- the rule only specifies the bindings for BOLT. (This illustrates the major drawback to single operator learning. The rest of the solution sequence must still be constructed, even after the control rule verifies that the remainder of the sequence will match.) In this case, at least, the benefits of knowing the bindings for BOLT are considerable, since this eliminates most of the search (at least in this example). So the utility question for this rule boils down to the following: does the condition reordering carried out by compression eliminate enough search to justify the cost of matching the preconditions of the entire sequence? The answer can only be found by determining just how many bolts are available in an average example, how likely it is that a bit of the correct width is available, and how often the preconditions of the sequence match. These factors are indirectly measured during PRODIGY's empirical utility evaluation.

```
(BINDINGS-SUCCEEDS node g op bindings)
if (AND (IS-EQUAL g (JOINED v9 v8 v7))
        (IS-EQUAL op BOLT)
        (IS-EQUAL bindings (v9 v8 v6 v5 v4))
        (KNOWN node
            (AND (IS-OBJECT v9)
                 (IS-DRILLABLE v9 v7)
                 (NOT (SURFACE-CONDITION v9 POLISHED))
                 (LAST-SCHEDULED v9 v75)
                 (IS-OBJECT v8)
                 (IS-DRILLABLE v8 v7)
                 (LAST-SCHEDULED v8 v23)
                 (CAN-BE-BOLTED v9 v8 v7)
                 (IS-BOLT v4)
                 (IS-WIDTH v3 v4)
                 (HAVE-BIT v3)
                 (LATER v1 v75)
                 (NOT (EXISTS (v89) SUCH-THAT
                         (SCHEDULED v89 DRILL-PRESS v1)))
                 (NOT (EXISTS (v37) SUCH-THAT
                         (SCHEDULED v37 DRILL-PRESS v2)))
                 (LATER v2 v23)
                 (NOT (EXISTS (v14) SUCH-THAT
                         (SCHEDULED v14 BOLTING-MACHINE v5)))
                 (LATER v5 v1)
                 (LATER v5 v2)
                 (COMPOSITE-OBJECT v6 v7 v9 v8)
                 (OR (NOT-EQUAL v8 v9)
                     (AND (NOT-EQUAL v23 v75)
                          (NOT-EQUAL v1 v23))))))))
```

Table 7-3: Learned Description

7.4.2. Gridworld Example

The preceding example illustrated how *constraint reordering* can increase the utility of learning from success. The following example will illustrate the utility of *constraint combination*, another effect of compression. The example is from the 3-D robotics gridworld described in appendix I. Consider the inference rule shown in table 7-5. It indicates that a square is occupied when there exists some object whose location in 3-space encompasses the square. This rule is actually a slight variation of a rule in appendix I, INFER-OCCUPIED-SQ. In fact, the variation in table 7-5 predates the rule in the appendix, and is much less efficient. The following example illustrates why the rule is inefficient and shows how PRODIGY learns a control rule that partially overcomes the inefficiency.

```
(PUTDOWN (ob new-loc rmg-loc)
    (PRECONDS
        (VACANT-LOC new-loc)
        (OBJECT ob ob-size)
        (NEXT-TO new-loc rmg-loc)
        (LOCATION-SIZE new-loc loc-size)
        (IS-EQUAL loc-size ob-size))
        (SUPPORTED-LOC new-loc)
        (SUPPORTED-LOC rmg-loc)
        (HOLDING ob)
        (AT RMG rmg-loc)
        (WITHIN-HEIGHT new-loc rmg-loc RMG-REACH)))))
    (EFFECTS
        ((DEL (HOLDING ob))
        (ADD (AT ob new-loc)))))
```

Table 7-4:   Definition of PUTDOWN in Gridworld

```
(INFER-OCCUPIED-SQ-VERSION1 (sq obj loc)
    (PRECONDS (AND (IN sq loc)
                   (AT obj loc)))
    (EFFECTS ((ADD (OCCUPIED-SQ sq)))))
```

Table 7-5:   Inefficient OCCUPIED-SQ Inference Rule

Let us suppose that PRODIGY is asked to achieve (OCCUPIED-SQ SQUARE1) where SQUARE1 is a particular square that we have named for the reader's convenience. (A real goal might be (OCCUPIED-SQ (0 2 0 0 2 0)). Let us assume that in the initial state, SQUARE1 is not occupied. We will also assume, for convenience, that the robot is holding some object and standing right next to SQUARE1, so that all it has to do is put the object down in SQUARE1. In other words, we will assume that all the preconditions of PUTDOWN (shown in table 7-4) are satisfied in the initial state.

The first thing that the system does when it is presented with this problem, is to backchain on INFER-OCCUPIED-SQ. The precondition (IN *sq loc*), is a static formula; IN is implemented by a function. Thus matching the formula with *sq* bound to SQUARE1 generates all the possible locations which contain SQUARE1.

Unfortunately, even in a small, finite world, there will be many, many such locations. For example, in a miniscule 4x4x4 "world", there will be 96 locations containing square (0 2 0 0 2 0). In general for an NxNxN world there may be from N^3 to $N^6/64$ encompassing locations, depending on whether the square is near a corner or in the middle of the "world". PRODIGY will pick one these possible bindings for *loc*, and subgoal on (AT *obj loc*). If it cannot put an object in the location *loc*, it will eventually try the next candidate *loc*.[22]

Subgoaling on (AT *obj loc*) involves trying the operator PUTDOWN, the only relevant operator. In almost all cases, PUTDOWN will fail, because there will be no object that has the same size as the *loc*. (The preconditions of PUTDOWN specify that the object that is being putdown can only be placed into a location of the same size.) Eventually an instantiation of PUTDOWN will be found that succeeds. This may take a very long time. (Of course, the user can interrupt PRODIGY and guide the problem solver, taking advantage of PRODIGY's learning apprentice capabilities. This does not interfere with PRODIGY's method for learning from success.)

Table 7-6 shows the learned description produced by analyzing the successful instantiation of PUTDOWN, before and after compression. (Actually, both descriptions have undergone partial evaluation.) In the uncompressed description, the conditions are listed in the same order as they are encountered by the problem solver (for illustrative purposes). Matching this description is expensive, because the matcher encounters the same generator problems as the problem solver did. Specifically, it generates all encompassing locations for *sq*, and then must test all of them. The problematic generator is highlighted in the description.

The compressed description is much more efficient to match. Two transformations were performed, in addition to some condition reordering. The first transformation, EQUAL propagation (see section 5.2.2), replaced the variable *loc-size* with *ob-size* and dropped the constraint (IS-EQUAL *loc-size ob-size*). The second transformation was to apply the simplification axiom shown below:

```
(COVERS loc size sq)
if (AND (IN sq loc)
        (LOCATION-SIZE loc ob-size))
```

The formula (COVERS *loc size sq*) is used to generate all locations with a

---

[22]It might be argued that the inefficiency in INFER-OCCUPIED-SQ is due to the fact that its two preconditions are badly ordered. First, this is not true, because if the order were reversed a similar problem would arise when backchaining on PUTDOWN. Secondly, even if it was true, I would argue that the whole purpose of the learning process is to recover from poor domain specifications. A perfect domain specification would require no learning.

```
Before:
(BINDINGS-SUCCEED node goal op bindings)
    (AND (IS-EQUAL goal (OCCUPIED-SQ sq)
         (IS-EQUAL op INFER-OCCUPIED-SQ)
         (IS-EQUAL bindings (sq ob loc))
         (KNOWN node
                (AND (IN sq loc)              <--- Bad Generator
                     (VACANT-LOC loc)
                     (OBJECT ob ob-size)
                     (NEXT-TO loc rmg-loc)
                     (LOCATION-SIZE loc loc-size)
                     (IS-EQUAL loc-size ob-size))
                (SUPPORTED-LOC loc)
                (SUPPORTED-LOC rmg-loc)
                (HOLDING ob)
                (AT RMG rmg-loc)
                (WITHIN-HEIGHT loc rmg-loc RMG-REACH))))

After:
(BINDINGS-SUCCEED node goal op bindings)
    (AND (IS-EQUAL goal (OCCUPIED-SQ sq)
         (IS-EQUAL op INFER-OCCUPIED-SQ)
         (IS-EQUAL bindings (sq ob loc))
         (KNOWN node
                (AND (OBJECT ob ob-size)
                     (COVERS loc ob-size sq)
                     (VACANT-LOC loc)
                     (NEXT-TO loc rmg-loc)
                     (SUPPORTED-LOC loc)
                     (SUPPORTED-LOC rmg-loc)
                     (HOLDING ob)
                     (AT RMG rmg-loc)
                     (WITHIN-HEIGHT loc rmg-loc RMG-REACH))))
```

Table 7-6: Learned Description Before and After Compression (Phase 2 & 3)

particular size that cover a given square.[23] The use of this generator can improve the matching process by orders of magnitude. Instead of generating all locations that encompass the square (which may increase by order N^6 as the size of the world increases), only the few locations with the correct dimensions need be generated. In effect, the COMPRESSOR has combined multiple constraints into a more efficient form.

---

[23]By expanding the definition of IN and LOCATION-SIZE, it is theoretically possible for the COMPRESSOR to produce a learned description that is as efficient as that using the COVERS predicate. Thus, strictly speaking, the COVERS axiom is not strictly necessary. However, the sequence of simplifications is quite complex, and depends on having exactly the right set of simplification axioms.

7.5. Problems

The two examples in the last section illustrate how learning from success is used in PRODIGY. They also demonstrate how the COMPRESSOR's ability to propagate and combine constraints increases the utility of the learned rules. However, as described in chapter 10, PRODIGY's strategy for learning from success performs rather poorly in practice. This section outlines some of the performance problems that arise when employing this strategy, and some potential solutions.

The first problem, commonly referred to as the "generalization-to-N" problem, has recently been addressed by Shavlik and DeJong [79], and Prieditis [71]. The generalization-to-N problem occurs when a solution sequence has a repeating subsequence.[24] For example, in gridworld, moving the robot to a location might involve a repeated sequence of MOVE operations that cover a path of length N. A good control rule would abstract away from the exact number of moves in the solution, so the rule would apply to paths of length N, N+1, N+2 and so on. The problem is called the generalization-to-N problem because one does not want to use any particular operator sequence as an explanation, but instead use an explanation indicating that the subsequence can repeat "N" times. The generalization-to-N problem arises in the gridworld (and the STRIPS domain) whenever path planning occurs, it arises in the blocksworld whenever a stack is built or dismantled, and it shows up in the scheduling domain whenever a schedule is iterated through. The problem poses a particular difficultly when PRODIGY is learning from success, because there will typically be an infinite, or very large, number of operator sequences that can solve a goal. Thus PRODIGY learns a large number of overly-specific rules (i.e. rules with low application frequency). For example, in the gridworld, one rule will indicate that a goal is solvable if there is a path of length one, another rule will indicate that the goal is solvable if there is a path of length two, and so on. Furthermore, although one would hope that this problem would be partially alleviated by inter-description compression, typically the learned rules cannot be successfully combined because they do not cover the complete set of possible solutions.

Both DeJong and Shavlik [79] and Prieditis [71] have described systems that address the generalization-to-N problem by identifying repeating sequences of rules, and creating a more abstract composite rule that need not be repeatedly applied. Although PRODIGY does not currently handle the generalization-to-N problem, Sridhar Mahadevan, Prasad Tadepalli and myself have jointly described a similar solution the generalization-to-N problem [45]. Our solution uses the mechanisms described in this thesis to produce and compress explanations that capture the

---

[24]More generally, one wants to say that there is some repeating substructure in the explanation. However, if one views explanations as operator sequences, one can speak in terms of repeating subsequences.

recursive structure of repeating operator subsequences. Unlike the other recent proposals to handle the generalization-to-N problem, our proposal employs compression to reduce recursive descriptions to closed form, and thus is quite general in this respect.

A second problem with that PRODIGY's method for learning from success is that the learned control rules only indicate preferences, and thus in the current implementation cannot be used as *generators*. In other words, preference rules can only be used to order a set of alternatives, however, if the set of alternatives is very large (as in the Gridworld example in the preceding section) it would be more efficient to employ the learned control rule to generate a small subset of alternatives to try first. Unfortunately, this is not possible to do within the current control rule framework.

7.6. Factors Influencing Utility

This section describes some of the factors that determine the utility of PRODIGY's strategy for learning from success. The purpose is to provide some analytical insight into the strengths and weaknesses of the strategy, complementing the empirical data in chapter 10. As the reader will observe, the factors listed below are not necessarily independent of each other. No particular significance should be attached to the order in which they are enumerated.

To aid in the discussion, let me first clarify a few points. Each domain is implicitly associated with a set of potential problems. Each potential problem is in turn implicitly associated with a search space (or problem space); the search space can be viewed as the set of operator sequences[25] that PRODIGY may consider when solving the problem (assuming no prior control knowledge). Thus, a domain is implicitly associated with a set of potential operator sequences that may be explored. (This view was first put forth in chapter 2, and although PRODIGY is more complex than the simple problem solving/learning model explored in that chapter, the same basic concepts are relevant.)

- Solution density and distribution: The solution density of a domain refers to the percentage of potential operator sequences that are solutions to potential problems. The more potential solutions there are, the more control rules one can expect to learn, and the lower the average benefit one can expect from learned preference rules. One can view the learned preference rules as introducing experiential bias into the system, so that previously successful sequences are tried before other sequences. In the extreme case if *all* operator sequences have been successful, then the learned preferences will have no

---

[25]Actually, a single operator sequence can be composed in several different ways, depending on how the effects and preconditions of the individual operators unify with each other. Thus a more accurate term would be "operator composition" rather than "operator sequence".

benefit, and only detract from the system's efficiency. On the other hand, if only a few of the potential operator sequences are potential solutions (a low solution density), then the experiential bias will prove highly effective.

Solution distribution is closely related to solution density, and refers the distribution of solutions throughout the search space. Even when the overall solution density is high, some learned control rules may still be useful if the solution distribution is nonuniform. For example, PRODIGY specializes its target concepts so that each control rule is relevant to a particular type of goal. Thus the utility of a given control rule is primarily dependent on the solution density for that particular goal type, rather than the overall solution density.

- Number of covering solutions: Consider a case where there are many solutions associated with a goal but one particular solution is at least as good as all the others. In other words, whenever any other other solution is appropriate, so is this particular solution. As soon as this "covering" solution is learned, no other control rules will be learned for this goal. (Furthermore, any previously learned rules should be eventually eliminated by utility analysis). If there are a relatively small number of solutions which cover the domain, then fewer control rules need to be learned, and the more useful learning from success is likely to be.

- Number of partitions: Normally, a conjunctive description is more efficient to evaluate than a disjunctive description, assuming the two are semantically equivalent. Thus, PRODIGY uses inter-example compression to combine multiple rules wherever possible. Specifically, inter-example compression takes preference rules for the same operator or goal, and attempts to combine them into a conjunctive expression (although the resulting expression need not be completely conjunctive). How well can inter-example compression work, in the best case? One indicative measure is the minimum number of disjuncts, or partitions, necessary to describe the preconditions of a covering set of solution sequences (see above) in a DNF formula. (This is a simplification, because DNF may not be the most efficient representation.) While the minimum partitioning is an indication of how well inter-example compression can do in the best case, there are other factors that influence how well it will do in practice. For example, the more operator sequences necessary to achieve a covering set, the more unlikely it is that inter-example compression will successfully produce the minimum number of partitions, due to the increased difficulty of the COMPRESSOR's job.

- Constraint distance: Let us say that two atomic formulii are *related constraints* if they share a variable. For example, (AT ROBOT x) and (NEAR x y) are related constraints. If the preconditions of a potential solution contain two conjuncts that are related constraints, then their distance is the number of conjuncts that separate them. (Assume that the preconditions have the same order as they are encountered by the problem solver.) If the average distance between related constraints is high, then the re-ordering accomplished by compression is more likely to be beneficial. This factor was illustrated by the scheduling example described earlier in this chapter.

- Capacity for constraint combination: If two constraints can be compressed into a more efficiently evaluated form by simplification axioms, then compression is likely to be more beneficial. Therefore if there are many solution paths that contain such compressable set of constraints, then learning from success is more likely to be useful. (Similarly the more simplification axioms that one can provide for the domain, the higher the likelyhood that compression will be beneficial. However, there is a tradeoff -- eventually the number of simplification axioms will overwhelm the theorem-prover.)

8. Learning from Failure

This chapter describes an explanation-based method for failure-driven learning. This strategy tends to be considerably more useful than the success-driven strategy described in the previous chapter. Following the outline established in the previous chapter, a description of the strategy will first be provided, followed by several illustrative examples. The chapter will conclude with a description of some of the factors that influence the utility of learning from failure.

8.1. How PRODIGY Learns from Failure

A control choice (of a node, goal, operator, or bindings) fails when it leads only to dead ends, rather than to a solution. As with all of PRODIGY's EBL learning strategies, failure-driven learning can either be interleaved with problem solving, or it may take place after the problem solver has finished. For purposes of discussion, I will assume that the learning is invoked post-hoc, although it makes little difference to the nature of the method.

After PRODIGY encounters a failure, the failed subtree is analyzed in order to produce rejection rules. In effect, learning from failure identifies necessary conditions (for success) that were missing. There are four target concepts that can be used to learn from failure: NODE-FAILS, GOAL-FAILS, OP-FAILS, BINDINGS-FAIL. These target concepts are defined in terms of one another, as shown by the schemas listed below (which have been simplified for readability). The schemas state that the failure of a node is implied by the failure of a goal at that node, which is in turn implied by failure of the available operators under all relevant bindings. The definition is recursive because a bound operator may fail if subgoaling generates a node that fails, or applying the operator generates a node that fails. Other failure-related schemas (not shown) indicate that a node can fail if a goal-stack cycle or state cycle is detected, and a node, goal, operator or bindings can fail if they are rejected by a control rule. The full set of schemas for describing failures take up several pages of text, as described in [53]. As with PRODIGY's schemas for analyzing success and goal-interference, the schemas for failure are believed to be complete (except for very minor implementation bugs), and thus can be used to explain *any* failure that the problem solver encounters.

```
Schema-F1: A node fails if a goal at that node fails.
(NODE-FAILS node)
if (AND (ATOMIC-FORMULA goal)
        (IS-GOAL node goal)
        (GOAL-FAILS goal node))


Schema-F2: A goal fails if all operators fail to achieve it.
(GOAL-FAILS goal node)
if (FORALL op SUCH-THAT (IS-OPERATOR op)
        (OPERATOR-FAILS op goal node))


Schema-F3: An operator fails if it is irrelevant to the goal.
(OPERATOR-FAILS op goal node)
if (FORALL effect SUCH-THAT (IS-EFFECT op effect)
        (DOES-NOT-MATCH effect goal))


Schema-F4: An operator fails if it is relevant, but all bindings
fail.
(OPERATOR-FAILS op goal node)
if (FORALL bindings
        SUCH-THAT (IS-RELEVANT-BINDINGS bindings op goal)
        (BINDINGS-FAIL bindings op goal))


Schema-F5: A set of bindings fail if the operator can not be
applied with those bindings, and subgoaling fails. (Simplified
for readability.)
(BINDINGS-FAIL bindings op goal node)
if (AND (NOT-APPLICABLE bindings op node)
        (CHILD-NODE-AFTER-SUBGOALING child-node bindings op node)
        (NODE-FAILS child-node))


Schema-F6: A set of bindings fail if applying the instantiated
operator leads to failure. (Simplified for readability.)
(BINDINGS-FAIL bindings op goal node)
if (AND (IS-APPLICABLE bindings op node)
        (CHILD-NODE-AFTER-SUBGOALING child-node bindings op node)
        (NODE-FAILS child-node))
```

In addition to the four target concepts for failure, there are four related target concepts that describe when a candidate is a "sole-alternative":

```
NODE-IS-SOLE-ALTERNATIVE
GOAL-IS-SOLE-ALTERNATIVE
OP-IS-SOLE-ALTERNATIVE
BINDINGS-IS-SOLE-ALTERNATIVE
```

The schemas defining these four target concepts are shown below. In general, a control choice is said to be a sole alternative if all other choices fail. For example, an operator is a sole alternative if all other operators fail. Learning about sole-alternatives produces selection rules. Sole-alternatives can be safely selected because all the other alternatives are guaranteed to fail.

```
(NODE-IS-SOLE-ALTERNATIVE node)
if (FORALL other-node SUCH-THAT (IS-NODE other-node)
       (OR (IS-EQUAL other-node node)
           (NODE-FAILS other-node)))

(GOAL-IS-SOLE-ALTERNATIVE goal node)
if (FORALL other-goal SUCH-THAT (IS-GOAL other-goal)
       (OR (IS-EQUAL other-goal goal)
           (GOAL-FAILS other-goal node)))

(OP-IS-SOLE-ALTERNATIVE op goal node)
if (FORALL other-op SUCH-THAT (IS-OPERATOR other-op)
       (OR (IS-EQUAL other-op op)
           (OPERATOR-FAILS other-op goal node)))

(BINDINGS-IS-SOLE-ALTERNATIVE bindings op goal node)
if (FORALL other-bindings SUCH-THAT (IS-BINDINGS other-bindings)
       (OR (IS-EQUAL other-bindings bindings)
           (BINDINGS-FAIL other-bindings op goal node)))
```

In practice, NODE-IS-SOLE-ALTERNATIVE is not a useful target concept, and therefore it is not used in the implementation. It is not useful because it is never true; the set of candidate nodes at any decision point includes the entire tree, and it can never be the case that all but one node fails, since all nodes on the solution path will succeed.[26]

8.2. Heuristics for Selecting Examples

PRODIGY employs several heuristics to determine which examples of failure should be analyzed. As mentioned in chapter 4, these heuristics help PRODIGY focus on the examples which are most likely to produce useful rules:

1. Highest-failure-per-node heuristic: In order to avoid the proliferation of examples, PRODIGY only considers the highest level failures that occurred at a node. For example, if an operator fails, then although all the sets of bindings for that operator must have failed, the bindings failures are not considered "interesting". In other words, even though they are analyzed in the course of explaining why the operator failed, they will not be considered training examples in their own right. A node-level failure is the highest level of failure, then goal-level failure, then an operator level failure and finally a bindings-level failure. When an entire subtree of nodes fails, then PRODIGY considers each of the node-level failures, but not the lower level failures at each node. Consider the case where an operator fails because it was impossible to achieve its preconditions -- there will be an entire subtree of failed nodes that arose while trying to achieve the operator's preconditions.

---

[26]The trivial case where the solution path only includes one node is uninteresting, in this case the problem is already solved at the start node.

PRODIGY will use the operator-level failure as an example, as well as all the node-leve failures that occurred in the subtree below it.

2. Ignore-Clone heuristic: As described in chapter 3, when PRODIGY achieves a subgoal it generates a child node, referred to as a *clone*, by "resetting" the higher level goals that led to the subgoal. It is typically not a good idea to learn about failures at clones when the higher level node which generated the clone is also a failure node. The higher level result will tend to be more general, subsuming the result produced by analyzing the clone node.

3. Sole-alternative-must-succeed heuristic: As stated earlier, a candidate is a sole alternative when all other candidates fail. Thus, technically speaking, an alternative may fail and still be an example of a sole alternative. To avoid this situation, PRODIGY filters out examples of sole-alternatives where the candidate fails.[27]

8.3. Examples of Learning from Failure

This section illustrates some prototypical cases in which learning from failure produces significant performance improvement. The first example is taken from the scheduling episode described in section 3.3, where the problem solver constructed a plan to lathe and polish an object in order to make it cylindrical and polished. The reader will recall that the problem solver did not immediately find this solution, but first explored the possibility of rolling the object and then polishing it. This possibility failed because the object could not be clamped to the polisher once it had been rolled due to its high temperature. From this experience PRODIGY will learn a control rule that enables it to avoid repeating the mistake in the future.

Figure 8-1 illustrates the portion of the search tree analyzed by PRODIGY as it explains the failure of ROLL. The final result of the analysis, describing why ROLL failed, is shown alongside Node1. In addition the figure shows the intermediate results describing why each of the lower-level nodes failed. As have seen, PRODIGY begins the learning process by starting at the bottom left-most portion of the search tree and working upwards. The lower-level results serve as lemmas in explaining the higher level failures.

Let us walk through the learning process. As shown in figure 8-1, PRODIGY identifies the failure at Node4 to the fact that there no way to change the temperature of an object so that it is not hot. (In other words, there is no way to cool an object.) This failure is propagated up the tree to Node3, at which point PRODIGY can state that CLAMPING an object will fail if the object is not cool.

---

[27]The target concept definitions for sole-alternatives do not specify that the sole alternative must succeed. Doing so would reduce the utility of the learned rules because it would introduce the problems (described in the previous chapter) that occur when learning from success.

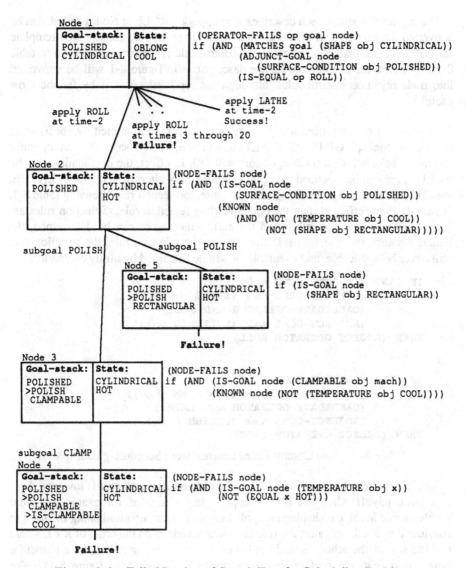

Figure 8-1: Failed Portion of Search Tree for Scheduling Problem

Continuing the postorder traversal of the failed subtree, PRODIGY concludes that the failure of Node3 is due to the fact that it is impossible to make an object rectangular. Thus Node2's failure is attributed to the fact that polishing an object is impossible if the object is not cool and not rectangular (thus it cannot be clamped and is not stable). This also immediately explains why the other attempts to apply POLISH at later time periods also failed. Finally, the top-level failure of ROLL is attributed to the fact the object had to be subsequently polished; as evidenced by the example, polishing is impossible after applying ROLL.

The top-level result, which describes why applying ROLL at Node1 failed, can be converted directly into an operator rejection rule via the rule construction template for OPERATOR-FAILS. The resulting control rule is the first rule shown in table 8-1). (In fact, all of the node-failure descriptions in figure 8-1 will be converted into node rejection control rules, although the top-level result is by far the most useful.)

However, a slightly more useful control rule can be constructed by specializing the target concept OP-IS-SOLE-ALTERNATIVE, which says that an operator should be selected if all other operators will fail. In effect, the explanation of why ROLL failed can be extended to explain why the only alternative operator, LATHE, should be selected. The resulting selection rule, the second rule shown in table 8-1, is slightly more efficient than the corresponding rejection rule. (Selection rules are checked before rejection rules, and the earlier the choice can be determined, the better. Because the selection rule fires before the rejection rule, the rejection rule will never be applicable, and eventually it will be discarded by utility evaluation.)

```
IF  (AND  (CURRENT-NODE node)
          (CURRENT-GOAL node (SHAPE obj shape))
          (CANDIDATE-OPERATOR node ROLL)
          (ADJUNCT-GOAL node (POLISHED obj)))
THEN  (REJECT OPERATOR ROLL)


IF  (AND  (CURRENT-NODE node)
          (CURRENT-GOAL node (SHAPE obj shape))
          (CANDIDATE-OPERATOR node LATHE)
          (ADJUNCT-GOAL node (POLISHED obj)))
THEN  (SELECT OPERATOR LATHE)
```

Table 8-1: Two Control Rules Learned from Scheduling Example

The learned selection rule is highly useful because its match cost is low, and there is a large payoff when the rule is applicable. Consider, for example, similar problems that involve reshaping and polishing an object. By eliminating the need to consider the ROLL operator, the rule produces a savings on the order of $n \times t$, where n is the size of the schedule, and t is the cost of considering ROLL for a particular time-period (e.g. the cost of searching nodes 2 through 5 in figure 8-1). For problems where there are intervening goals that are achieved after rolling the object but before attempting to polish it, the benefit can be as high as $O(n^k)$ where k is the number of intervening top-level goals. Empirically speaking, this rule has been observed to increase the performance of the system by over an order of magnitude on certain problems.

In general, failure-driven learning is most beneficial when the reason(s) for the failure can be expressed by a concisely, easily evaluated description. Our example also demonstrates that it is not always necessary to analyze the entire search tree in order to learn from failure. To learn why applying ROLL at Node1 failed, it was only necessary to analyze the subtree rooted at Node2. Once the reason for the failure was discovered, it immediately followed that the other applications of ROLL (at TIME-2 through TIME-20) would fail for the same reason. In fact, had learning been interleaved with problem solving, PRODIGY could have avoided these subsequent attempts to apply ROLL. In effect, when learning and problem solving are interleaved, PRODIGY's strategy for learning from failures results in a very general form of dependency-directed backtracking.

8.3.1. An In-Depth Look at Explaining a Failure

Because the schemas for explaining failures are very complex, there is a sense in which learning from failure is significantly more complex than learning from success. One reason for the complexity is that to explain a failure it is necessary to explain why *all* the branches in the subtree failed, whereas to explain success, one only has to explain why a single branch succeeded. The description of the scheduling example in the previous section skimmed over the complexity of the explanation process. In this section, a detailed view of the explanation process is presented, focusing on the failure of Node4.

As was described above, Node4 failed because the goal was (TEMPERATURE OBJECT-A COOL), and no operator was available for cooling objects. In fact, the only operator that changes an object's temperature is ROLL, and ROLL heats an object. Table 8-2 lists the relevant lower-level architectural schemas needed to explain why no operators were relevant at Node4. These schemas state that an operator fails if its postconditions do not match the goal. Normally, as we will see, much of this detail is simplified away by the compressor during the explanation process. In particular, as described earlier in chapter 5, partial evaluation plays an important role.[28]

The EBS process begins with the following target concept and example:

```
Target concept: (NODE-FAILS node)
Example: (NODE-FAILS NODE4)
```

NODE-FAILS is specialized by architectural level schemas F1 and F2 (see section 8.1), to arrive at the following:

---

[28]In fact, the reader may refer back to section 5.2.1 of chapter 5, and note the similarity between the schemas which describe when two atomic formulas match, and the schemas in table 8-2 which describe when two atomic formulas don't match. Unfortunately, although there is a single matcher in PRODIGY, both sets of schemas are necessary for the explanation process. Conceivably, the schemas describing why two formulas don't match could be automatically derived from the schemas describing when they do match. However, since the form of the schemas influences the system's bias, as discussed in section 4.3.1, this would require a system that could reason about bias.

The following schemas are used to explain why a match failed.
The arguments to the matcher are a pattern, which is an atomic formula
with variables such as (TEMPERATURE y x), a list, which is a
ground formula such as (TEMPERATURE OBJECT-A COOL) and an
initial set of bindings for the variables in the pattern. A
match fails if the list cannot be unified with the pattern.

Schema MATCH-FAIL-1: A match fails if the head element of
the pattern is a constant that is not equal to the head
element of the list.
(DOES-NOT-MATCH *pattern list bindings*)
if (AND (IS-CAR *list-head list*)
        (IS-CAR *pat-head pattern*)
        (IS-CONSTANT *pat-head*)
        (NOT (EQUAL *list-head pat-head*)))

Schema MATCH-FAIL-2: A match fails if the head element of
the pattern is a variable, and its binding is not equal
to the head element of the list
(DOES-NOT-MATCH *pattern list bindings*)
if (AND (IS-CAR *list-head list*)
        (IS-CAR *pat-head pattern*)
        (IS-VARIABLE *pat-head*)
        (IS-BINDING *value pat-head bindings*)
        (NOT (EQUAL *value list-head*)))

Schema MATCH-FAIL-3: A match fails if the head element of
the pattern matches the head element of the list, but the
remainder of the list does not match the remainder of the
pattern.
(DOES-NOT-MATCH *pattern list bindings*)
if (AND (IS-CAR *list-head list*)
        (IS-CAR *pat-head pattern*)
        (IS-CDR *rest-of-list list*)
        (IS-CDR *rest-of-pattern pattern*)
        (UPDATE-BINDINGS *new-bindings list-head pat-head bindings*)
        (DOES-NOT-MATCH *rest-of-pattern rest-of-list new-bindings*)))

Table 8-2:   Architecture-level Schemas for DOES-NOT-MATCH

(NODE-FAILS *node*)
if (AND (ATOMIC-FORMULA *goal*)
        (IS-GOAL *node goal*)
        (FORALL *op* SUCH-THAT (IS-OPERATOR *op*)
          (OPERATOR-FAILS *op goal node*))

After specializing and simplifying ATOMIC-FORMULA and IS-OPERATOR,
we have the expression shown below.   The description of the goal
(TEMPERATURE *obj temp*), comes from the expansion of ATOMIC-FORMULA.
The references to the particular operators come from expanding IS-OPERATOR.

```
(NODE-FAILS node)
if (AND (IS-GOAL node (TEMPERATURE obj temp))
        (OPERATOR-FAILS LATHE (TEMPERATURE obj temp) node)
        (OPERATOR-FAILS POLISH (TEMPERATURE obj temp) node)
        (OPERATOR-FAILS IS-CLAMPABLE (TEMPERATURE obj temp) node)
        ....
        (OPERATOR-FAILS ROLL (TEMPERATURE obj temp) node))
```

Except for ROLL, no operator or inference rule has a postcondition that can match (TEMPERATURE *obj temp*). Therefore after specialization, all of the other operator failures simplify to TRUE, and we are left with:

```
(NODE-FAILS node)
if (AND (IS-GOAL node (TEMPERATURE obj temp))
        (OPERATOR-FAILS ROLL (TEMPERATURE obj temp) node))
```

After specializing OPERATOR-FAILS by Schema-F3, and a domain-level schema listing the effects of ROLL, we have:

```
(NODE-FAILS node)
if (AND (IS-GOAL node (TEMPERATURE obj temp)
        (DOES-NOT-MATCH (TEMPERATURE obj HOT)
                        (TEMPERATURE obj temp)
                        op node)))
        (DOES-NOT-MATCH (SHAPE obj CYLINDRICAL)
                        (TEMPERATURE obj temp)
                        op node)))
        (DOES-NOT-MATCH (SCHEDULED obj ROLLER time)
                        (TEMPERATURE obj temp)
                        op node))
        (DOES-NOT-MATCH (LAST-SCHEDULED obj time)
                        (TEMPERATURE obj temp)
                        op node)))
```

The first of the DOES-NOT-MATCH expressions is successively specialized by schema MATCH-FAIL-3 (two applications) and MATCH-FAIL-2, because it was the fact that HOT was not equal to COOL (in the example) that was responsible for the failure of the match. The remaining DOES-NOT-MATCH terms are specialized by MATCH-FAIL-1, because the predicates are not equal. After simplifying we have the following, the final result of the analysis for Node4:

```
(NODE-FAILS node)
   (AND (IS-GOAL node (TEMPERATURE obj temp))
        (NOT (EQUAL HOT temp)))
```

8.3.2. The Utility of Learning from Failure: An Example

This section provides an example contrasting learning from failure with learning from success. The example, taken from the blocksworld (whose specification is given in the appendix), illustrates a situation in which learning from failure performs significantly better than learning from success.

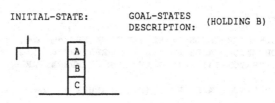

Figure 8-2: An Example Problem

The goal and initial state are shown in figure 8-2. To solve the problem, PRODIGY considers applying the operators PICKUP or UNSTACK to achieve (HOLDING B), as illustrated in figure 8-3. PICKUP is inappropriate, because a block can only be picked up from the table. However, this is only discovered during the course of solving the problem. In attempting to PICKUP B, PRODIGY is forced to subgoal on (CLEAR B) and (ONTABLE B), the unsatisfied preconditions of PICKUP. These are added to the goal-stack, and then PRODIGY attempts to solve (CLEAR B). Unstacking A from B achieves (CLEAR B), but then a goal-stack cycle occurs in attempting to achieve (ONTABLE B). PRODIGY then attempts other ways to (CLEAR B) at Node2, but these also result in failure. (The problem solver has no way of knowing that UNSTACKING A from B did not cause the failure of Node3.) Eventually backtracking to Node1, PRODIGY attempts UNSTACKING B from C, which leads to a solution.

To explain why the selection of PICKUP at Node1 failed, PRODIGY must explain why the subtree rooted at Node2 failed. The failure of PICKUP at Node2 can then be used to explain why UNSTACK, the only alternative operator relevant to (HOLDING B) was the appropriate operator at Node1. The first control rule shown in table 8-3 results from specializing of OP-IS-SOLE-ALTERNATIVE, using the training example:

    (OP-IS-SOLE-ALTERNATIVE UNSTACK (HOLDING B) NODE1)

How much does the rule save? In some cases, the savings are exponential in the number of blocks in the problem. Experimental results show that solving the problem shown in figure 8-2 with no control knowledge, takes 1.3 CPU seconds (23 nodes), and with the addition of the learned rule, .8 CPU seconds (12 nodes). If there are additional blocks on the table in the initial state then the problem is only slightly more difficult; the system will require approximately 2 nodes more per block. However, if a *single* block is added on top of block A, the system takes 15.9 CPU seconds (290 nodes) without the rule, and 2.0 CPU seconds (26 nodes) with the rule. Even more dramatically, with two blocks stacked on block A, the figures increase to 61.1 CPU seconds (1114 nodes) without the rule, and 10.9 CPU seconds (158 nodes) with the learned rule. The obvious utility of the rule in this case is amplified by the fact that the system has no other control knowledge; once the system makes the initial mistake of attempting to use PICKUP, its problems are compounded by the subsequent mistakes it makes. (As described previously, the

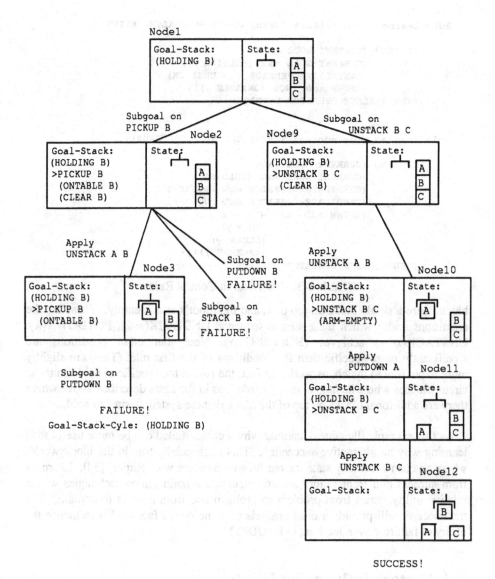

Figure 8-3: Search Tree

system tries *all* alternatives that can clear B, such as unstacking C from B.) Because the search space is exponential and PRODIGY's default search strategy is depth-first, it may take a long time until the problem solver backtracks over the initial mistake.

We can contrast this control rule with the rule learned from analyzing why UNSTACK succeeded, also shown in table 8-3. This latter rule indicates that UNSTACK is appropriate when the goal is to be holding a block *x*, *x* is on another

```
Rule learned from failure (using OP-IS-SOLE-ALTERNATIVE):

    IF (AND (CURRENT-NODE node)
            (CURRENT-GOAL node (HOLDING x))
            (CANDIDATE-OPERATOR node UNSTACK)
            (KNOWN node (NOT (ONTABLE x))))
    THEN (SELECT OPERATOR UNSTACK)


Rule learned from success (using OPERATOR-SUCCEEDS):

    IF (AND (CURRENT-NODE node)
            (CURRENT-GOAL node (HOLDING x))
            (CANDIDATE-OPERATOR node UNSTACK)
            (CANDIDATE-OPERATOR node other-op)
            (KNOWN node (AND (ON w x)
                             (ON x y)
                             (CLEAR w)
                             (ARMEMPTY))))
    THEN (PREFER OPERATOR UNSTACK TO other-op)
```

Table 8-3: Two Search Control Rules

block, there a single block on top of x, and the robot's arm is empty. These are the conditions under which the operator sequence UNSTACK(w x), PUTDOWN(w), UNSTACK(x y) achieves (HOLDING x). Note that these conditions are significantly more specific than the conditions of the first rule. (They are slightly more expensive to match, as well.) In fact, the rule is too specific to apply in those circumstances where its help is really needed, as in the cases described above where there are additional blocks on top of the block that the system desires to hold.

As this example illustrates, learning why a choice failed can be more useful than learning why an alternative succeeded. This is especially true in the blocksworld, where one can succinctly state the reason why a choice was "stupid" [38]. Learning from success and from failure are complementary optimization techniques whose relative utility varies from problem to problem and from domain to domain. The next section will provide a brief analysis of some of the factors that influence the utility of failure-driven learning in PRODIGY.

8.4. Factors Influencing Utility

This section describes some of the factors that determine the utility of PRODIGY's strategy for learning from failure. Some of these factors are related to the the factors described previously with respect to learning from success, and I adopt the same terminology.

- Solution density and distribution: If the solution density is high, then learning from failure is more likely to be useful, because fewer rules will be learned. (In contrast, a low solution density is preferable for learning from success for the complementary reason.) In the blocksworld, the solution density is high -- most operator sequences that PRODIGY explores tend to be useful under some circumstances -- and this contributes to the relative utility of learning from failure in the blocksworld. Similarly, if the solutions are distributed so that particular goals, operators, or bindings are associated with many potential solution sequences, then learning from failure will tend to be most useful for these particular candidates.

- Subtree size: The utility of learning from failure depends partly on how long it takes the problem solver to discover that a candidate fails. If the problem solver can quickly explore the subtree in question, then it may not be worth learning a control rule to avoid that search. Thus the rejection rules that are most useful tend to reject candidates that would generate large subtrees.

- Capacity for constraint combination: In general, if the reasons why a candidate fails can be compressed into an inexpensive description, then learning from failure is likely to be quite useful. This typically happens when a candidate fails and the failures at each leaf in the subtree all reflect a single underlying cause of failure.

- Number of Partitions: The number of partitions refers to the number of conjunctive descriptions necessary to express the specializations of a target concept. In general, if the learned descriptions can be combined into a small set of conjunctive descriptions (that are efficient to match) this will improve the performance of the learning system. However, as pointed out in the previous chapter, other considerations can effect the influence of this factor. For example, if a large number of examples are required to "cover" the target concept, then it is less likely that compression will be able to find the best way to combine these descriptions.

9. Learning from Goal Interactions

Goal interactions are ubiquitous in planning. They may be either beneficial or detrimental to the planning process. Beneficial goal interactions occur when solving one goal makes a second goal easier to solve; this is generally termed *goal concord*. Similarly, detrimental goal interactions happen when solving one goal makes a second goal harder to achieve; this case is referred to as *goal interference*.

This chapter describes an explanation-based method for learning from goal interference. (Learning from goal concord is not addressed, although presumably it could be implemented similarly.) Much of the previous work in planning has focused on methods for avoiding goal interferences. For example, Sacerdoti's NOAH system [75] constructs plans separately for each goal and then attempts to merge them, avoiding interferences where possible, and patching the plans if necessary. In contrast, PRODIGY reasons about observed interferences in order to *learn* search control rules that enable the system to handle similar interactions efficiently. This approach was first pioneered by Sussman's HACKER [83] program. In the following sections I describe how the approach can be implemented using EBL. As in the previous two chapters, I first describe some prototypical cases where learning produces improved behavior, and give a brief analysis of some of the factors involved.

9.1. How PRODIGY learns from Goal Interference

A well-known example of goal interference occurs in the blocks world problem shown in figure 9-1. If the goal (ON A B) is addressed before (ON B C), then the two goals interfere. Specifically, if A is placed on B there is no way to then achieve (ON B C) without first unstacking A from B. The resulting plan involves stacking A on B twice.

In the general case, we say that a plan exhibits goal interference if there is a goal in the plan that has been negated by a previous step in the plan. There are two complementary forms in which a goal interference may manifest itself during planning. A *protection violation* occurs when an action undoes a previously achieved goal, requiring the goal to be re-achieved. A *prerequisite violation* occurs when an action negates a goal that arises later in the planning process. In our example, a prerequisite violation occurs when stacking A on B deletes (CLEAR B),

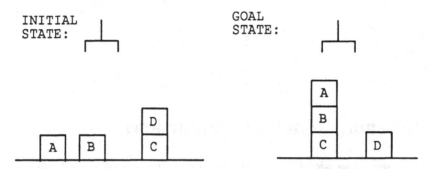

Figure 9-1: A Blocks World Problem Illustrating Goal Interference

since (CLEAR B) is a goal that arises when attempting to achieve (ON B C). (Furthermore, a protection violation will follow when picking up B deletes the previously achieved goal (ON A B). The two phenomena can also occur independently.) Goal interferences may result in sub-optimal plans or the outright failure to find a plan. In this section we will only consider the first case, since learning from failure is covered by the schemas described the the previous chapter.

Since goal interferences may be unavoidable in some problems (and may even occur in optimal plans) PRODIGY learns preference rules, rather than selection or rejection rules. This enables solutions to be found that minimize the adverse effects of interferences even when avoiding all interferences proves impossible. In those cases when goal interferences can be avoided, search time is typically reduced, and in addition, better solutions (i.e., shorter in length) tend to be found. Learning to avoid goal interference is an optimization technique specifically designed for planning domains; In other types of domains (e.g., theorem-proving) where interferences do not occur, this technique is not applicable.

The four target concepts relevant to explaining goal interferences are the following:

```
NODE-RESULTS-IN-GOAL-INTERFERENCE
GOAL-RESULTS-IN-GOAL-INTERFERENCE
OP-RESULTS-IN-GOAL-INTERFERENCE
BINDINGS-RESULTS-IN-GOAL-INTERFERENCE
```

In general, a candidate (node, goal, operator or bindings) results in a goal interference if all paths resulting from that candidate's selection result in either a failure, a prerequisite violation or a protection violation. Table 9-1 shows some of the proof schemas that are used to define goal-interactions. The schemas for goal interactions capitalize on the schemas for failure in two ways. First, many of the schemas are identical in structure to the schemas for failure, as can be seen be referring back to the previous chapter. Secondly, they make direct use of (i.e., are a superset of) the failure schemes, as illustrated by schema-I6. (In fact, the target concept for goal-interference is essentially a generalization of the target concept for failure. Goal-interferences can be regarded as a "soft failures", as opposed to "hard failures".)

9.2. Heuristics for Selecting Examples

PRODIGY uses two heuristics to determine which examples of interference should be analyzed. These training example selection heuristics enable PRODIGY to focus on the examples which are most likely to produce useful rules. The two heuristics are described below:

1. Highest interaction per node heuristic: This heuristic is essentially the same as the "highest failure per node" heuristic described in the previous chapter. In order to avoid the proliferation of examples, PRODIGY restricts its attention to the highest level goal interaction it can find at each node. So, for example, if all sets of bindings for an operator result in interaction, PRODIGY will analyze why the operator resulted in an interaction, but it not learn rules for each of the individual examples at the bindings level, and so on.

2. Ignore-standard-failures heuristic: Technically speaking, every example of a failure qualifies as an example of a goal interaction, since the definition of a goal interaction subsumes that of failure. However PRODIGY does not consider a failure to be an interesting example of a goal interaction unless there is at least one prerequisite violation or protection violation in the failed subtree.

9.3. A Blocksworld Example

The blocksworld problem described earlier, shown in figure 9-1, provides a simple example illustrating the power of the learning technique. As we have described, putting A on B before putting B on C leads to a suboptimal solution. After observing such a solution, PRODIGY will notice that putting A on B created a prerequisite violation with respect to putting B on C. (This "noticing" is done by a target concept recognition function.) However, to explain why the decision to solve (ON A B) before (ON B C) caused a goal-interaction, PRODIGY must show that *all* paths on the search tree subsequent to that decision terminate in a protection violation, a prerequisite violation or a failure. Thus, the search tree must be expanded until this can be proved for each path below the decision point. In this example, only a few extra nodes must be explored. The expanded search tree is shown in figure 9-2. (The top-level goals are shown as an unordered conjunction at Node1 to emphasize the fact that PRODIGY will actually consider both possible orderings of the top-level goals. For simplicity, previous diagrams have only shown one ordering of the top-level goals.)

The target concept for this example is GOAL-RESULTS-IN-INTERFERENCE. This concept is appropriate for goal ordering examples, where choosing a particular goal (to be solved first) results in goal interference. The learned rule will be a goal

Schema-I1: A node results in goal interference if there exists a set of goals at that node that mutually interfere.
```
(NODE-RESULTS-IN-GOAL-INTERFERENCE node)
if (AND (SET-OF-GOALS goals node)
        (FORALL goal SUCH-THAT (MEMBER goal goals)
           (AND (GOAL-RESULTS-IN-GOAL-INTERFERENCE goal node)
                (INTERFERENCE-DEPENDS-ON-GOAL-SET goal node goals))))
```

Schema-I2: A goal results in goal interference if all operators result in goal interference once that goal is selected.
```
(GOAL-RESULTS-IN-GOAL-INTERFERENCE goal node)
if (FORALL op SUCH-THAT (IS-OPERATOR op)
        (OPERATOR-RESULTS-IN-GOAL-INTERFERENCE op goal node))
```

Schema-I3: An operator results in goal-interference if all bindings for that operator result in goal-interference.
```
(OPERATOR-RESULTS-IN-GOAL-INTERFERENCE op goal node)
if (FORALL bindngs SUCH-THAT (IS-RELEVANT-BINDINGS bindings op goal)
        (BINDINGS-RESULT-IN-GOAL-INTERFERENCE bindings op goal))
```

Schema-I4: A set of bindings for an operator results in goal-interference if the operator cannot be applied with those bindings, and subgoaling results in goal-interference. (Simplified)
```
(BINDINGS-RESULT-IN-GOAL-INTERFERENCE bindings op goal node)
if (AND (NOT-APPLICABLE bindings op node)
        (IS-CHILD-NODE-AFTER-SUBGOALING child-node bindings op node)
        (NODE-RESULTS-IN-GOAL-INTERFERENCE child-node))
```

Schema-I5: A set of bindings for an operator results in goal-interference if applying the instantiated operator results in goal-interference. (Simplified)
```
(BINDINGS-RESULT-IN-GOAL-INTERFERENCE bindings op goal node)
if (AND (IS-APPLICABLE bindings op node)
        (IS-CHILD-NODE-AFTER-SUBGOALING child-node bindings op node)
        (NODE-RESULTS-IN-GOAL-INTERFERENCE child-node))
```

Schema-I6: A node results in goal-interference if the node fails.
```
(NODE-RESULTS-IN-GOAL-INTERFERENCE: node)
if (NODE-FAILS node)
```

Schema-I7: Defines a prerequisite violation (for top-level goals).
```
(NODE-RESULTS-IN-GOAL-INTERFERENCE node)
if (AND (IS-TOP-LEVEL-GOAL node goal)
        (OR (AND (IS-NEGATIVE-FORMULA goal)
                 (WAS-ADDED-AT-NODE node goal))
            (AND (IS-POSTIVE-FORMULA goal))
                 (WAS-DELETED-AT-NODE node goal)))))
```

Table 9-1: Illustrative Architecture-level Schemas for GOAL-INTERFERENCE

preference rule.

The intermediate results that PRODIGY produces as it specializes the target concept are shown alongside the nodes in the search tree. The key point in the learning process occurs at Node3, where EBS reveals that achieving (ON *v1 v2*) before (ON *v3 v4*) results in an interaction if *v2* equals *v3*. (The names of the variables are changed for expository purposes.) The equality constraint arises because achieving (ON *v1 v2*) must delete (CLEAR *v3*) for the prerequisite violation to occur. In other words, the fact that *v2* and *v3* were incidently bound to the same constant in the example is *not* the reason for the equality constraint.

It is also worth pointing out that the result at Node3 eliminates the necessity of having to analyze the branch labeled UNSTACK(A *underob*) emanating from Node2, because this result at Node3 immediately holds for Node2.

The preference rule learned from this example is shown below. This rule not only improves search time, but does so by producing shorter solutions. In the best case, the rule may produce a speedup that is exponential in the number of goals. This case occurs when the default ordering of goals is such that, without the rule, the system explores every possible ordering before it is successful. This can be illustrated empirically as follows. The example problem takes 3.0 CPU seconds (32 nodes) to produce a solution of length 10 without the learned rule, and 1.5 CPU seconds (14 nodes) to produce the optimal (length 6) solution. If the goal is changed to (AND (ON A B)(ON B C)(ON C D)), with the same initial state, the results change dramatically. Without the rule, PRODIGY takes 38.9 CPU sections (236 nodes) to find a solution of length 18, but with the learned rule only 5.3 CPU seconds (18 nodes) to find the optimal solution of length 8.

```
IF (AND (CURRENT-NODE node)
        (CANDIDATE-GOAL node (ON x y))
        (CANDIDATE-GOAL node (ON w x)))
THEN (PREFER GOAL (ON x y) TO (ON w x))
```

9.4. A Scheduling Example

Our second example is taken from the scheduling problem described in section 3.3, where the problem solver constructs a plan to lathe and polish an object in order to make it cylindrical and polished. However, we will modify the problem slightly in order to illustrate how PRODIGY learns to avoid goal interferences. Let us assume that PRODIGY first attempted to solve the goal (SURFACE-CONDITION OBJECT-A POLISHED) before the goal (SHAPE OBJECT-A CYLINDRICAL), as shown in figure 9-3. (Again, as in the previous example, the top-level goals are shown as an unordered conjunction at Node1 to illustrate that PRODIGY will actually consider both possible goal orderings.) After successfully polishing the object, the system attempts to reshape it. Both lathing the object and rolling the object have the unfortunate side effect of deleting (SURFACE-CONDITION

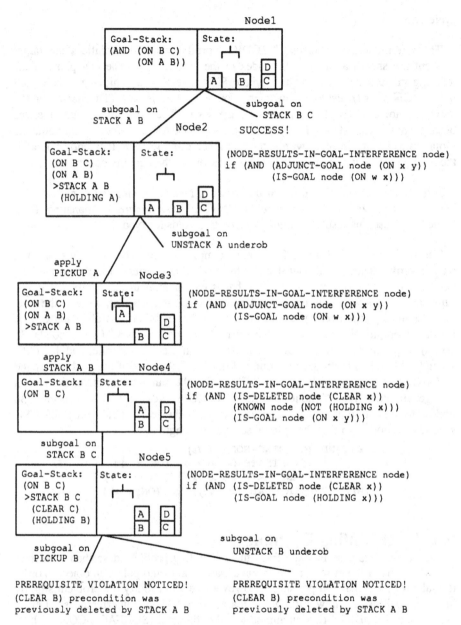

Figure 9-2: Search Tree for Blocksworld Problem

OBJECT-A POLISHED). Of course, PRODIGY can re-polish the object, in which case the resulting plan will involve polishing the object twice. However, by noticing the goal protection violation that occurs when (SURFACE-CONDITION OBJECT-A POLISHED) is deleted, PRODIGY can learn to avoid this interaction by ordering the goals correctly[29].

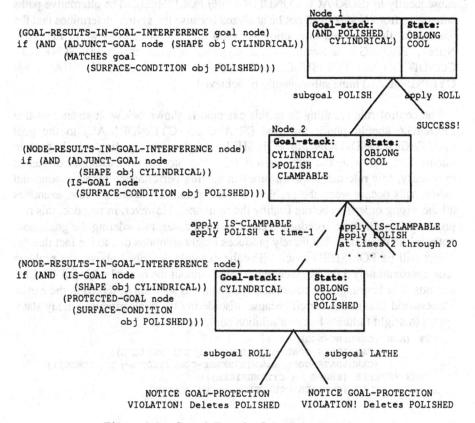

```
(GOAL-RESULTS-IN-GOAL-INTERFERENCE goal node)
if (AND (ADJUNCT-GOAL node (SHAPE obj CYLINDRICAL))
        (MATCHES goal
            (SURFACE-CONDITION obj POLISHED)))
```

```
(NODE-RESULTS-IN-GOAL-INTERFERENCE node)
if (AND (ADJUNCT-GOAL node
            (SHAPE obj CYLINDRICAL))
        (IS-GOAL node
            (SURFACE-CONDITION obj POLISHED)))
```

```
(NODE-RESULTS-IN-GOAL-INTERFERENCE node)
if (AND (IS-GOAL node
            (SHAPE obj CYLINDRICAL))
        (PROTECTED-GOAL node
            (SURFACE-CONDITION
                obj POLISHED)))
```

Figure 9-3: Search Tree for Scheduling Problem

In order to explain why the initial goal ordering resulted in goal interference, PRODIGY must show that all paths in the search tree subsequent to that goal choice point resulted in either a failure or goal interference. To formulate its explanation, PRODIGY will use the target concept GOAL-RESULTS-IN-GOAL-INTERFERENCE, which describes why choosing a goal at a node results in goal interference.

---

[29]Note that not all examples of goal interactions involve learning about goal orderings. For example, learning why an operator causes an interaction will result in an operator preference rule.

The tree shown in figure 9-3 is annotated with the results derived during the EBS process. As the figure illustrates, PRODIGY notices that both ROLL and LATHE result in a goal interaction once the POLISHED condition becomes a protected goal. Then, at Node2, the interaction is attributed to the fact that (SHAPE *obj* CYLINDRICAL) was an adjunct goal, and therefore slated to be achieved subsequently to (SURFACE-CONDITION *obj* POLISHED). The alternative paths emanating from Node2 need not be analyzed because the system determines that the reasons for the observed interaction are valid for each of them as well. Finally at Node1, PRODIGY determines that selecting a goal matching (SURFACE-CONDITION *obj* POLISHED) will result in an interaction if (SHAPE *obj* CYLINDRICAL) must subsequently be achieved.

The control rule resulting from this example is shown below. It states that that PRODIGY should prefer the goal (SHAPE *obj* CYLINDRICAL) to the goal (SURFACE-CONDITION *obj* POLISHED) when it is deciding which goal to pursue first. As with the rule learned from the blocksworld example discussed previously, this rule can improve problem solving performance by an exponential factor. This occurs when the problem solver, operating without the rule, examines all the wrong orderings before finding the right one. However, in practice, this rule produces less dramatic speedups because in most cases, misordering the goals does not result in dead ends, but merely produces longer solutions due to the fact that the object will be POLISHED twice. (For the example described above, the problem took approximately 3.0 CPU seconds to solve without the control rule, and 1.2 CPU seconds after learning.) In contrast, the tremendous speedup observed in the earlier blocksworld example occurred because misordering the goals produced many state-cycles (outright failures) before a solution could be found.

```
IF (AND (CURRENT-NODE node)
        (CANDIDATE-GOAL node (SHAPE obj CYLINDRICAL))
        (CANDIDATE-GOAL node (SURFACE-CONDITION obj POLISHED)))
   THEN (PREFER (SHAPE obj CYLINDRICAL)
               TO (SURFACE-CONDITION obj POLISHED))
```

9.5. Factors Influencing Utility

The learning strategy described in this chapter is in certain respects quite different from the strategies of learning from success and failure. The rules that are learned not only improve the efficiency of the problem solver, but also tend to produce better quality solutions. The solutions are generally shorter and require less resources, characteristics which may be more important in some domains than in others. Thus, while I have primarily ignored the quality issue in order to focus on search time efficiency, it must nevertheless be mentioned as a potentially significant factor impacting the usefulness of a learning strategy. Having said this, I will now proceed to describe some of the factors that determine whether PRODIGY's strategy for learning from goal interactions improves search time efficiency. Unfortunately, the factors appear to be much more complex than for learning from success and failure, and so I mention only the more obvious:

- Density and distribution of interactions: If there are never any goal interactions encountered when solving problems, then obviously no rules will be learned, and thus there will be no effect on behavior. At the other extreme, if along *every* path in the problem space a goal interaction can arise, then all the learned preference rules will conflict with one and other. This will dramatically slowdown the problem solver. The best situation arises when at every decision point, there is a single "good" path -- one that does not involve a goal interaction. This will maximize the benefit of the learned rules. Thus, the distribution of interactions appears to be a crucial factor in determining how effective this learning strategy is.

- Difference in Solution Length: If, for a particular decision, there are solution paths with interactions and solution paths without interactions, learning to avoid interactions will provide the most power when the solution paths with interactions are typically much longer than the solution paths without interactions.

- Subtree size/Distance between decision and violation: With respect to a given path, the benefit of the learned rules increases with the number of intervening operators between the place where the violation occurs, and the place were the decision leading to the violation is made. The more intervening operators there are, the more time that is wasted, since their effects are undone. This factor is closely related to the "subtree size", the number of nodes in the subtree below the interaction.

10. Performance Results

This chapter presents the results of a set of experiments designed to measure the performance of PRODIGY's EBL subsystem. Although the previous chapters have described individual examples for which learning produces exponential speedup, as I have argued earlier, the real test of a learning method is whether it produces improvement with extended usage in a problem solving domain. Producing performance improvement on isolated examples is a necessary condition, but not a sufficient condition. Consequently the tests described in this chapter measure PRODIGY's performance improvement over populations of problems. Equally important, the experiments were conducted in several different domains, since the utility of the learning process varies from domain to domain. The emphasis on performance improvement over a large population examples is relatively new in machine learning, and therefore this chapter also considers what constitutes an appropriate methodology for evaluating programs with respect to this criterion. Finally, this chapter evaluates the relative contributions made by individual components of the learning system.

10.1. Randomly Generating Problems

How does one empirically measure the performance of a general problem solver that learns? Since a general problem solver can supposedly be employed in *any* domain, ideally one would like to measure the improvement produced by learning in a set of "randomly selected domains". Unfortunately, the concept of a "random domain" is difficult to pin down. It is analogous to the concept of a "random integer" -- there is no such thing. It seems that the best we can do do is to evaluate a system's performance on a set of standard, or "typical", test domains. The situation is quite similar to that found in the fields of program optimization and performance evaluation. Normally one tests an optimization technique on a suite of test programs that are acknowledged standards. This approach has its limitations; the optimizer may be tailored to the test suite, since it is known in advance, and the test suite may or may not accurately reflect the population of programs that are written. However, this is probably the most practical and convincing way to test performance.

Unfortunately, at the present time there is no standard methodology for comparing problem solving systems, nor are there many standard task domains (for reasons discussed in the next section). Nevertheless, there do exist several domains that are well-known throughout the AI community, including the blocksworld and STRIPS robot world. Thus these were used as two of the test domains for the experiments described in this chapter (although additional operators were added to the original STRIPS domain to increase its complexity). The other test domain, the scheduling domain, was created specifically for PRODIGY. The three domains have a variety of different characteristics.[30] For example (given the domain specifications in appendix A) solving blocksworld problems typically requires deep subgoaling, while solving scheduling problems usually involves shallow subgoaling. The characteristics of each domain are discussed later in this chapter when the relevant experiments are described.

A domain can be viewed as a *population* of problems, each with a given probability of being selected on any particular trial. To properly evaluate a learning system, it is essential that the suite of test problems be an unbiased sample of the domain. For the experiments described in this chapter, test problems were randomly generated by fixed procedures. The procedures each take several parameters dictating the maximum "size" of the generated problems. For example, the procedure for generating blocksworld problems takes a maximum number of blocks, and a maximum number of goals. Thus, properly speaking, the procedures do not actually generate examples from the domain as a whole, but rather from a subdomain dictated by the size parameters.

To enable the experiments reported here to be replicated, the description of each domain in the appendix includes the procedure for generating problems. In practice, randomly generating problems appears to be quite important for measuring the utility of learned rules. At least in my own experience, the distribution of "easy" and "hard" problems was often surprising.

10.2. Standards for Comparisons

Another difficulty in evaluating the effectiveness of an EBL problem solver is that there are no obvious standards against which the system should be compared. One can compare problem solving performance after learning to optimal performance, but this is impractical in many domains where it is not clear what constitutes an optimal problem solver. One can define optimality in terms of the worst case complexity of solving problems in the domain, however, this ignores constant factors which may be quite important in practice (especially in cases where the match cost and benefit of learned rules are constant factors).

---

[30]Originally, the 3-D gridworld domain was also slated to be a test domain for the experiments. Unfortunately, however, without adequate control knowledge, even the simplest problems in this domain could not be solved by the problem solver. This presented a serious difficultly for the large-scale experiments described in this chapter. At the present time, only isolated examples have been tested in this domain.

A more reasonable alternative is to compare the rules learned by the system to rules generated by human experts. In the ideal case, the system should learn control rules that are at least as good as the rules coded by experts. Therefore, for each of the test domains, a set of control rules was written by other members of the PRODIGY group (Craig Knoblock and Yolanda Gil), with my help. To help generate the rules they were given the same set of problems that PRODIGY was given as its training set. Constructing and debugging the rules was time-consuming; for both the STRIPS domain and the scheduling domain several hours (approximately 4 to 7) were required.

A third possibility for evaluating the system's performance is to compare it against other EBL problem solvers. Unfortunately, there are very few implemented EBL systems besides PRODIGY that are sufficiently robust to operate in multiple domains and solve many problems. Furthermore, these EBL systems are typically embedded in radically different problem solvers, which use very different representations for their input. Comparing PRODIGY to SOAR, for instance, is akin to comparing an optimizing Lisp compiler to an optimizing C compiler. As pointed out in chapter 3, even minor differences in a domain specification, such as the inclusion of an additional precondition, can dramatically effect the performance of a problem solver. It is the *specification* of the domain which determines the complexity of that domain for a problem solver, not the domain itself. For example, the blocksworld specification used in this thesis creates search trees that grow exponentially in the size of the problem for PRODIGY. However, it is possible to code the blocksworld domain so that all problems are solved in linear time, by building control knowledge into the specification. (In fact, because PRODIGY is equivalent to a universal turing machine, it is possible to make the system simulate any other system merely by tinkering with the domain specification.)

Furthermore, even if two problem solvers use a similar representation (e.g., STRIPS operators) they may operate quite differently, in which case it is difficult to compare their learning mechanisms. For example, comparing the effect of learning on a linear problem solver and a non-linear problem solver may be quite difficult, even though the same representation is used. This is because the two problem solvers may differ dramatically in what constitutes a hard problem.

Given the difficulties in comparing PRODIGY directly with other existing EBL systems, the approach adopted here was to write a traditional EBL macro-operator learning component for PRODIGY, and compare its performance against the "new" EBL component described in this book. This was straightforward to implement, since macro-operator learning is a simple variation of PRODIGY's strategy for learning from success. However, as described in section 10.8, even this comparison was more complex than one would expect.

10.3. Methodology

For each of the three test domains the following experimental methodology was used. First, a training set of 75-100 problems was generated. The training set was purposely biased by filtering out problems that were judged too difficult or too easy as the system was learning. This was done in order to speed up the learning process. If this had not been done, many more problems would have been needed in order to achieve the same level of performance. Biasing the training set is not inconsistent with the use of PRODIGY as a learning apprentice. However, if the set is too biased, it will not be representative of the real population of problems and consequently the usefulness of PRODIGY's empirical utility evaluation will suffer. Section 10.9 discusses in detail why biasing the training set can produce more effective learning, and the reasons why this was done for the experiments.

When processing the first ten training problems in each domain, the problem solver was instructed to completely expand the search tree until all paths either succeeded or failed. Normally, of course, the problem solver immediately terminates after finding a solution. By having the problem solver completely expand the tree, the learning system could quickly learn about the many outrightly "stupid" alternatives that immediately failed. Normally, on simple problems, the problem solver's default heuristics are smart enough to avoid these alternatives. Thus they are only expanded when solving complex problems (when the problem solver backtracks) and then they greatly complicate both the search and the learning process. Consequently, by learning about simple failures early, the learning process is greatly facilitated.

After the training phase, learning was turned off, except for utility evaluation, and the system was put through a shorter "settling" phase. This phase, consisting 15-25 randomly generated problems, was included so that the rules learned at the end of the training phase could undergo empirical utility evaluation. Furthermore, the settling phase provided a completely unbiased set of problems, partially compensating for any bias in the the problem distribution that might have been introduced in the training phase.[31]

Finally, in the test phase, a test set of 100 randomly generated problems was presented to the system. When generating the problems, the parameters setting the maximum size of the problem were gradually increased. This was done for illustrative purposes. For all problems, a time limit of 80 CPU seconds was employed, after which search was terminated. (All of the experments were

---

[31]At the end of the settling phase, utility validation was turned off, and all learned rules that had never fired were eliminated from the system, despite having a positive utility value. This was done because a positive utility value for any such rules could have come about only because of an extremely high original savings estimate. In other words, since the rules had never fired, the system must not have been running long enough for the rules' match cost to accumulate to the break-even point. Therefore the system was programmed to discard them, a cautious measure.

conducted using the Franzlisp version of PRODIGY, fully compiled, running on a MicroVax II with 8 megabytes of main memory.)

10.4. Performance in the Blocksworld Domain

The blocksworld training phase consisted of 90 problems, followed by a settling phase of 25 problems. Over the course of the blocksworld training phase 328 training example/target concept pairs were expanded via the EBS algorithm, and 69 of the resulting descriptions were converted into rules. Of these, 50 were eventually discarded on the basis of empirical utility measurements, resulting in a final rule set containing 19 rules.

Problem	sol length	search time with cntrl	search time no cntrl	learning time
BW-TRN5	1	0.3	0.2	8.8
BW-TRN10	2	1.4	0.3	0.3
BW-TRN15	4	2.7	0.5	0.4
BW-TRN20	3	10.5	6.0	77.1
BW-TRN25	6	5.3	1.0	11.2
BW-TRN30	4	5.5	1.8	31.0
BW-TRN35	18	21.7	30.8	31.5
BW-TRN40	5	4.4	1.5	1.1
BW-TRN45	5	3.5	1.6	12.6
BW-TRN50	1	1.9	0.6	11.4
BW-TRN55	2	1.3	0.2	0.2
BW-TRN60	4	3.0	0.7	0.4
BW-TRN65	5	21.1	80.1	45.7
BW-TRN70	6	5.5	1.5	12.0
BW-TRN75	12	12.4	22.5	4.7
BW-TRN80	9	9.8	3.0	7.4
BW-TRN85	7	8.4	57.8	5.9
BW-TRN90	10	6.7	6.8	2.2

Table 10-1: Sample Data from the Blocksworld Training Phase

Table 10-1 shows the results for every fifth training problem. The first column lists the problem number, the second column gives the number of operators on the solution path, the third lists the time spent solving the problem (in CPU seconds), and the fourth column shows the time necessary for the system to solve the example without any control rules. The final column shows the learning time (not including the time necessary to expand the tree to verify goal interferences).

The test phase consisted of 100 problems. The MAX-BLOCKS and MAX-GOALS factors were gradually increased from three blocks and three goals to twelve blocks and ten goals. Table 10-2 lists performance results for every fifth test problem. The table indicates the time to solve each problem without the learned

Problem	no cntrl rules		learned rules		hand-coded rules	
	time	nodes	time	nodes	time	nodes
BW-TST5	0.6	10(10)	1.9	10(10)	1.0	10(10)
BW-TST10	0.2	4(4)	0.4	4(4)	0.3	4(4)
BW-TST15	0.6	15(4)	1.2	8(4)	0.8	10(4)
BW-TST20	1.2	10(10)	2.8	10(10)	1.9	10(10)
BW-TST25	7.1	175(12)	4.4	12(12)	2.1	12(12)
BW-TST30	0.5	10(10)	1.7	10(10)	1.0	10(10)
BW-TST35	10.9	173(40)	25.0	68(24)	5.4	24(24)
BW-TST40	28.5	684(30)	13.0	26(26)	6.0	26(26)
BW-TST45	80.0	2142(*)	6.1	12(12)	2.7	12(12)
BW-TST50	0.6	4(4)	1.2	4(4)	0.5	4(4)
BW-TST55	3.0	30(14)	6.7	14(14)	3.2	14(14)
BW-TST60	80.0	1794(*)	13.6	14(14)	5.4	14(14)
BW-TST65	0.4	4(4)	0.7	4(4)	0.5	4(4)
BW-TST70	0.2	4(4)	0.7	4(4)	0.3	4(4)
BW-TST75	1.8	43(10)	2.1	10(10)	1.2	10(10)
BW-TST80	80.0	1701(*)	41.8	28(28)	15.0	28(28)
BW-TST85	80.0	1764(*)	34.3	30(30)	13.5	30(30)
BW-TST90	3.8	46(10)	5.8	10(10)	2.5	10(10)
BW-TST95	33.9	839(14)	7.0	14(14)	3.2	14(14)
BW-TST10	80.0	1886(*)	32.7	44(34)	8.9	22(22)

Table 10-2: Sample Data from the Blocksworld Test Phase

rules, with the learned rules and with the rules that were hand-coded by the human expert. In addition, the table indicates the number of nodes expanded by the problem solver for each condition and next to this, in parenthesis, the number of nodes on the solution path[32]. (A asterisk indicates that no solution was found within the allotted time.) A complete table of results for all training and test problems is given in [53].

Figure 10-1 graphically illustrates the test phase performance results for each of the three conditions. The top graph shows how the *cumulative problem solving time* grew as the number of examples increased. The cumulative time is the total problem solving time *over all examples* up to that point. (This is the value that the learning system attempts to minimize.) Thus, the slopes of the curves are positive because the y-axis represents cumulative time. The fact that the problems were progressively more difficult is reflected in the fact that the *second derivatives* of the curves are positive. The bottom graph shows how the *average problem* solving

---

[32]Typically the number of nodes on the solution path is approximately twice the solution length plus two. The multiplier of two comes from the fact that for each operator that cannot be directly applied, PRODIGY must subgoal, and then rematch the operator. The extra two nodes are the initial and final nodes, which the system always generates.

time varied as the problems became more difficult; the one hundred test problems were divided in into ten groups of ten and the problem solving time for each group of problems was averaged. (In both graphs, problems that were not solved in the 80 CPU second time limit were counted as taking 80 CPU seconds). Notice that the curves (in the bottom graph) are generally rising, which is due to the fact that the problems were, in general, progressively more difficult. However, the curves do not rise monotonically which indicates that the later problems were not *necessarily* more difficult. This is due to two factors. First, although the MAX-BLOCKS and MAX-GOALS parameters were increased as the problems were generated, they to not directly correspond to the difficulty of the problem as far as the problem solver is concerned. Secondly, the problems were randomly generated (within the range specified by the parameters) so that the number of blocks and number of goals for a particular problem could be less than the maximum.

An examination of the results shows that overall learning produced a large performance improvement over non-learning, but not unexpectedly, the hand-coded rules produced even better improvement. Notice that for the first thirty problems, which could all be solved very quickly, the system performed slightly better without the learned rules than with then.

In general, the payoff from learning grew with the difficulty of the problem. Interestingly, if one only compares the problems that the non-learning system solved within the 80 second time limit, one finds that the total speedup over these problems due to learning is close to zero. This suggests that the problems that the system solved, it solved relatively quickly. The real benefit from learning comes when the problem solver gets lost; in particular, if the size of the problem is large the problem solver quickly becomes swamped by the exponential size of the search tree whenever it makes a mistake.

The factor that best illustrates the knowledge/search tradeoff is the average time per node expansion. Over all problems, the average time per node without learning is 0.044 seconds, whereas with learning the time per node is 0.553 seconds. With the hand-coded rules, the time per node is 0.245 seconds. Thus the learned rules slow the problem solver down by over a factor of ten, and the human coded rules by a factor of five. The slowdown is highly correlated to the number of rules in the system. Only nine rules were employed in the hand-coded set, as compared to nineteen learned rules. (A certain percentage of this slowdown may be attributable solely to the overhead of calling the search control code, which in general has not been as highly optimized as the problem solving code. This is believed to be a minor factor.)

The coverage of the learned rules was largely adequate, since only two problems were unsolved within the given time limit. The hand-coded rules successfully solved all the problems, whereas without control rules, nineteen problems remained unsolved. Another measure of coverage is the total number of nodes that were

Figure 10-1: Relative Performance on Blocksworld Test Phase Problems

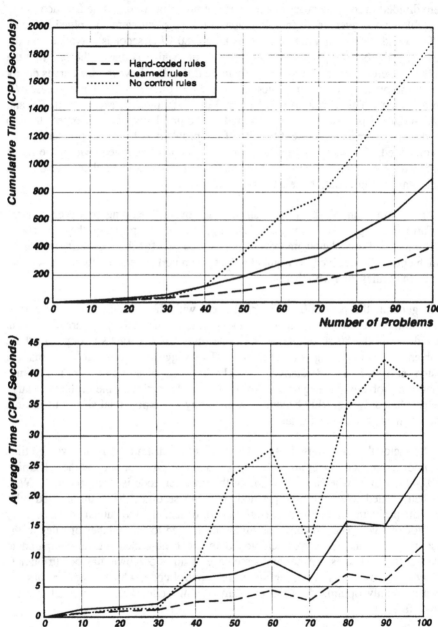

explored during the test phase. Without control rules, 42,792 nodes were explored. In contrast, the learned rules focused the search so that only 1,641 nodes were explored. Similarly, with the hand-coded rules only 1,644 nodes were explored. This is another indication that the learned rules were as powerful, with respect to their coverage, as the hand-coded rules.

The fact that the learned rules had the same coverage as the hand-coded rules, but were twice as expensive to use, indicates that despite the actions of the compressor, a better representation of the learned rules could probably be found. A careful comparison of the actual rule sets appears to support this conjecture. In my opinion, the knowledge expressed by the learned rules was not significantly different in character than the knowledge expressed in the hand-coded rules. The hand coded rules accomplished the same results more concisely and parsimoniously.

In comparing the learned and hand-coded rules, it should be mentioned that it took several passes to debug the final version of the hand-coded rules. Interestingly, a number of bugs were discovered only·after the test phase experiments were run, and the results for the hand-coded rules were compared to those for the learned rules. It was then discovered that the learned rules performed suspiciously better on a number of problems. After the bugs responsible for the poor performance of the hand-coded rules were corrected, the experiments were re-run to generate the final results described above. This illustrates an potential advantage of the learned rules, in that they are "guaranteed" to be correct, or at least as correct as the axioms used to construct them. In a simple, intuitive domain like the blocksworld this advantage may be slight, but for more complex domains, such as the scheduling domain (for which it is more difficult to correctly code control rules) the benefit is corresponding greater.

One additional point should be considered when evaluating the system's performance in the blocksworld. The hand-coded rules, as well as the learned rules, are missing (at least) one obvious rule. Given two goals, (ON A B) and (ON C D), and the initial state shown in figure 10-2 the problem solver should achieve (ON C D) before (ON A B), because D is under B. However, the vocabulary of the blocksworld only includes the relations ON, CLEAR, ON-TABLE, ARM-EMPTY, HOLDING and OBJECT, and there is no way to express the general relation UNDER without defining it as a separate predicate.[33] Thus, one can indicate that block A is on block B, or that block A is on block x which is on block B, but cannot express the fact that there may be "n" blocks separating A and B. (This expressiveness problem is reminiscent of the "generalization-to-N problem" discussed in chapter 7.)

---

[33]In fact, there are ways to define such predicates in PRODIGY, but to do so one must either make use of mechanisms not described in this book, or reformulate the domain specification. The authors of the hand-coded rules were asked to use only the predefined relations for writing control rules.

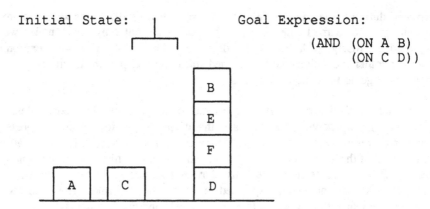

Figure 10-2:   Blocksworld Problem Illustrating Unexpressible Control Rule

10.5. Performance in the STRIPS Domain

This STRIPS domain is a version of the original STRIPS robot problem solving domain [25], augmented by several additional operators for locking and unlocking doors, and picking up and carrying objects. The operators are more complex than those in the blocksworld; their left-hand sides have multiple generators and the right-hand-sides contain deletions with universally quantified variables. This provided a more complex test for the learning, in that a greater variety of proof schemas were utilized.

The training phase for the STRIPS domain consisted of 83 problems, followed by a settling phase of 15 problems. Over the course of the training phase, 588 training example/target concept pairs were expanded via the EBS algorithm. Of these, 130 were estimated to have positive utility as control rules. Eventually 100 of these were discarded on the basis of empirical utility measurements, leaving a final rules set of 30 rules.

The test phase consisted of one hundred problems. In generating these problems the MAX-BOXES and MAX-GOALS parameters were gradually increased from two boxes and two goals up to five boxes and five goals. Furthermore as described in the appendix, three different ROOM-CONFIGURATIONS were used, from two rooms to five rooms. Table 10-3 indicates the performance results for every fifth test problem, in the same format used in the previous section. The full table of results can be found in the appendix.

Figure 10-3 graphs the test phase performance results for the system running with the learned control rules, with a set of twenty-six hand-coded control rules, and without any control rules. The results are quite similar to those of the blocksworld, however, the difference between the level of performance without any control rules and with the learned control rules is more pronounced. The performance of the

Problem	no cntrl rules		learned rules		hand-coded rules	
	time	nodes	time	nodes	time	nodes
SW-TST5	13.6	142(32)	8.3	32(32)	7.2	32(32)
SW-TST10	0.9	6(6)	1.2	6(6)	1.0	6(6)
SW-TST15	1.0	8(8)	1.6	8(8)	1.4	8(8)
SW-TST20	16.3	222(14)	4.7	14(14)	3.8	14(14)
SW-TST25	19.5	252(18)	4.6	18(18)	3.7	18(18)
SW-TST30	80.0	843(*)	12.9	42(42)	11.3	43(42)
SW-TST35	25.4	291(10)	6.9	19(10)	8.8	40(10)
SW-TST40	80.0	955(*)	9.8	30(30)	16.0	70(30)
SW-TST45	80.0	840(*)	20.2	52(52)	25.3	99(52)
SW-TST50	80.0	872(*)	16.1	46(46)	18.7	77(46)
SW-TST55	31.3	332(26)	9.3	26(26)	8.8	34(26)
SW-TST60	65.0	593(50)	20.4	52(50)	14.0	51(50)
SW-TST65	80.0	912(*)	14.6	38(38)	1.8	39(38)
SW-TST70	80.0	588(*)	4.6	12(12)	3.3	12(12)
SW-TST75	80.0	742(*)	27.7	55(30)	26.4	81(30)
SW-TST80	80.0	753(*)	19.3	43(34)	13.6	46(34)
SW-TST85	44.8	486(14)	6.0	14(14)	4.2	14(14)
SW-TST90	41.9	397(14)	6.8	14(14)	7.5	26(24)
SW-TST95	2.1	6(6)	1.9	6(6)	1.5	6(6)
SW-TST100	80.0	793(*)	30.6	67(60)	22.7	66(60)

Table 10-3: Sample Data from the Test Phase for the STRIPS Robot Domain

system without control rules was quite poor. In part this is because the STRIPS problems were correspondingly more difficult than the blocksworld problems. The average time for solving the test problems was significantly higher in this domain.[34]

In examining the results for the non-learning condition, it should be remembered that the problem solvers's performance is sensitive to the encoding of the domain. In particular, during the process of writing and debugging the STRIPS domain specification I found that the problem solvers's performance was very sensitive to the ordering of the operators' preconditions. In the end, the preconditions were ordered so that the problems were typically solvable, but no special attempt was made to find the optimal ordering.(The learning process is supposed to compensate for poor precondition orderings.)

Compared to the hand-coded rules, for problems SW-TST30 through SW-TST60 the learned rules did approximately as well as the hand-coded rules. For the remainder of the problems, figure 10-3 shows that performance was on the order of

---

[34]The large increase in average problem solving time shown in figure 10-3 that occurs after problems 21-30 is due to the fact that the ROOM-CONFIGURATION changed at that point from the two-room configuration to the four-room corridor.

Figure 10-3: Relative Performance for STRIPS Robot Domain Test Phase

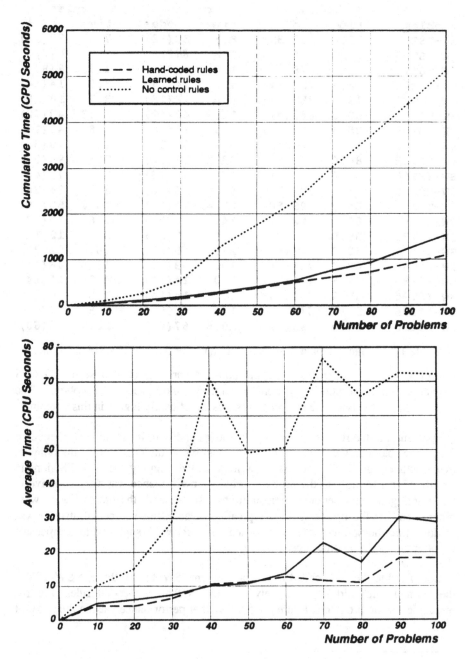

50% worse for the learned rules, although far better than without control rules. The average time per node without control rules was 0.098 seconds, with the hand-coded rules 0.274 seconds, and with the learned rules 0.379 seconds. The differences are not as great as in the blocksworld, but again, the learned rules were more expensive to use than the hand-coded rules. If one examines the coverage of the rules, as in the blocksworld, one finds that the learned rules and the hand coded rules did not differ significantly. Over the course of the test phase, 3,992 nodes were explored using the hand-coded rules and 4,038 nodes were explored using the learned rules. In contrast, 52,821 nodes were explored without control rules, illustrating the tremendous focusing effect of (both sets of) control rules.

As in the blocksworld domain, the expressiveness of both the learned rules and the hand-coded rules was limited by the available vocabulary. In particular, no concept of "distance" exists in the STRIPS domain vocabulary. In some cases, one would like to indicate that the robot should move a particular direction because the goal is to be in a particular room. Because this concept was not available, the system had to perform some search even with the hand-coded rules. (Had a single, fixed configuration of rooms been used this vocabulary limitation would not have been a problem; interestingly, it seems that for a fixed configuration of rooms a very specific set of rules would be best, indicating the appropriate routes from room to room. Neither the EBL method described in this book nor standard macro-operator techniques are capable of adjusting their bias to change the specificity of the learned rules.)

10.6. Performance in the Scheduling Domain

The scheduling domain is in many respects more complex than either of the two previous domains. The domain specification includes both operators and inference rules. The syntactic complexity of the domain description is increased further by the use of both disjunction and universal quantification in their preconditions.

Problem solving in this domain has a quite different character than in either the blocksworld or STRIPS domain. First of all, unsolvable problems are legal in the scheduling domain. Secondly, in the other domains, solving a goal typically requires recursively subgoaling to depths of ten or twenty in some cases. The scheduling domain rarely requires subgoaling to a depth of more than four. The key to solving problems in this domain is to avoid interactions between goals. In most cases, such interactions lead to failures, as illustrated by the original scheduling problem described in chapter 3.

Over the course of the training phase, 946 training example/target concept pairs were expanded via the EBS algorithm. 243 of the resulting descriptions were converted to rules, 204 of which were eventually discarded on the basis of empirical utility measurements, leaving a final rule set consisting of 37 rules.

	no cntrl rules		learned rules		hand-coded rules	
Problem	time	nodes	time	nodes	time	nodes
SC-TST5	1.7	20(14)	4.2	17(14)	7.3	21(14)
SC-TST10	2.1	22(18)	4.9	21(18)	8.1	23(18)
SC-TST15	0.6	7(6)	1.3	6(6)	1.4	6(6)
SC-TST20	3.3	54(0)	0.1	1(0)	0.2	1(0)
SC-TST25	63.1	911(0)	0.1	1(0)	0.2	1(0)
SC-TST30	80.0	1128(*)	12.6	24(20)	9.4	25(20)
SC-TST35	4.7	55(12)	3.9	13(12)	2.7	13(12)
SC-TST40	13.8	222(0)	0.1	1(0)	0.2	1(0)
SC-TST45	0.9	7(6)	1.5	6(6)	1.5	6(6)
SC-TST50	80.0	1261(*)	0.2	1(0)	0.2	1(0)
SC-TST55	34.0	426(14)	80.0	326(*)	6.3	15(14)
SC-TST60	80.0	1304(*)	0.3	1(0)	0.3	1(0)
SC-TST65	4.7	64(0)	0.2	1(0)	0.2	1(0)
SC-TST70	3.3	11(10)	5.0	10(10)	3.6	11(10)
SC-TST75	2.3	13(12)	3.3	12(12)	4.0	12(12)
SC-TST80	80.0	1025(*)	16.8	27(26)	15.6	33(32)
SC-TST85	80.0	651(*)	0.3	1(0)	0.4	1(0)
SC-TST90	80.0	771(*)	0.2	1(0)	0.6	1(0)
SC-TST95	80.0	605(*)	80.0	86(*)	33.0	39(36)
SC-TST100	8.6	17(16)	14.2	14(14)	8.9	16(16)

Table 10-4:   Sample Data from the Test Phase for the Scheduling Domain

The test phase again consisted of one hundred problems. While generating these problems the number of objects was increased from two to four, the number of available bolts from one to four, the maximum number of goals from one to ten, and the number of available time-slots from four to twelve. Some of the results from the test phase are shown in table 10-4, and the full table of results for the experiments can be found in [53].

Figure 10-4 graphically illustrates the test-phase performance results for the system. The results are similar to those for the previous domains; the learned rules provided significant performance improvement, but not quite as much as did the hand-coded rules. As before, the trends become more pronounced as the problems increase in difficulty. A closer inspection at the data reveals that when the system was able to solve a problem without control rules, its performance on that problem was frequently superior to its performance with control rules (both learned and hand-coded). The use of control rules, in effect, trades off search speed for the ability to quickly recognize unsolvable problems.

Comparing the learned rules to the hand-coded rules (a set of thirteen), one finds that there were five problems that could not be solved (within the 80 second time limit) with the learned rules, compared to two (different) problems that could not be

Figure 10-4: Relative Performance for Scheduling Domain Test Phase

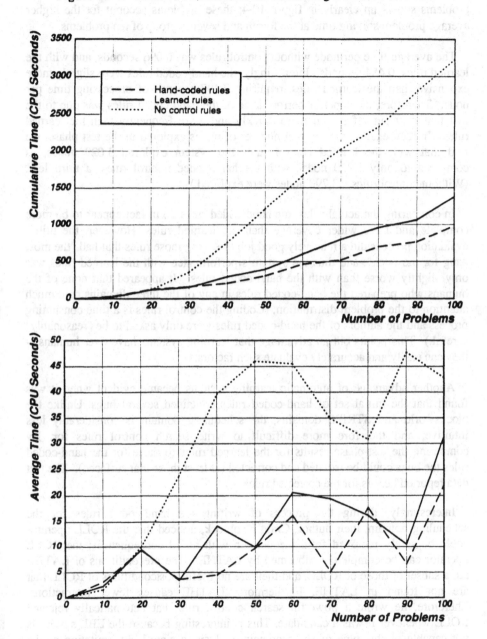

solved with the hand-coded rules. The fact that the learned rules missed three more problems shows up clearly in figure 10-4; these problems account for the higher average problem solving time at the fourth and seventh group of ten problems.

The average time per node without control rules was 0.096 seconds, and with the learned rules, 0.454 seconds. Interestingly, the hand-coded rules were slightly more expensive than the learned rules, requiring 0.497 seconds of processing time per node. Therefore, the superior performance of the hand-coded rules was due to the fact that they cut off search more quickly and more frequently than the learned rules. In fact, examining the total number of nodes explored in the test phase, we find that with the learned control rules the system explored 3,029 nodes, as compared to only 1,970 nodes with the hand-coded control rules, a third less. (Without control rules, 33,790 nodes were explored.)

In comparing the actual rules, the hand-coded rules do in fact appear to be more complete and have wider coverage than the learned rules. However, the utility evaluation process did a relatively good job of saving those rules that had "the most bang for the buck", and thus the system's performance with the learned rules was only slightly worse than with the hand-coded rules. It appeared that none of the humans who prepared the hand-coded rules in any of the three domains paid much attention to the problem distribution. (Coding the control rules is a time consuming process and the authors of the hand-coded rules were only asked to be "reasonably" careful.) This points out an advantage that learning systems have over humans -- they can easily and accurately evaluate such factors.

Another advantage of automatic learning systems became evident when it was found that the initial set of hand-coded rules contained several bugs. Unlike the blocksworld and STRIPS domains, the scheduling domain is considerably less intuitive, and therefore more difficult to write search control rules for. By comparing the test-phase results for the learned rules to those for the hand-coded rules the bugs could be isolated and corrected (at least those that surfaced). The test data reported here is for the corrected rules.

Interestingly, during the process of writing the hand-coded rules for the scheduling domain, their author, Craig Knoblock, noticed that the ROLL operator could be safely removed from the domain with no ill consequences; the ROLL operator can be completely subsumed by LATHE. The preconditions of LATHE are a subset of those of ROLL, and their are no useful postconditions of ROLL that are not found in LATHE. Furthermore, LATHE causes fewer interactions. Therefore, he wrote a powerful search control rule that automatically rejected ROLL whenever it was a candidate. This is interesting because the EBL system is not capable of this type of static domain analysis, a significant limitation of the system.

10.7. Evaluating the Components of the Learning System

The following sections evaluate the contributions made by each of the three primary components that are the keynotes of the PRODIGY/EBL system: multiple target concepts, compression analysis and utility evaluation. Of course, as in any complex system, it is impossible to completely separate out the components due to their symbiotic relationship. The purpose of the following sections is to consider the relative degree to which each component improved the total performance of the system.

10.7.1. Target Concepts

Table 10-5 shows the number of rules learned in each domain for each of the four types of target concepts. This gives a rough indication of the relative contribution provided by each target concept, since the table includes only those rules that were determined to be of positive utility (i.e., the table does not include rules removed from the system by utility evaluation). As the table indicates, no individual target concept alone accounted for the improvement in problem solving performance. Learning from success appeared to be the least useful strategy (especially since the resulting rules were preferences, which are relatively weak).

	Blocksworld	Stripsworld	Schedworld
Succeeds	1	6	6
Fails	14	12	10
Sole-Alternative	4	6	4
Goal-interaction	1	6	17

Table 10-5: Breakdown of Learned Rules by Target Concept Type

10.7.2. Compression Analysis

Determining the exact contribution made by the compression process is difficult. As described in chapters 4 and 5, PRODIGY interleaves specialization and compression, so that the specialization process relies heavily on the first phase of compression, partial evaluation. If the partial evaluator is turned off, the specialization process will frequently fail to terminate. (See the example in chapter 5, section 5.2.1, illustrating the relationship between specialization and partial evaluation.) Similarly, phase two of the compression process cannot be completely turned off either, because the resulting rules are frequently so bad that the matcher will run out of space when testing them (e.g., a stack overflow will occur).

Given these difficulties, the best that could be done to test the effectiveness of compression (and have the system still run) was to turn off the third phase of compression and the non-critical transformations carried out by phase two. Figure 10-5 shows the performance results for the blocksworld test phase with the system running in this configuration. The graph also shows the performance of the system with only phase three of the compression process (the theorem prover) eliminated. Finally, for comparison, the figure includes the curves indicating the performance of the system without control rules and with the rules learned by the complete PRODIGY/EBL system as originally shown in table 10-2.

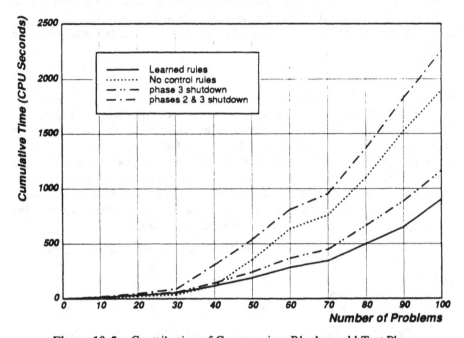

Figure 10-5: Contribution of Compression, Blocksworld Test Phase

As might be expected, without phase three the learning system's performance is significantly worse, although performance is still much better than the non-learning condition. With both phase three shutdown and phase two partially shutdown, performance is actually worse than if no learning had been done, illustrating the usefulness of compression.[35]

These results are corroborated by examining the effect of compression on the size of the learned descriptions. Specifically, we can measure the average number of atomic formulas in each description before and after the second and third stages of compression. (The size of a description tends to be correlated with its match cost.)

---

[35]The fact that performance is actually worse that without learning also demonstrates that PRODIGY's utility evaluation process is not perfect. Theoretically, the system's performance should never be worse than if it had not done any learning. In the worst case, all learned rules should be eliminated by utility evaluation. Unfortunately, in this experiment the system overestimated the savings produced by rejection rules, illustrating a problem discussed in section 10.9.

In the blocksworld, the second phase of compression reduces the number of atomic formulas in each description by an average of forty-five percent, and the third phase of compression reduces each description further by an average of six percent. (For almost two-thirds of the descriptions the third phase of compression produced no change, but when it did produce a change the reductions averaged nineteen percent).

An analysis of the actual descriptions shows that compression was most useful when learning from failures and goal-interactions, and least useful when learning from success. This appears to be due to two factors. First, PRODIGY's method of learning from success is significantly simpler than the other strategies, in that many fewer schemas are employed. Whereas learning from success requires analyzing only a single path in the search tree, the other strategies analyze subtrees. Moreover, multiple paths in a subtree often fail (or interact) for the same reason, allowing ample opportunity for compression.

Similar results were produced when the experiments reported in this section were repeated in the STRIPS robot problem solving domain and the scheduling domain.

10.7.3. Utility Evaluation

The contribution made by utility evaluation can be directly measured by simply removing the module which performs this function. Once this is done, PRODIGY will retain every rule it has learned. Unfortunately, because some of the learned rules are so horrendous, the learning process quickly spirals out of control as poorer and poorer rules are learned (due to the cascading effect described in chapter 6). Thus, it proved impossible to provide comprehensive results, because the system became quickly bogged down, resulting in technical problems (thrashing, stack overflows in the matcher, etc.). However, if only utility validation is turned off, so that utility estimation alone is used to screen undesirable rules, it is possible to run complete experiments.

Figure 10-6 shows how performance in the blocksworld degrades without utility validation. The system's performance was significantly worse, although not as bad as if it had done no learning. The system saved sixty-nine rules, as compared to the nineteen rules that were originally learned. The extra coverage provided by the additional rules was insignificant, and the system did not manage to solve either of the two problems that had remained unsolved with the original rule set. Over the course of the one hundred test problems, the system expanded 1641 nodes with the original rules, compared to 1615 nodes with the additional rules, illustrating how little the additional rules helped focus the search. In fact, the difference is largely due to the two problems that remained unsolved within the 80 CPU second time limit, where the system examined more nodes with the learned control rules only because it was running faster. Specifically, the time taken to expand a node slowed from an average of .553 seconds to .883 seconds, accounting for the poorer performance of the system with the additional rules. (Similar results were produced when these experiments were repeated in the STRIPS robot problem solving domain and the scheduling domain.)

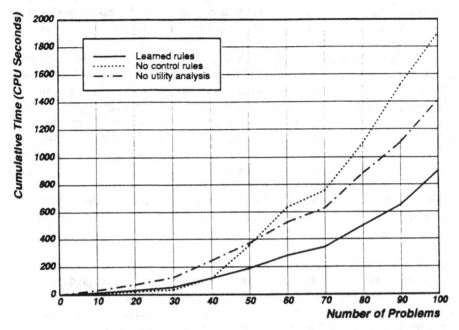

Figure 10-6: Contribution of Utility Analysis, Blocksworld Test Phase

10.8. Comparison with Macro-Operator Learning

Figure 10-7 compares the performance of two macro-operator learning versions of PRODIGY on the blocksworld test problems (the same set of problems used in the previous blocksworld experiments). For comparative purposes, the figure also shows the performance of the system without control rules, and with the control rules learned by the PRODIGY/EBL component. One of the macro-operator versions is a *selective* learner, which uses the same example selection heuristics as PRODIGY's strategy for learning from success. The other version, which performed much more poorly, uses a more traditional macro-operator learning technique similar to the STRIPS MACROPS method [25]. Whereas the selective macro-operator learning system only learns macro-operators for solving subgoals where the problem solver made a mistake, the other system learns macro-operators for each subgoal on the solution path.[36] In the blocksworld, the selective system learned 17 macro-operators, whereas the non-selective system learned 134 macro-operators. To produce a fair comparison between the various systems, both macro-operator learning systems employed compression analysis (although it is not particularly useful when learning from success). Neither employed utility evaluation; selectivity levels were adjusted purely through the use of selection heuristics.

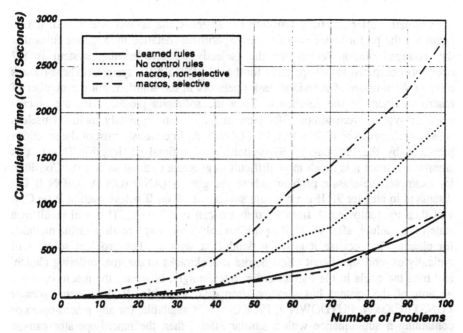

Figure 10-7: Relative Performance of Macro-Operator Learning in Blocksworld

As would be predicted, in this experiment selective learning outperformed non-selective learning, but surprisingly, the selective macro-operator learning system appeared to perform as well as the PRODIGY/EBL system. At first this seems

---

[36]In addition, the selective macro learning system is more restrictive when determining whether a macro-operator is relevant in a problem solving context. If an operator sequence was used to solve goals A and B, the selective system will only consider the corresponding macro-operator to be relevant when goals A and B are both present. The non-selective system will consider using the macro when either A or B is present. In either case, both of these systems are more selective in this regard than the original STRIPS MACROPS system, which will consider using a macro-operator when any of its effects unify with a goal. Furthermore, neither system will backchain on the preconditions of macro-operators. Thus both of these systems differ in several respects from the the STRIPS MACROPS system and the author's MORRIS system [49]. The sole purpose of the macro-operator experiments reported here was to provide a comparison of learning methods within the PRODIGY architecture, rather than a replication of the STRIPS and MORRIS results.

especially difficult to understand since, as reported in section 10.7.1, the EBL system's strategy for learning from success produced only a single useful rule in the blocksworld. The strategy for learning from success is identical to the selective macro learning method, except that it performs "single operator learning", as discussed in chapter 7. Consequently, the left-hand sides of the learned control rules are, for all intents and purposes, identical to the preconditions of the learned macro-operators, although the right-hand sides are less powerful. For this reason, one would not expect the macro-operator learning system to perform so well.

Eventually, after carefully profiling the systems, the answer was found. If one examines the performance data for this experiment (detailed in [53], one finds that the average solution length for the (selective) macro-learning system is 8.7 operators compared to 6.0 operators for the PRODIGY/EBL system. (These figures refer to the number of individual task operators in the solution, not the number of macro-operators in the solution.) Thus the solutions produced by the macro-operator system were almost fifty percent longer, and typically included useless subsequences such as PICKUP A, PUTDOWN A. In contrast, most of the solutions produced by the PRODIGY/EBL system were optimal (in length). This fact is significant, since it is much more difficult to generate optimal solutions. Consider, for example, the classic problem where the goal is (AND (ON A B)(ON B C)) discussed in chapter 9. If the problem solver puts A on B before putting B on C, it will then try removing A from B so that it can put B on C. This will result in a state-cycle failure, after which the problem solver will explore all possible methods for clearing B, because it is using depth-first search. The problem solver will typically expend significant effort before it backtracks to the goal ordering choice, and tries the goals in the correct order. Interestingly, however, the macro-operator version of the system has another alternative available. If the macro-operator <UNSTACK x y, PUTDOWN x, PICKUP y> is available, (or any macro-operator containing a subsequence with a similar effect) then the macro-operator can be immediately applied after stacking A on B, with the effect that A will be put back on the table, and the problem solver will end up holding B. The problem solver will never notice the state-cycle, since it has "jumped" over the repeated state. At this point the problem can be quite simply solved, although the solution will be suboptimal. The key point is that the the macro-operator system has a greater variety of solutions available, and thus it is searching in a less constrained, and in practice, much less difficult space. In a sense, the macro-operator system is trading off solution quality for problem solving time.

Interestingly, this effect was much less significant in the other two test domains. Figures 10-8 and 10-9 show the performance results for the STRIPS robot domain and scheduling domain comparing the selective macro-operator system to the normal EBL system, and to the system running without learned control rules. Performance of the macro-operator learning system was considerable poorer in these domains. It is not immediately clear why selective macro-operator learning did not perform better in the STRIPS robot domain, but at least its performance was

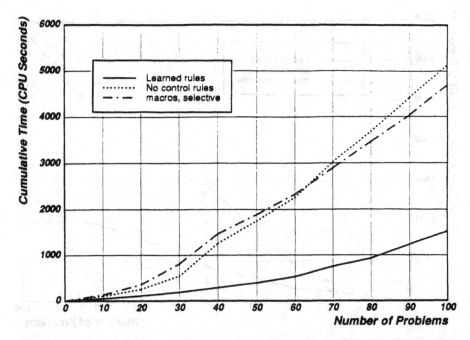

Figure 10-8: Performance of Macro-Operator Learning in STRIPS Robot Domain

slightly better than without learning. For the scheduling domain, the performance of macro-operator learning was even worse. There appear to be (at least) two factors that are responsible. First, no state-cycles can occur in the scheduling domain, since the schedule grows monotonically, and therefore the tradeoff effect described above is absent. Secondly, macro-operator learning cannot be used to learn from failures or goal interactions; if one looks closely at the performance of the PRODIGY/EBL system in this domain, one finds that most of its performance improvement comes from learning about problems which are unsolvable.

This results in this section have illustrated the difficulty of comparing learning systems. As we have seen, even when comparing similar learning methods for the same problem solver, subtle effects may manifest themselves and muddy the waters.

10.9. Discussion of Performance Results

Although the PRODIGY/EBL system did dramatically improve the problem solver's performance, a number of difficulties manifested themselves during the experiments. First, as pointed out earlier, it became clear that the learning process was sensitive to both the ordering and choice of training problems. Therefore, in order to speed up the learning process, the sequences of training problems were biased by gradually increasing their difficulty. The sensitivity to problem difficulty arises because the system typically generates better explanations (i.e., higher in

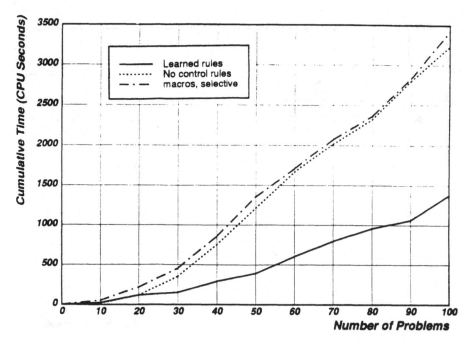

Figure 10-9:   Performance of Macro-Operator Learning in Scheduling Domain

utility) for simpler problems. An example will help to illustrate why. Let us suppose that a node fails, and in analyzing the subtree below it, the EBL subsystem finds that nine of the node's ten children failed for reason "A", and the tenth failed for reason "B". Consequently the EBL subsystem reports that the node failed because both "A" and "B" were true. Now, it might have been that the tenth child would have also eventually failed because of reason "A", but "B" manifested itself first. In this case, the learned rule is overspecific, since "A" alone is sufficient to insure failure.   This phenomenon is more likely to occur on more difficult problems because the explored search tree will be larger.

A concrete example will show how this problem arises in practice.   Let us suppose that the system is solving a blocksworld problem, and the subgoal (ON BLOCKA BLOCKA) arises, which the system has not yet learned is impossible. If there are many blocks in the initial state and few control rules in the system, the problem solver may expend quite a bit of effort in trying to achieve this goal, and generate a correspondingly large subtree. The problem solver will try all possible methods for simultaneously achieving (CLEAR BLOCKA) and (HOLDING BLOCKA) in its attempt to stack BLOCKA on itself. Let us suppose that in analyzing why the subtree failed, the EBL component finds a leaf node that failed because there was a goal-stack cycle with a *supergoal* of (ON BLOCKA BLOCKA). Even without the goal-stack cycle, this node would have failed eventually, since there is no way (ON BLOCKA BLOCKA) can be achieved.

Because the goal-stack cycle manifested itself first, the learned rule will be too specific -- the explanation will include an extraneous reference to the existence of the supergoal, which has nothing to do with the fact that (ON BLOCKA BLOCKA) is unachievable. In other words, the system will learn only that (ON x x) is unachievable in certain contexts (i.e., when the supergoal is present).

The probability that the system will become "distracted" in this way grows as the size of the subtree that it is analyzing grows[37]. If the system has learned "enough" search control rules, the subtrees expanded during the problem solver's search will be relatively small, decreasing the likelihood that the system will become distracted and produce an over-specific rule. Thus, in this way the system behaves similarly to a human; learning is most effective when the system is trained on increasingly difficult problems. I would conjecture that there is more than a surface similarity here. A human cannot carry out complex analyses unless he has previously learned the simpler tools that allow him to deal with the complexity.

Before leaving this discussion, let us take a moment to consider what happens if the system does learn an over-specific rule. In theory; eventually a simpler problem illustrating the same principle will arise, and the system will learn a better rule. How quickly this will happen depends partially upon whether the over-specific rule remains in the system, or is thrown out on the basis of utility evaluation. If the rule remains in the system, it may be general enough so that it fires on (some of) the simpler problems when they show up, preventing re-learning. This can be a serious problem. More likely, the over-specific rule will be of negative utility, and it will be quickly discarded, enabling the system to learn the better rule. The more quickly this occurs the better, since, as pointed out in chapter 6, control rules have a tendency to become incorporated in other rules that are subsequently learned.

Another issue that arose during the experiments concerns PRODIGY's method of utility evaluation. As explained in chapter 6, PRODIGY estimates the benefits of a rule rather taking direct measurements. The estimate is based on the savings that the rule would have produced when solving the original problem where it was learned. Unfortunately, I observed several cases where PRODIGY's savings estimates appeared to be quite poor. Frequently the estimated savings were too low, and a valuable rule was discarded. Typically this happened when a rule was learned on a very simple problem, where the savings were low. Thus, even though the rule was quite valuable when it was used to solve more complex problems, the system

---

[37]The problem is serious, but is frequently alleviated by the following practice. After explaining why a target concept is true at a node, the system checks whether the explanation holds at the parent node or any brother node. If the explanation holds at the parent or brother it eliminates the need to generate a new explanation. This not only improves the efficiency of the learning process, but increases the probability of finding a simple explanation for a target concept (one that involves only a single reason explaining why the target concept holds). This practice was illustrated in several of the examples described in chapters 7 through 9 (e.g., see section 9.3.)

could not correctly appraise its true benefit. Ironically, the most valuable rules are typically learned when solving relatively simple problems, as observed above.

Theoretically speaking, this is not a significant issue, since a rule can presumably be re-learned on a subsequent example where a more realistic savings estimate may be made. However, in practice there may not be much opportunity for re-learning unless the training set is very large.

Another problem I observed with PRODIGY's method of utility evaluation is that the system appears too liberal in its method for determining the savings for rejection rules. Whenever a rejection rule fires, the system increments the cumulative savings by the estimated savings for that rule. However, in many cases a rule rejects an alternative that the system would not have explored anyway, because another alternative would have succeeded first. In this case the rule does not really save the system anything. Presumably, this could be corrected by being more careful when attributing savings for a rejection rule, but further analysis is necessary to determine how this can be implemented.

11. Proofs, Explanations, and Correctness: Putting It All Together

This chapter presents a formal, non-procedural description of explanation-based learning. My aim is to provide a theoretical model that complements the experimental work described in the previous chapters. The model will characterize the term "explanation" precisely, enabling us to prove that the EBS algorithm is correct with respect to the model.

EBL is usually described as a knowledge-intensive learning approach in which one analyzes *why* an example is a positive instance of a target concept. EBL programs are typically described either in English at a intuitive-level of description, or algorithmically. The first is a very-high level of description and the second is a very low-level of description. This chapter aims for something intermediate in order to bridge the gap. The descriptive model developed in this chapter is based on the non-algorithmic notion of weakest preconditions. The intent is to provide a level of description that is both intuitive and precise.

The chapter begins by discussing the relationship between proofs, derivations and explanations and then defines EBL as a method for finding the weakest premises of an explanation. Using this definition, a proof is outlined that proves the correctness of a simplied version of the EBS algorithm. The chapter concludes by describing how compression fits into the model.

11.1. The Missing Level of Description

In the past five years there have been a variety of EBL algorithms designed and demonstrated in a wide variety of task domains, including game-playing [47, 84], planning [25, 78], and circuit design [44, 23]. Although recently there have been several useful comparisons of EBL systems at the algorithmic level [61, 73], the specification of what these systems are supposed to compute has been incompletely addressed. Interestingly, however, there appears to be wide agreement (at least among the researchers who designed them) that the algorithms are in many respects equivalent. For example, Mooney and Bennet, in comparing abstract versions of three EBL algorithms, the EGGS algorithm, the STRIPS algorithm, and the EBG algorithm (all of which are discussed in the next chapter), state the following:

"It is reasonably clear that all of the above algorithms compute the same desired generalized explanation. They all perform a set of unifications and substitutions to constrain the explanation structure into one in which equated patterns unify directly without requiring any substitutions. The difference between them lies in the number of unifications and substitutions required and the order in which they are performed."

In other words, the three algorithms *appear to* compute the same thing, but have different efficiencies. Unfortunately, Mooney and Bennett's brief analysis, worthwhile as it is, is very informal. This is perhaps the best that could be expected, since they were working from incomplete and sometimes vague descriptions of algorithms that operated on different types of data-structures. In fact, they constructed their own abstract versions of the algorithms in order to compare them.

The central problem remains that there is still no specification describing *what* it is that these algorithms are supposedly computing. The actual algorithms are difficult to compare; it took many years before researchers noted and discussed their similarities. More intuitive high-level descriptions tend to be very vague, oftening relying on anthropomorphic statements such as "The system explains why the goal is achievable....". In the next section, I propose that we can bridge the ground between these two distant levels of specification by appealing to the notion of weakest preconditions.

11.2. Explanations, Proofs and Weakest Preconditions

In a 1984 paper [47] I introduced the following domain-independent characterization of explanation-based learning (at the time referred to as constraint-based generalization):

> "**INPUT:** A set of rules that can be used to classify an instance as either positive or negative, and a positive instance.
>
> **GENERALIZATION PROCEDURE:** Identify a sequence of rules that can be used to classify the instance as positive. Employ backward reasoning to find the weakest preconditions of this sequence such that a positive classification will result. Restate the preconditions in the description language."

While I believe this definition is still a good informal characterization EBL, it can be improved in several respects. For example, the reliance on backward reasoning now seems unnecessary. Most importantly, to provide a precise formal statement the terms must be better specified and grounded in a well understood formalism.

The need for such a formalism has also become evident from subsequent questions raised by other researchers regarding the adequacy of "weakest preconditions". For example, Kibler and Porter [69] pointed out that the weakest preconditions of a given rule sequence may not be expressible in the description language. They claimed that this limits the applicability of analytic EBL techniques.

Furthermore, Mitchell, Keller and Kedar-Cabelli [57] specifically designed their
EBG method so that it would not in fact produce the weakest preconditions, but
only sufficient preconditions. I will return to both of these points later in this
chapter, after introducing the formalism.

11.2.1. Proofs as Explanations

In their influential work on EBG, Mitchell, Keller, and Kedar-Cabelli
[57] explicitly equated explanations with proofs. Although, as DeJong has
correctly pointed out, operator sequences or rule sequences are equivalent to proofs,
adopting logic as a formalism allows us to take advantage of a well-understood and
fairly standardized formal framework.[38] However, because Mitchell et al. did not
explicitly define the notion of weakest preconditions with respect to proofs, it is
necessary expand on their proposal.

Before doing so, a minor terminological point must first be addressed. A proof is
generally defined as a sequence of statements, such that each statement is either an
axiom or an immediate consequence of an earlier statement in the sequence. A
derivation resembles a proof, but the initial statements may include *premises* as well
as axioms. Premises are assumptions; whether or not they are true is immaterial to
the validity of the derivation. Thus in a derivation the last statement is not
necessarily a theorem, because it is contingent on the truth of the premises. If the
formula (Q x) is derived from the premises (P x) and (R x), the resulting theorem is
not (Q x), but "(P x) and (R x) implies (Q x)". In EBL, we are actually concerned
with derivations rather than proofs. Although an example may provide a proof that
(Q A) is true, the real point of interest is that (Q A) was derived from some set of
assertions, e.g., (P A) and (R A). By analyzing the derivation the general case can
be identified, e.g., "(P x) and (R x) implies (Q x)".

11.2.2. Proof Systems

A *proof system* consists of a language and a set of inference rules. The inference
rules specify what formulas in the language can be derived from other formulas.
The analysis in the following sections is relevant to proof systems in general,
including resolution systems, Hilbert style systems, etc.

For the proof system we consider first, the language is essentially a subset of
PDL. All formulas are either atomic formulas, simple conjunctions, or simple

---

[38]One might argue that equating explanations with proofs unnecessarily limits what can constitute an
explanation. For example, what if an explanation refers to default or probabilistic knowledge? Clearly, it
is inconvenient in most currently available logics to formulate such knowledge. But the alternatives are
usually specialized languages that merely reduce the inconvenience. In any even, this issue should
probably be considered a knowledge representation problem, rather than an EBL problem.

conditionals. A simple conjunction is a conjunction where all the subformulas are atomic, e.g.:

$$\text{(AND (GREATER-THAN } x \text{ 7) (INTEGER } x \text{))}$$

A simple conditional is a conditional with the following properties: all variables are universally quantified (and their scope extends over the entire conditional), the antecedent is an atomic formula or a simple conjunction, and the consequent is an atomic formula. For technical purposes (without loss of generality) we will require that the consequent be a *fully general* atomic formula; that is, it has no constants other than the predicate (only variables), and all the variables are distinct. Two simple conditionals are shown below. (In this chapter, for simplicity, the syntax is slightly revised. Conditionals are represented using an IMPLIES connective, so that F1 implies F2 is written (IMPLIES F1 F2) and all variables in conditionals are implicitly universally quantified).)

$$\text{(IMPLIES (GREATER-THAN } x \text{ 7) (FOOBAR } x \text{))}$$

$$\text{(IMPLIES (AND (GREATER } x \text{ 7) (ODD } x \text{) (EQUAL } y \text{ 8))}$$
$$\text{(GREATER } x \text{ } y \text{))}$$

Our proof system will use two standard rules of inference, modus ponens and conjunction introduction. This is an interesting subset of PDL because many EBL systems are restricted to just this language. Later I will discuss extending this subset to include all of PDL. Below, a derivation in this proof system is shown.

Axioms
```
Axiom1: (IMPLIES (AND (B x) (C x w))
                 (D x))
Axiom2: (IMPLIES (A y)
                 (B y))
```

Assertions		Explanation
Line1:	(A 1)	PREMISE
Line2:	(B 1)	M-PONENS, Axiom2, Line1
Line3:	(C 1 2)	PREMISE
Line4:	(AND (B 1)(C 1 2))	CONJ-INTRO line2, line3
Line5:	(D 1)	M-PONENS, Axiom1, Line4

A derivation consists of a sequence of formulas, such that each formula is either a premise, or derived by an inference rule from axioms[39] and previous formulas. Each formula in the derivation is accompanied by a *justification* indicating either that the formula is a premise, or specifying the inference rule and the formulas that

---

[39]The convention of not including the axioms in the sequence of assertions has been adopted for two reasons. First, we assume that the axioms characterize the domain, and do not change, whereas the assertions may change as the state changes. Secondly, if we adopt this convention, our proofs appear similar to the proofs in the EBG paper [57], while adopting a natural deduction framework. An alternative would be to make each axiom a separate inference rule.

support the inference. Finally, an explanation is defined to be a sequence of justifications.

11.2.3. The EBL Process

In general, we can describe EBL as the composition of two functions: The first function takes an example and a target concept and produces an explanation and the second function determines the most general conditions under which the sequence of justifications in the explanation can derive the target concept.[40] It is this second function that is typically referred to as the generalization algorithm in a given EBL system, and which is the subject of this chapter. The term "generalization algorithm" is perhaps a bit of a misnomer -- in PRODIGY the second function is carried out by EBS, which I have described as a specialization algorithm. Either term is acceptable; it depends on whether one focuses on the fact that the example is being generalized, or the fact that the target concept is being specialized. For consistency with the rest of the EBL community, I will refer to the second function as the generalization algorithm for the remainder of the chapter.

To be specific, a formula Q is defined to be more general, or *weaker* than formula P iff $P \models Q$ but $Q \not\models P$. In other words, Q is weaker than P if the models of Q are a proper superset of the models of P.

Let us now define exactly what the generalization algorithm computes. Suppose E is an explanation, TC is a target concept and PRE is a formula. We say that $PRE \vdash_E TC$ if there is a valid derivation with TC as the last assertion, E as its explanation, and premises PS, such that $PRE \models PS$. Intuitively, $PRE \vdash_E TC$ indicates that TC can be derived via explanation E using the premises described[41] by PRE. Then the generalization algorithm, given TC and E, computes a *weakest* formula WPRE such that such that $WPRE \vdash_E TC$. By weakest formula, I mean that there is no formula W such that $W \vdash_E TC$ and W is weaker than WPRE.

Note that more than one such weakest formula may exist. In fact, there will normally be infinitely many such formulas (e.g., all alphabetic variants of WPRE).

---

[40]Alternatively, one can have the first function produce a derivation, and then have the second function compute the most general derivation of the target concept that has the same justifications (but weaker assertions) and return the conditions under which this more general derivation applies. The two definitions are essentially the same. I point this out because previous researchers in EBL have referred to the process of "generalizing the explanation".

[41]In this chapter, as in the preceding chapters, I treat logical formulae as descriptions of states. Following standard practice, I say that a formula describes a state iff the formula is true in the state. More formally, a formula describes a state iff the state is a model for that formula. (Every logical formula has a set of models, which are the interpretations in which that formula is true.) We can extend this idea of formulas as descriptions, and say that P describes Q if $P \models Q$. Thus in the definition of $PRE \vdash_E TC$, we say that PRE describes premises PS which allow TC to be derived via E.

The generalization algorithm only needs to produce one such formula.

Given this definition, we can now prove that an EBL algorithm is correct, in that it produces a formula describing the weakest premises under which an explanation derives the target concept.

11.2.4. Correctness of EBS

While the explanations described in this chapter may appear to be a distant idealization of the explanations in the PRODIGY/EBL system, in reality there is a close connection. To make this more explicit we need to break down the EBS algorithm (described in chapter 4) into its component parts. As it is implemented, EBS operates by recursively specializing the target concept in accordance with the problem solving trace. Although the resulting description represents the weakest premises of an explanation, that explanation is never explicitly created. However, it is quite simple to break EBS into a two-phase algorithm that creates the explanation as an intermediate data structure. To do so, we can divide EBS into two component procedures, EBS-EXPLAIN and EBS-WP, as shown below.

```
                               EBS
implementation: TRACE   ===================> LEARNED-DESCRIPTION


                    EBS-EXPLAIN          EBS-WP
equivalently:    TRACE  ==> EXPLANATION ==> LEARNED-DESCRIPTION
```

Table 11-2 and table 11-1 show versions of the EBS-EXPLAIN procedure and the EBS-WP procedure[42] that are appropriate for the subset of PDL introduced in this chapter. Comparison of these with the original EBS procedure (table 4-3 in chapter 4) reveals how the two components were distilled from the original.

EBS-EXPLAIN operates by recursively expanding the target concept, the same way EBS does. However, instead of saving the primitive atomic formulas to create the learned description, EBS-EXPLAIN creates a derivation. (The procedure EBS-EXPLAIN actually returns the last line created; the derivation is created as a side effect of repeatedly calling the subprocedure CREATE-NEW-LINE-IN-DERIVATION). Each line in the derivation corresponds to a level in the tree expanded in recognizing the target concept. Specifically, each AND connective corresponds to an application of conjunction introduction, each non-primitive atomic formula corresponds to an application of modus ponens, and each primitive atomic formula corresponds to a premise. Once the derivation is constructed by EBS-EXPLAIN, EBS-WP can find the weakest premises of the explanation

---

[42]The description of EBS-EXPLAIN has been somewhat abstracted, as was the original description of the EBS algorithm presented in chapter 4. The description of EBS-WP is more detailed so that the proof can be carried out.

associated with the derivation. EBS-WP operates by recursively sweeping through the explanation, starting with the last line and working forward.

Procedure (Ebs-explain *TC example*) =

- **If** *TC* **is a conjunctive expression, i.e. (AND** *F1 F2...FK*)

```
Then let support-1 = (Ebs-explain F1 F1-example)
          support-2 = (Ebs-explain F2 F2-example)
          ....
          support-k = (Ebs-explain F2 F2-example)
Return (Create-new-line-in-derivation
          line-num: (get-next-available-line-number)
          assertion: (AND F1 F2...FK)
          justification = CONJ-INTRO
          supports: support-1, support-2...support-k)
```

- **If** *TC* **is atomic, and primitive, then:**

```
Return (Create-new-line-in-derivation
          line-num: (Get-next-available-line-number)
          assertion: TC
          justification: PREMISE)
```

- **If** *TC* **is atomic, and not primitive:**

```
Let axiom-nm = (Call-discriminator-function TC example)
    schema-body = (Get-left-hand-side axiom-nm)
    schema-body-example = (Find-instantiation schema-body example)
    support-1 = (Ebs-explain schema-body schema-body-example)
Return (Create-new-line-in-derivation
          line-num: (get-next-available-line-number)
          assertion: TC
          justification = M-PONENS
          axiom: axiom-nm
          supports: support-1)
```

Table 11-1: Description of EBS-EXPLAIN Procedure

This chapter is primarily concerned with EBS-WP, the "generalization" function in EBS. EBS-WP examines the last line of the explanation, recursively calling itself to find the weakest premises of the shorter sub-explanations that support the last line, and then transforming those descriptions so that inference rule used by the last line will apply.

To prove that EBS-WP is correct, we must prove that, given an explanation E and a target concept TC, EBS-WP produces a description of the weakest premises under which E derives TC. This can can be reduced to proving the following two statements:

1. (EBS-WP TC E) $\vdash_E$ TC.

2. If there exists a description PRE such that PRE $\vdash_E$ TC, then PRE $\models$ (EBS-WP TC E)

The first statement specifies that (EBS-WP TC E) correctly describes some set of premises under which E derives TC. The second statement specifies that if another

Procedure (Ebs-wp *TC E*) =
Let *line-n* **be the last line in the explanation E.**

- **if the justification for** *line-n* **is PREMISE then return** *TC*

- **if the justification for** *line-n* **is CONJ-INTRO then**

```
Let F₁, F₂...Fₖ be the conjuncts in TC.
Let E₁, E₂...Eₖ be the subexplanations for
    each of the k lines supporting line-n.
Return (AND (Ebs-wp  F₁ E₁)
            (Ebs-wp  F₂ E₂)
            ....
            (Ebs-wp  Fₖ Eₖ)
```

- **if the justification for** *line-n* **is M-PONENS then**

```
Let ∀ v₁,v₂...v_q [F_lhs → F_rhs] be the axiom used by line-n.
Let σ_u be the following substitution:
    For each variable v in v₁,v₂...v_q
        if v is the jth member of F_rhs
            then v←u where u is the jth member of TC.
        Otherwise v← unique-variable-name.
Let E-SUB be the subexplanation for the line
    supporting line n.
Return (Ebs-wp (σ_u  F_lhs) E-SUB)
```

Table 11-2: Descriptions of EBS-WP Procedures

formula PRE describes a set of premises under which E derives TC, (EBS-WP TC E) is at least as weak as PRE. The following paragraphs briefly outline a proof for these statements; the complete proof is presented in [53].

Let us consider the first statement first. The proof is by induction on the length of the explanation. We can show that if (EBS-WP TC E) $\vdash_E$ TC holds for all explanations of length less than n, then it holds for explanations of length n. There are three cases. The justification for the last line in E is either PREMISE, CONJ-INTRO, or M-PONENS. For each of these three cases there is a corresponding IF clause in the EBS-WP algorithm.

The first case, in which the line is a premise, is quite simple. Since (EBS-WP TC E) returns TC, we merely have to show that TC $\vdash_E$ TC, which immediately follows from the fact that any concept is a legal premise. The other two cases are more complex. Consider the case in which the justification is CONJ-INTRO. In this case, TC must be have the form (AND $F_1...F_k$). We use the induction hypothesis to show that the recursive calls to EBS-WP, (EBS-WP F_1 E_1)....(EBS-WP F_k E_k), describe the premises for deriving $F_1...F_k$ using the respective sub-explanations $E_1...E_k$ (the sub-explanations that support the last line of E). Then we show that these results, $F_1...F_k$, can be used to derive (AND $F_1...F_k$) via CONJ-INTRO as specified in the last line of E. Since (AND $F_1...F_k$) is exactly TC, we have shown that (EBS-WP TC E) $\vdash_E$ TC. The case for MODUS-PONENS is handled similarly.

The second part of the proof shows that the description returned by (EBS-WP TC E) is at least as weak any other description of the premises under which E derives TC. We assume that PRE $\vdash_E$ TC, for some arbitrary description PRE, and from this deduce that PRE $\models$ (EBS-WP TC E). Again, the proof is by induction on the length of E, and there are three cases, depending on whether the justification for the last line in E is either PREMISE, CONJ-INTRO, or M-PONENS.

If the justification is PREMISE, then (EBS-WP TC E) returns TC, so we merely have to show that from PRE $\vdash_E$ TC we can deduce PRE $\models$ TC. This follows directly from soundness. The remaining two cases, are more complex, but also rely on soundness. Consider the case for CONJ-INTRO. The target concept must be of the form (AND $F_1...F_k$). Again, we assume that PRE $\vdash_E$ TC is true. Therefore, since the last assertion is derived by CONJ-INTRO, it must be the case that PRE $\vdash_{E_1} F_1$, ...and PRE $\vdash_{E_k} F_k$. (Again, $E_1...E_k$ are the sub-explanations that support the last line of E.) Then the induction hypothesis an be used to establish that the statement we wish to prove holds for the recursive calls to EBS-WP. Thus PRE $\models$ (EBS-WP F_1 E_1) ...and PRE $\models$ (EBS-WP F_k E_k). Therefore, applying conjunction introduction, we have:

```
PRE |= (AND (EBS-WP F₁ E₁)
        ...
        (EBS-WP Fₖ Eₖ))
```

By the definition of EBS-WP, when the last line of TC is conjunction introduction, then (EBS-WP TC E) is exactly (AND (EBS-WP F_1 E_1) ... (EBS-WP F_k E_k)). Thus we have now deduced PRE $\models$ (EBS-WP TC E) from PRE $\vdash_E$ TC, proving our result. The case for M-PONENS is carried out similarly, concluding the entire correctness proof.

Because the correctness proof operates by cases, where each case corresponds to a type of PDL expression, it is straightforward to extend the result to a complete version of EBS-WP that handles the full PDL language. Adding a new case simply requires molding the same general argument to that specific case. The main difficulty is that the use of embedded quantifiers complicates the details of the proof.

11.3. Generality

One of the questions regarding the proposed formalization is whether the notion of weakest premises is in fact appropriate for describing EBL. As stated previously, in a 1985 paper Kibler and Porter [69] pointed out that the actual weakest preconditions of a given rule sequence may not be expressible in the description language, which they claimed limits the applicability of EBL (and specifically, my own version of EBL presented in 1984). To illustrate their point, let us suppose our description language allows only conjunction and existential quantification of atomic formulas, and there exists a rule sequence <R2, R3> whose weakest preconditions are (AND (P a)(P b)(Q b)). If there exists a rule R1 which states that (R x) => (P x), then the preconditions of <R1, R2, R3> must be expressed disjunctively, as shown below, because (P x) can unify with either (P a) or (P b).

```
(OR (AND (R a) (P b) (Q b))
    (AND (P a) (R b) (Q b))
```

Whether or not this is an important problem is open to debate. The definition of weakest premises presented earlier allows one to compute the weakest "expressible" preconditions. Therefore, technically speaking, either disjunct satisfies the definition of weakest premises. Moreover, if this is not acceptable, one can simply choose a description language powerful enough to exactly express the weakest preconditions of any legal operator sequence. For example, if the description language in the above example allowed disjunction, there would be no problem. In fact, the *real* issue is that, traditionally, machine learning research has relied on restricted languages to express bias for inductive learning mechanisms (e.g., [54]), and thus disjunction and other powerful language constructs have been viewed as undesirable. However, this view is anachronistic, since the bias in EBL comes directly from the explanation, not the language.

This issue is directly relevant to this chapter, since Mitchell, Keller, and Kedar-Cabelli's well known EBG method [57] (and several earlier methods, notably Mahadevan's Verification-Based Learning method [44]) is specifically biased not to compute the weakest preconditions, but instead to compute a less general expression. In this way, EBG avoids learning disjunctive expressions. I will argue that even if one wants to limit oneself to conjunctive expressions (for whatever the reason), it can and should be done within the weakest preconditions framework.

The EBG method operates by regressing a target concept through an explanation. To avoid producing disjunctive descriptions, the EBG regression algorithm considers only the specific variable bindings used in the explanation of the training instance. Furthermore, if any rule used in the explanation has disjunctive preconditions, the algorithm considers only the particular disjuncts satisfied by the training example. One reason that EBG avoids disjuncts is that the weakest preconditions may contain unsatisfiable disjuncts, as pointed out by Mahadevan [44]. For example, the STRIPS operators GOTO-LOC and PUSH-BOX (whose definitions are shown in table 11-3) can be applied in sequence to have a robot move to a box and push the box to another location; the weakest preconditions of the operator sequence <GOTO-LOC, PUSH-BOX> are shown below:

```
    GOTO-LOC (end-loc)
     Preconditions:  (AT ROBOT start-loc)
     Additions:  (AT ROBOT end-loc)
     Deletions:  (AT ROBOT start-loc)

   PUSH-BOX (bx end-loc)
    Preconditions:  (TYPE bx BOX)
                    (AT bx start-loc)
                    (AT ROBOT start-loc)
    Additions:  (AT bx end-loc),  (AT ROBOT end-loc)
    Deletions:  (AT bx start-loc),  (AT ROBOT start-loc)
```

Table 11-3: STRIPS Operators

```
(OR (AND (TYPE ROBOT BOX)
         (AT ROBOT locx)))
    (AND (TYPE bx BOX)
         (AT bx locy)
         (AT ROBOT locx)))
```

The disjunction occurs because there are two ways to unify the (AT ROBOT end-loc) postcondition of GOTO-LOC with the goal expression.[43] The first disjunct in this expression is unsatisfiable because (TYPE ROBOT BOX) can never be made true (although in a different domain it might be possible that a robot can double as a box, and push itself). EBG would ignore this disjunct because only the unification that is consistent with the example is considered. The price paid, of course, is that for some examples EBG may produce overly-specific rules, because satisfiable disjuncts will also be ignored. Additional examples will be necessary to produce these alternative descriptions. However, this approach is consistent with the philosophy of EBL -- the example serves as a focus for producing useful generalizations.[44]

The EBG method, while it avoids producing unsatisfiable disjuncts, sacrifices the elegance of weakest preconditions; there is no a clear description of exactly what the output will be. Instead of abandoning the notion of weakest preconditions, another alternative is to revise our notion of what we consider an acceptable explanation. For example, given our example above, our original explanation might be paraphrased in English as "*Applying the GOTO-LOC operator resulted in a state where the preconditions of PUSH-BOX were satisfied.*" An alternative explanation is "*Applying the GOTO-LOC operator satisfied the (AT ROBOT start-loc) precondition of PUSH-BOX, which was then applicable.*" This latter explanation is

---

[43]Actually the weakest preconditions includes a third disjunct that is not shown, representing the case where (AT ROBOT *end-loc*) does not unify with any of the preconditions of PUSH-BOX.

[44]In fact, EBG can, in theory, be accomplished by a transforming the complete target concept definition into a disjunctive normal form expression, and then eliminating useless disjuncts.

more specific, because it specifies how the postconditions of the first operator compose (i.e. unify) with the preconditions of the subsequent operator. We can extend this idea to arbitrary operator sequences, so that instead of explaining why an operator sequence achieves some goal state, we explain why a particular *composition* of operators achieves some goal state. By taking the weakest preconditions of such compositions, we can avoid producing useless disjuncts. This illustrates a general principle: To modify the results of an EBL program (i.e., to adjust its bias) one can either tailor the algorithm that generalizes explanations, or one can change the explanations that are generalized.

I would argue that second approach is more elegant and more appropriate. It allows us to compare EBL systems in terms of the explanations they produce, rather than comparing the generalization algorithms they use. In practice, this allows us to focus our comparisons on the knowledge used by the systems, rather than on the knowledge *and* the generalization algorithms. To illustrate the approach, let us consider how we can do away with EBG's "modified" regression algorithm, and replace it with a true regression algorithm (one that finds the weakest conditions of the explanation). Consider the safe-to-stack example originally discussed by Mitchell, Keller, and Kedar-Cabelli. The derivation in table 11-4 shows that a particular object, OBJ1, is SAFE-TO-STACK on another object, OBJ2.

```
Axiom1:  (IMPLIES (AND (VOLUME p1 v1) (DENSITY p1 d1) (PRODUCT w1 v1 d1))
                  (WEIGHT p1 w1))
Axiom2:  (IMPLIES (AND (WEIGHT p1 w1) (WEIGHT p2 w2) (LESS-THAN w1 w2))
                  (LIGHTER p1 p2))
Axiom3:  (IMPLIES (ISA p1 ENDTABLE)
                  (WEIGHT p1 5))
Axiom4:  (IMPLIES (LIGHTER x y)
                  (SAFE-TO-STACK x y))
Axiom5:  (IMPLIES (NOT (FRAGILE y))
                  (SAFE-TO-STACK x y))
```

Assertions	Explanation
1 (VOLUME OBJ1 1)	Premise
2 (DENSITY OBJ1 .1)	Premise
3 (PRODUCT .1 .1 1)	Premise
4 (AND (VOLUME OBJ1 1) (DENSITY OBJ1 .1) (PRODUCT .1 .1 1))	CI: 1,2,3
5 (WEIGHT OBJ1 .1)	MP: 4, Axiom1
6 (ISA OBJ2 ENDTABLE)	Premise
7 (WEIGHT OBJ2 5)	MP: 6, Axiom3
8 (LESS-THAN .1 5)	Premise
9 (AND (WEIGHT OBJ1 .1) (WEIGHT OBJ2 5) (LESS-THAN .1 5))	CI: 5,7,8
10 (LIGHTER OBJ1 OBJ2)	MP: 9, Axiom2
11 (SAFE-TO-STACK OBJ1, OBJ2)	MP: 10, Axiom4

Table 11-4: Safe-to-Stack Derivation

Given the target concept (SAFE-TO-STACK *x* *y*), the weakest premises of this derivation can be described as follows:

```
        (EXISTS v, d, w  SUCH-THAT
            (AND (VOLUME x v) (DENSITY x d) (PRODUCT w v d)
                (LESS-THAN w 5) (ISA y ENDTABLE)))
```

Now let us introduce a disjunction in the theory. Suppose that axioms 4 and 5 were replaced by the axiom shown below:

```
Axiom6:  (IMPLIES (OR (LIGHTER x y)
                       (NOT (FRAGILE y)))
            (SAFE-TO-STACK x y))
```

Now, even though this axiom contains an OR, we can still construct a proof for SAFE-TO-STACK without introducing disjunction into the weakest premises. Our modified proof will require the Disjunction Introduction (DI) inference rule of natural deduction. (Since we have expanded our language to allow disjunction, we need an appropriate rule of inference for dealing with disjunctions.) DI enables us to prove assertions of the form (OR A B) from A. As with Conjunction Introduction, CI, we will assume that the rule DI is sensitive to the order of disjuncts so that from P we can infer (OR P Q) but not (OR Q P).[45] Using this rule, we could redo the last few lines of our SAFE-TO STACK proof as follows:

```
10 (LIGHTER OBJ1 OBJ2)                              MP: Axiom2, 9
11 (OR (LIGHTER OBJ1 OBJ2)(NOT (FRAGILE OBJ3)))     DI: 10,
12 (SAFE-TO-STACK OBJ1, OBJ2)                       MP: Axiom6 10
```

Using this derivation, we arrive at the same conjunctive set of weakest premises as in the previous section. Noticed that the justification for DI specifically indicates the previous line from which each disjunct was deduced (since the rule is sensitive to the order of disjuncts). Thus, even though we have introduced disjunction into the language, we can retain the notion of weakest premises and still eliminate useless disjuncts. By a syntactic restriction we have insured that our explanations will indicate which disjunct the derivation hinges on. In other words, we have achieved the same effect as EBG within the weakest premises framework merely by tailoring the explanation language. (See also [53] for an illustration of how the same technique can be used to eliminate the disjunction problem in the STRIPS <GOTO-LOC, PUSH-BOX> example.)

The important point illustrated by this example is that we can tailor the axioms and/or inference rules so that appropriate explanations are produced. There are many reasons for doing so, because in general, the form that an explanation takes influences the utility of the results that are produced. The utility of learned knowledge may be gauged by its generality, or its effectiveness for search control, but in any case having the right explanation is crucial for achieving good results.

---

[45] If necessary, a commutative rule for disjunctions can also be introduced, or some similar mechanism.

11.3.1. Transforming Explanations to Improve the Utility of EBL

This chapter has presented a two-phase model of EBL in which an explanation is constructed, and then its weakest premises are found. PRODIGY's compression process would appear to involve a third phase, in which the learned description is re-represented. In actuality, this complication is unnecessary. Compression is actually equivalent to modifying the original explanation, and so no third phase is needed in the model.

To illustrate this point, let us consider straightforward compression of a blocksworld description:

```
(AND (ON x y)            reduces to:   (AND (ON x y)
     (NOT (ONTABLE x))                      (CLEAR x))
     (CLEAR x))
```

This reduction is made possible by the following axiom, which we will refer as SIMP-AXIOM-1, stating that if a block is on another block then it is not on the table:

```
SIMP-AXIOM-1: (IMPLIES (ON x y) (NOT (ONTABLE x)))
```

Let us assume the unsimplified description represents the weakest premises of some initial explanation, shown schematically in table 11-5. By modifying this explanation to reflect the application of SIMP-AXIOM-1 (as shown by line 2 of the modified proof) the simplified description becomes the weakest premises. In the general case, any simplification can be incorporated into an explanation. Therefore, PRODIGY's simplification process is equivalent to modifying the initial explanation so that the match cost of the weakest premises is reduced. The perspective is valid even though in PRODIGY the simplification process occurs after the process of computing the weakest premises of the original explanation.

```
                    INITIAL DERIVATION
        1  (ON BLOCKA BLOCKB)           Premise
        2  (NOT (ONTABLE BLOCKA))       Premise
        3  (CLEAR BLOCKA)               Premise
        4  ..........


                    MODIFIED DERIVATION
        1  (ON BLOCKA BLOCKB)           Premise
        2  (NOT (ONTABLE BLOCKA))       MP: 1, SIMP-AXIOM1
        3  (CLEAR BLOCKA)               Premise
        4  ..........
```

Table 11-5: Modifying an Explanation to Reflect a Simplification

One of the benefits of the model put forth in this chapter is that it provides a framework for comparing EBL systems. For example, consider DeJong and Mooney's EBL method [15], which generates an initial explanation and then improves it by eliminating various overspecific facts. Notice that, under our model, compression is also viewed as modifying an initial explanation. This viewpoint helps to clarify the relationship between DeJong and Mooney's EBL method and PRODIGY's EBL method.   Both include mechanisms for modifying an initial explanation.   DeJong and Mooney's method changes the generality of the learned description because their modifications are not equivalence preserving. In contrast, PRODIGY's compression method merely re-represents the learned description, because only equivalence preserving axioms are added to the explanation.   (The relationship between DeJong and Mooney's work and PRODIGY is discussed further in chapter 12.)

11.4. Conclusion

One of the surprising aspects of the history of EBL is that many independently developed systems have turned out to be quite similar in structure [47, 61, 73]. Typically, similarities to earlier programs have been noticed and analyzed only after the design or implementation process has been completed. Partly, this is due to the imprecise and ad-hoc manner in which EBL programs have been described. This chapter presents a simple, non-procedural model of generalization in EBL that is both clear and precise.

12. Related Work

The past few years has seen a resurgence of interest in knowledge-intensive learning methods. In particular, there has been a great deal of recent research on explanation-based learning methods and related approaches. In this chapter I review this research and briefly describe its historical development, focusing on the aspects most relevant to this dissertation. For each learning method I will consider two questions: "For what types of problem solving situations is the method appropriate?" and "How does the method fare with respect to utility?". As we will see, the utility issue is often sidestepped, ignored, or "assumed away". Most researchers have not directly considered the cost and benefits of the methods they have proposed.

The chapter is organized into two sections. The first section reviews explanation-based methods and the second considers other knowledge-intensive methods. Since, under some broad definitions of EBL, all of these methods might be considered explanation-based, the classification relies primarily on how they have been presented in the literature. The chapter concludes with a summary describing some of the themes that became evident while comparing the various learning methods.

12.1. Explanation-Based Approaches

The development of explanation-based learning has been a collaborative, evolutionary effort, marked by a gradual transition from exploratory research to more general and well-defined methods. The roots of EBL can be traced back to early learning programs such as STRIPS [25], HACKER [83], and Waterman's poker player [89], that could improve their performance by analyzing single examples. In the early eighties a number of researchers, including DeJong [16], Silver [81], Mitchell [58], Carbonell [10] and others [91, 76, 2], were independently working on projects in a variety of different domains where learning depended on analyzing why observed examples had some significant property. These projects all emphasized knowledge-based learning from single examples, in contrast to much of the research on inductive (similarity-based) learning that was being conducted at the time. From 1983 to 1986 it gradually came to be realized that these approaches all shared a very similar philosophy, and in some cases the actual methods were quite similar.[46]   Eventually a series of comparison papers [47, 57, 15, 61, 73] were written that attempted to unify these approaches within a single paradigm. The term *explanation-based learning*, which was suggested by DeJong, has come to be identified with this paradigm.

In the following subsections, I will review some of the more prototypical approaches to EBL, including Mitchell, Keller, and Kedar-Cabelli's EBG method [57] (and related work), the schema-acquisition method developed by DeJong and his colleagues [15], the STRIPS macro-operator learning method [25], and my own earlier work on the Constraint-Based Generalization (CBG) method [47]. Later I will review other approaches that can be mapped into EBL, such as the SOAR chunking method [73], and Carbonell's Derivational Analogy [9].

12.1.1. The EBG Approach

In 1986, Mitchell, Keller and Kedar-Cabelli described a unified approach to EBL, called Explanation-Based Generalization (EBG) [57], which clarified many of the common threads in the various systems that had previously been developed. There were at least three major contributions of the EBG paper. First, explanations were explicitly identified with proofs. While earlier work (including [47]) had alluded to the relationship between EBL and deduction, making the relationship explicit give a more precise meaning to the term "explanation". (This precision was capitalized on and extended in the preceding chapter.) Furthermore, Mitchell *et al.* suggested a clear specification of the input and output of EBL, as shown in table 12-0. The input consists of a target concept,[47] a theory for constructing explanations, an example, and an operationality criterion that defines what it means for a description to be useful. Finally, Mitchell *et al.* described several open problems that have become active areas of research. These include the following:

- Imperfect theory problems: What if the domain theory is incomplete, inconsistent, or specified in a manner such that forming explanations is intractable?

- Automatically formulating learning tasks: Where do the inputs to EBL system (i.e. target concepts, theory, operationality criterion and examples) come from? Can they be automatically formulated by the system?

---

[46]Discussions at the 1983 and 1985 Machine Learning workshops contributed to the gradually development of a unified paradigm. In particular, during the 1983 workshop it became evident that there was some similarity between the approaches, and during the 1985 workshop, many of the similarities between the actual methods were identified.

[47]I have slightly modified Mitchell et al.'s terminology for consistency with the previous chapters of this book. In particular, I have substituted the term *target concept* for *goal concept*, to avoid confusion with the goals of the problem solver. The term *target concept* has been previously used by Keller [36] and others in the same fashion.

• Combining explanation-based and similarity-based methods: How can explanation-based methods be combined with less knowledge-intensive methods so as to gracefully accommodate varying degrees of knowledge?

The EBG method operates by first constructing a proof, and then generalizing it using a modified regression algorithm, as discussed in the previous chapter. The EBG method was presented primarily as a unifying theoretical model of previous work in EBL, and only recently has EBG itself been implemented (e.g. [33]). I will therefore defer a discussion of the applications of EBG until the next section on EBG-related work. However, is appropriate at this point to briefly compare EBG to the EBS algorithm used by PRODIGY. For the most part, EBS is quite similar to EBG (and in fact EBS was heavily influenced by EBG). However, there are at least two interesting differences:

1. A significant practical requirement for any EBL system is that it be able to construct explanations from examples efficiently. PRODIGY's EBS method uses discriminator functions which examine the search tree generated by the problem solver to control the explanation construction process. In contrast, the EBG method does not specify any particular mechanism for identifying or constructing explanations. Recent implementations of EBG [34, 64], have relied on a theorem prover to construct explanations, which may be prohibitively costly; it may be necessary for the theorem prover to re-explore the search space traversed by the problem solver. In other words, the theorem prover does not make use of the problem solver's experience. Thus, as mentioned by Mostow and Bhatnager [64], when explaining why an operator failed, for instance, their theorem prover can discover a reason for the failure that is different than the one encountered by their problem solver.

2. Unlike EBG, which first constructs a proof and then generalizes it, EBS simultaneously constructs the proof and finds its weakest premises. Thus, EBS will be more efficient when there is no search involved in constructing the proof (as in PRODIGY), because generalizing the proof repeats much of the work (i.e. the substitutions) involved in the construction phase.

While Mitchell *et al.* did not explicitly discuss the utility problem, one can view their operationality criterion as a static binary test of an explanation's utility [37]. There are two basic problems with this, however. First, their operationality criterion is only a test on the *form* of the explanation, as pointed out by DeJong and Mooney [15], and not necessarily a real utility test. In their examples, Mitchell *et al.*'s operationality criteria specify that the explanation must refer only to directly computable or observable features. In reality, such criteria would not guarantee that the explanations are actually useful. Only the individual costs of evaluating the features is considered, rather than the cumulative cost. Furthermore, no measurement or estimate of expected benefits (search savings) is considered. Costs are only one half of the utility issue. Secondly, in order to produce useful explanations, one needs more than a test that simply throws out poor explanations.

Given:

- **Target Concept Definition: A concept definition describing the concept to be learned. (It is assumed that this concept definition fails to satisfy the Operationality Criterion.)**

- **Training Example: An example of the target concept.**

- **Domain Theory: A set of rules and facts to be used in explaining how the training example is an example of the target concept.**

- **Operationality Criterion: A predicate over concept definitions, specifying the form in which the learned concept definition must be expressed.**

Determine:

- **A generalization of the training example that is a sufficient concept description for the the target concept and that satisfies the operationality criterion.**

Table 12-1:   Mitchell *et al.*'s Specification of EBL

In practice one needs to be able to generate good explanations in the first place. This is why PRODIGY uses multiple target concepts and compression in addition to utility evaluation. As we have seen, in certain domains learning from failure or from goal interactions can produce much more useful explanations than just learning from success.

12.1.2. Other EBG Related Research

In addition to the EBG paper itself, there has been a significant amount of related work (primarily at Rutgers) by Mitchell [58, 55, 60], Kedar-Cabelli [33], Keller [35, 36, 37], Utgoff [87], Mahadevan [44], Tadepalli [84], Mostow and Bhatnager [64], Prieditis [71, 72] and others. Rather than discussing each of these research projects in depth, I will simply focus on some of the issues they have raised that overlap with this thesis.

The EBG method grew out of earlier work on the LEX2 system [58]. LEX2 operated in the domain of symbolic integration; it learned heuristics indicating when to apply its operators for transforming integrals. As mentioned in chapter 7, LEX2 used single-operator learning. Each heuristic indicated circumstances when a single operator should be applied, even though the learning was based on analyzing solution sequences. Since no experimental results for LEX2 were ever published (the system was never completely tested), it is difficult to analyze how it fared with respect to the utility of the heuristics it learned, and what the effect of scaling up the number of problems would be.   There are two interesting factors that bear mentioning. First, it is significant that the problem solver relied on a brute force forward search. Thus one can assume that the system, before learning, must have been quite inefficient. There is a general principle that may be relevant here: the less efficient the program is to start with, the easier it is to improve. A second factor that is of interest when considering LEX2's utility is the generalization language in which the learned heuristics were expressed. In PRODIGY, the longer the macro-operator, the more preconditions it tends to have, and hence the more expensive it is to match. In LEX2, a generalization hierarchy of concepts was employed, so that the preconditions of longer operator sequences were not necessarily more expensive to match. It appears that descriptions in LEX2 were specialized primarily by descending the generalization hierarchy, rather than by adding preconditions. This restriction limits the complexity and cost of the learned control knowledge.

A more recent EBG-related system is Mostow and Bhatnager's FAILSAFE [64]. FAILSAFE employs the EBG method to learn from problem solving failures in a room layout domain. Thus FAILSAFE is one of the few systems other than PRODIGY that can learn from failure. One of the significant differences between PRODIGY and FAILSAFE is that FAILSAFE uses a theorem prover to determine why a failure occurred, while PRODIGY employs discrimination functions which map directly from the search tree to a proof. Mostow and Bhatnager do not address this issue, but I conjecture that their approach may be computationally expensive as the system scales up. (FAILSAFE had only a single problem solving operator.) On the other hand, because their approach can be extended to allow the learning system to explore the space of proofs, it is possible that better proofs will be found, although Mostow and Bhatnager have not yet addressed this possibility.

As for the the utility issue, Mostow and Bhatnager have shown that learning in FAILSAFE can produce vast performance improvement. However, FAILSAFE largely ignores the utility issue. Thus, it appears unlikely that performance improvement can be maintained as the system (and number of examples) is scaled up. Furthermore, the maxim that less efficient systems are easier to improve may be relevant here. Before learning, the FAILSAFE problem solver performed exceptionally poorly because it generated room layouts without considering that rooms should not overlap. This helps explain the tremendous improvement that Mostow and Bhatnager observed.

Prieditis and Mostow's PROLEARN [72] employs both EBG and partial evaluation to optimize Prolog programs. Of all the work in EBL, PROLEARN comes closest to being a practical tool for real applications. However, as it currently exists, PROLEARN has several limitations which prevent it from being of real use. For instance, Prieditis and Mostow have indicated that the utility problem does arise in PROLEARN, and that it can be a serious problem. Because of the utility problem, PROLEARN will speed up some queries while slowing down others.

Keller's META-LEX system [36] is one of the few systems other than PRODIGY that attempts to analyze the utility of learning. While not strictly an EBL program, META-LEX does begin with a target concept, and a domain theory for recognizing the target concept. Both PRODIGY and META-LEX can be viewed as concept operationalization systems. However, unlike PRODIGY which uses specialization and compression to rewrite a target concept, META-LEX operates by applying simple transformations to a target concept description, such as changing terms to TRUE. The system heuristically searches the space of transformed concept descriptions for a description that maximizes utility. Because META-LEX's transformations can alter the correctness and coverage of a concept description in addition to its efficiency, these factors are taken into account by the utility function. In PRODIGY only efficiency is considered, because the learned rules are guaranteed to be correct. In part, the difference between PRODIGY and META-LEX can be attributed to the different mechanisms that they use for rewriting target concepts.

12.1.3. Constraint-Based Generalization

In 1984 I described an early domain-independent form of EBL called Constraint-Based Generalization (CBG). CBG was demonstrated in a game-playing program which learned by analyzing why its opponent was able to force it into a trap. The program learned rules enabling to detect and avoid future instances of the trap.

Game-playing is a fertile domain for EBL because games are well-defined, so that clear-cut explanations of why a move was appropriate can often be found [84, 3, 88]. Consider the chess diagram in figure 12-1, which illustrates a simple chess combination called a "skewer". The black bishop has the white king in check. After the king moves out of check, as it must, the bishop can take the queen.

The game-playing program learned about tactical combinations of this type, where one opponent forces the other into a loss, a capture, or some other undesirable state. After falling into a trap, the program could deduce an appropriate generalization by analyzing why the trap succeeded. The analysis proceeded by reconstructing the causal chain of events responsible for the trap, so as to identify a sequence of rules explaining why the trap succeeded. CBG computed the weakest preconditions of the composed sequence of rules, thus identifying the general constraints necessary for the trap to succeed.

In the above example, CBG can establish that, while the pawns are irrelevant, the queen must be "screened" by the king for the plan to succeed. Thus, it is possible to learn a rule such as that shown below which enables traps of this type to be recognized, and indicates the appropriate move for completing the trap. (The rule is only illustrative, being somewhat simplified, but is representative of the type of rules that the program learned. See [48] for a detailed description of the implementation and its limitations.)

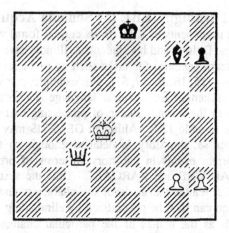

Figure 12-1: A Skewer

```
RECOGNITION-RULE:
    IF is-empty (attack-sq)
       & is-my-piece (attack-piece)
       & can-move-to (attack-sq, attack-piece)
       & can-attack (attack-piece, attack-sq, OPPONENT-KING)
       & is-screened (attack-sq, attack-piece, OPPONENT-KING,
                        opponent-piece)
       & worth-more (opponent-piece, attack-piece)
    THEN move (attack-piece, attack-sq)
```

The differences between the CBG and EBS algorithms are primarily technical differences. In fact, CBG was used for an early version of PRODIGY. One reason that I designed EBS was simply to explore the space of possible EBL algorithms. Both algorithms compute the weakest preconditions of a sequence of rules, with minor variations. CBG is a two-phase algorithm that first isolates an instantiated sequence of rules and then generalizes, whereas EBS computes the weakest preconditions as it builds the explanation.

The significant difference between PRODIGY and the game-playing program is *not* the different generalization algorithms employed, EBS vs. CBG. Rather, the difference lies in the context -- the programs in which the algorithms are embedded. For instance, PRODIGY has a much more expressive language than the game-playing implementation of CBG (which was limited to conjunctive rules). Even more importantly, PRODIGY can take advantage of meta-level target concepts, compress explanations, and analyze the utility of the rules it learns. The game-playing program included none of these capabilities and consequently it tended to slow down dramatically as more and more rules were learned.

12.1.4. DeJong's Paradigm: EBL for Schema Acquisition

One of the earliest proponents of EBL (in its current form) was Gerald DeJong. Over the past six years, DeJong and his students at Illinois have developed series of EBL programs that learn schemas for tasks such as problem solving and natural language understanding [15, 16, 66, 17, 61]. For example, one well-known system, GENESIS [62], is a schema-based natural language understanding system that learns new schemata in the normal course of processing narratives. Consider the first kidnapping story in table 12-2. Although GENESIS may not know anything about kidnappings per se, the story is detailed enough so that GENESIS can understand the important events in the story in terms of pre-existing low-level schemata such as CAPTURE and BARGAIN. Thus the system can build up a causal explanation that relates the goals of the characters and the actions in the story. The explanation can then be generalized by eliminating details incidental to the explanation, such as the names of the particular characters involved. The resulting schema reflects only the constraints necessary to preserve the causal structure of the explanation, and serves as a general schema for understanding kidnappings.

Using the learned schema, GENESIS is able to understand sketchy stories such as the second story shown in table 12-2. This sketchy story could not have been understood by the system had it not seen the first, causally complete, kidnapping story. Notice that the sketchy story leaves out information such as why Bob imprisoned Alice. Without the learned schema, the inferencing necessary to understand the sketchy story is combinatorially explosive. The learned schema thus enables GENESIS to connect the events in the sketchy story without incurring the cost of the combinatorial explosion.

Story1: Fred is the father of Mary and is a millionaire. John approached Mary. She was wearing blue jeans. John pointed a gun at her and told her he wanted her to get into his car. He drove her to his hotel and locked her in his room. John called Fred and told him John was holding Mary captive. John told Fred if Fred gave him $250,000 at Treno then John would release Mary. Fred gave him the money and John released Mary.

Story2: Ted is the husband of Alice. He won $100,000 in the lottery. Bob imprisoned Alice in his basement. Bob got $75,000 and released Alice.

Table 12-2: Two Kidnapping Stories

DeJong and his colleagues' research strategy has been to produce implementations, often domain-specific, that illustrate general principles of EBL. However, they have also recently begun to describe detailed domain-independent algorithms for EBL [15, 61]. For example, the domain-independent generalization algorithm used in the GENESIS system, called Explanation-Based Generalization Using Global Substitution (EGGS) was described by Mooney and Bennet in a subsequent paper [61]. Mooney and Benett demonstrated that the EGGS algorithm could produce the same generalizations as the STRIPS method and the EBG method, and analyzed the strong similarities between these various generalization methods. In fact, the EGGS method is also quite similar to both the CBG method and the EBS method (although, again, EGGS is a two-pass algorithm and EBS is a one-pass algorithm). Of course, these similarities should not be surprising; As I claimed in the previous section, these algorithms all can be viewed as taking the weakest premises of some explanation.

If one examines the various EBL methods that have been developed, one finds that their significant differences are due to the differing contexts in which the methods are applied, rather than to the generalization algorithms that they use. For example, in comparing the basic approach shared by the Illinois EBL systems [15] with the approach used in PRODIGY, one of the most significant differences is in the type of explanations employed. DeJong and Mooney's theories primarily consist of the domain operators used by the problem solver (and additional domain inference rules). The target concepts correspond to goals of the problem solver, and the explanations are sequences of operators that solve the goals (augmented by inference rules). In contrast, PRODIGY's theory is a meta-level theory that describes both the domain operators and the problem solver. Thus PRODIGY can explain meta-level phenomena such as failures and goal interactions, whereas presumably the Illinois systems are limited to explaining only domain-level concepts.[48]

The utility question has been addressed tangentially by DeJong and his colleagues. In their approach, a goal is considered to be operational if there exists a schema that can be easily instantiated to achieve that goal. The definition of operationality is dynamic, in that it depends on the pre-existing schemas in the system's knowledge base. However, they assume that all such schemas are equally good; they do not consider the relative costs and benefits of learned schemata. To my knowledge, there have been no experimental results describing the performance of any of the Illinois systems over large sets of examples.[49]

---

[48]DeJong and Mooney have proposed using their schema to refine over-general concepts, and their proposal has been extended and implemented by Chien [13], but this is essentially an extension of the standard approach for learning from success. No meta-level theory is used in Chien's scheme; the system initially produces incomplete explanations which can later be extended if they do not adequately explain subsequent events.

[49]O'Rorke [67] has recently described experimental results for an EBL system based on Newell, Shaw and Simon's LOGIC-THEORIST, running on the first 52 examples of Principia Mathematica. However, it is difficult to draw conclusions about O'Rorke's work with respect to the utility issues, because the sequence of examples was specifically designed so that the solutions to the earlier problems would be useful for solving subsequent problems.

While DeJong and Mooney do not directly address the utility issue, they have in fact described a method for improving the generality of overspecific explanations (which can be considered one manifestation of the utility problem). In their scheme, one can prune over-specific aspects of the explanation. Specifically, if the explanation refers to a state or action that is irrelevant to the goal (that the schema is supposed to achieve) then that part of the explanation can be dropped. In addition, if the explanation includes information derivable from previously acquired schemas, then that part of the explanation can be eliminated. Finally, if the explanation indicates that an action or object is a member of a more abstract category, only the reference to the abstract category is kept. This eliminates all but the most abstract actions and states which support the goal. In each case, these techniques make the resulting schema more general. DeJong and Mooney do not consider the possibility of improving an explanation by making it more specific.

DeJong and Mooney's method for improving explanations is philosophically similar to compression. However, their method takes an explanation and changes its generality. In contrast, compression takes an explanation and changes its representation (or more accurately, the representation of its preconditions). Inter-example compression can combine multiple explanations, in effect, creating a single general explanation from several more specific explanation.

More recently, Segre [77] has considered another aspect of the utility issue within DeJong's framework -- the operationality/generality tradeoff. Segre discusses the fact that more general schemas (i.e., learned descriptions) in his ARMS system are typically more expensive to apply. In particular, the more general the schema, the more work that must be done to instantiate it. Segre presents empirical results illustrating the tradeoff, and demonstrates that the operationality of learned schemas may be characterized in terms of the structure of the explanation. Although the schemas learned by Segre's systems are quite different than PRODIGY's search control rules, his observations regarding the expense of using more general knowledge is quite relevant to the utility issue. However, in PRODIGY, at least, more general rules are *not* necessarily more difficult to evaluate. While one must often trade off generality for efficiency, the curve relating the two factors is not necessarily monotonic.

12.1.5. STRIPS and MORRIS

The STRIPS macro-operator formation method [25] is widely regarded as one of the precursors of EBL. In fact, as previously mentioned, Mooney and Bennett [61] have argued that their EGGS algorithm is equivalent to the STRIPS generalization algorithm (except for some efficiency differences).

After the STRIPS planner solved a problem, it would take the resulting plan and convert it into a general macro-operator for solving similar problems in the future. In the STRIPS task domain a robot could move from room to room and push boxes together. Consider the problem of achieving (NEXT-TO BOX1 BOX2) when the robot is in ROOM1 and BOX1 and BOX2 are in an adjacent room, ROOM2. One plan that STRIPS might construct to solve this problem is:

GOTO-DOOR(ROOM1, ROOM2)
GOTHRU-DOOR(ROOM1, ROOM2)
GOTO-BOX(BOX1)
PUSH-BOX(BOX1, BOX2)

By analyzing why the plan achieved the goal of getting BOX1 next to BOX2, STRIPS could generalize the plan, producing a macro-operator can be used to achieve the general goal (NEXT-TO box-x box-y):

GOTO-DOOR(rm-w,rm-v)
GOTHRU-DOOR(rm-w, rm-v)
GOTO-BOX(box-x)
PUSH-BOX(box-x, box-y)

The procedure for generalizing the plan involved more than simply replacing constants by variables. STRIPS analyzed why each step in the plan was necessary so that, for example, two identical constants could be replaced by distinct variables if doing so did not disturb the structural integrity of the plan. Once the plan was generalized, the preconditions of the resulting operator sequence described conditions under which the goal (NEXT-TO box-x box-y) could be solved.

The EBL perspective on this process is that the successful plan explains why the goal (NEXT-TO BOX1 BOX2) was achievable. The generalized plan, or macro-operator, is useful for achieving goals of the form (NEXT-TO box-x box-y). Thus, the target concept is the class of situations in which (NEXT-TO box-x box-y) is achievable. Macro-operator formation computes sufficient conditions for membership in this class, represented by the preconditions of the macro-operator. Note that the theory that is employed to construct macro-operators consists completely of the domain operators. Therefore, STRIPS is limited to explaining why a goal was achievable.

As mentioned in previous chapters, the MORRIS project demonstrated that blindly employing the STRIPS approach may be pointless, due to the large numbers of non-effective macro-operators that can be learned. When using the STRIPS learning method to acquire macro-operators, it was found that performance tended to deteriorate as more and more macro-operators were learned. In effect, the cumulative benefits of the macro-operators were outweighed by the costs of matching their preconditions, and thus the average utility of the learned macro-operators was negative. It was also demonstrated that over a series of twenty-five examples, saving only the best macro-operators led to improved performance.

We can view PRODIGY's utility analysis as a more sophisticated, empirical method of selecting the "best" learned rules. MORRIS used two simple utility metrics for determining whether a macro-operator was useful. The first was application frequency; only the most frequently used macro-operators were saved. Note that PRODIGY takes application frequency into account during utility evaluation. The second metric had to do with MORRIS' heuristic evaluation function, which it used when traversing the search space. If a macro-operator crossed a "valley" in the evaluation space, then it was considered useful because it enabled the problem solver to exit from a local maximum in the direction of a global maximum. Although PRODIGY, unlike MORRIS, does not include a built-in evaluation heuristic, if it did then a similar utility metric could be implemented using a training example selection heuristic. (Even without such a heuristic PRODIGY's utility analysis would eventually produce the same end result, since it measures the overall benefit of the learned rules.) MORRIS did not include any method for measuring the cost of testing a macro-operator's preconditions.

One of the problems with the MORRIS system is that it could only throw out useless macro-operators -- it had little control over the macro-operators that were generated or the form of their preconditions (except for the ordering of the preconditions). In retrospect, this appears to be a crucial weakness. Throwing out useless macro-operators is a very weak strategy. Although this strategy is better than learning all macro-operators without regard to their utility, I have observed that in many cases MORRIS's performance was still much worse than one could produce by manually creating a good set of macro-operators (or, even better, control rules), or encoding control knowledge directly into the program. PRODIGY attempts to address this weakness by employing multiple target concepts and compression, so that relatively good control rules will be generated in the first place.

12.2. Other Knowledge-Intensive Learning Methods
In this section we consider knowledge-intensive learning methods that are related to EBL, but are typically not considered "explanation-based".

12.2.1. Chunking in SOAR
The SOAR system, developed by Laird, Newell, and Rosenbloom [43, 42] employs a learning method called "chunking". Chunking operates by summarizing the information examined while processing a subgoal. The mechanism bears a strong resemblance to EBL, because chunking not only identifies the conditions that determined the result for the subgoal, but also groups them into a composite rule. The relationship between chunking and EBL has been analyzed in detail by Rosenbloom and Laird [73].

There are a number of important philosophical differences with respect to learning in SOAR and PRODIGY. These include the following:
    1. SOAR is intended to be a general cognitive architecture. As such, its

learning mechanism, chunking, must be capable of learning all that a human can learn. The members of the SOAR project have made a continuing effort to demonstrate that chunking can act as a completely general learning mechanism [82]. In contrast, PRODIGY is not intended to be a general cognitive architecture; instead, we view PRODIGY as a problem solving tool that is particularly well-suited to problems that involve planning and/or means-end analysis. Similarly, the EBL subsystem in PRODIGY is not intended to be a general learning mechanism, it is intended to be a tool for improving PRODIGY's efficiency as it solves problems in a given domain. Thus, while generality is of utmost importance in SOAR, it is not quite as important in PRODIGY. On the other hand, efficiency and ease of use are both very important criteria in PRODIGY, and perhaps less so in SOAR.

2. Laird, Rosenbloom and Newell have characterized SOAR as a *simple experience learner*, rather than a *deliberate* learner. By this they mean that there is a single learning mechanism, which is fixed and does not perform any complex problem solving. PRODIGY, on the other hand, actively selects target concepts, compresses explanations, and analyzes their utility, all of which can be considered complex problem solving. (This is especially true of compression.) Thus PRODIGY can be considered a much more deliberate learner than SOAR.

3. Laird, Rosenbloom and Newell specifically state that SOAR uses a single learning mechanism and thus cannot be considered a "multi-strategy learner", one that uses a variety of mechanisms. PRODIGY, on the other hand, uses a variety of target concepts, each of which represents a different learning strategy. However, if one looks a little bit deeper, the differences become less obvious. For example, we might equally well say that PRODIGY has single learning strategy (EBS followed by compression and utility evaluation) since the various target concepts and the theory can all be viewed as data. And conversely, SOAR's chunking mechanism can be viewed as implementing multiple learning strategies. For example, if SOAR has a problem space in which it reasons about goal interferences, it can in principle chunk and store the conditions under which two goals are observed to interfere.

4. In SOAR all knowledge is represented in terms of problem spaces. Thus the effectiveness of chunking is directly dependent on the encoding of the problem space that it operates in. In PRODIGY, the domain description used by the problem solver constitutes one source of knowledge, and the axioms used by the EBL subsystem constitute another source of knowledge. Thus, in PRODIGY, it is intended that the effectiveness of learning *not* be completely dependent on the domain specification. In fact, I regard learning to be a means for recovering from poor domain specifications (in particular, those that result in inefficient problem solving).

In addition to these philosophical differences, there are a number of technical differences that distinguish chunking from EBL. For example, chunking operates by identifying the working memory elements that were examined while processing a subgoal, rather than by identifying the sequence of rules that fired. Because chunking does not operate by finding the weakest preconditions of the rules that fired, it may overgeneralize. Consequently chunking is not guaranteed to preserve correctness.

The utility issue has largely been ignored in SOAR, at least until recently. In part, this is because performance in SOAR is measured by the number of decisions necessary to perform a task. Since chunking will generally reduce the number of decisions that are made whenever there is any overlap between tasks, it does very well according to this performance metric. However, making a decision may involve complex processing in its own right. For example, the cost of matching chunks is ignored in this simplistic metric, and therefore adding arbitrarily many and arbitrarily complex chunks can never hurt performance according to this metric. For this reason the number of decisions does not necessarily correlate with actual CPU time, at least on conventional machines. The relationship between CPU time and decision cycles is a complex issue that depends in part upon the assumptions about the type of chunks typically formed. This issue has only recently begun to be investigated by Tambe and Newell [85], who found that SOAR can learn very expensive chunks that dramatically slow it down. We note that within the SOAR framework, questions regarding realtime performance are not necessary critical. SOAR has been proposed as a psychological model and its performance metric stems partially from this model.

12.2.2. Analogical and Case-Based Reasoning
There have been a number of methods developed for learning from experience that fall outside of the explanation-based learning paradigm. Many of these are forms of analogical reasoning (e.g., [9, 11, 6, 74, 6]) or case-based reasoning(eg. [40, 29]), which for the present I will group together. There are a number of key differences between these forms of reasoning and EBL.

- *When does the generalization process occur?* As soon as a single example is encountered, EBL systems create an explicit generalization. Analogical systems tend to generalize later, when an example is encountered that is similar to an earlier example.

- *What knowledge drives the generalization process?* In EBL systems an explicit target concept and domain theory drive the generalization process. Analogical systems generally include some sort of built-in method for assessing similarities that drives the learning, or "analogical mapping" process [12].

- *What is the result of the learning process?* EBL systems typically learn a knowledge structure that is used to improve the efficiency of a problem solver. Analogical systems tend to modify their behavior directly on the basis of previous experience without necessarily storing an explicit generalization.

Perhaps the analogical method that is closest to EBL is Carbonell's derivational analogy. Derivational analogy [9, 10] is an approach to problem solving in which operator sequences and their entire subgoal structure are stored away and re-used to solve similar problems. However, the operator sequences are not generalized before they are stored. Instead, while solving a new problem, the system retrieves stored operator sequences if the current (partial) analysis of the problem is similar to the analysis that occurred while solving the stored problem. This approach is similar to EBL because transfer between problem solving episodes is achieved via explanations describing *why* operator sequences were useful. However, in derivational analogy, a similarity metric is used to match explanations (or partial explanations) that are generated for each example. In EBL, a pre-existing target concept is used to generate a complete generalization as soon as an example is encountered.

The utility problem arises in analogical and case-based learning systems when the cost of matching examples exceeds the benefit that those examples produce. I am aware of no analogical or case-based system that has been systematically tested on a large number of examples, in part perhaps because the analogical reasoning problem is exceedingly complex, and progress has been slow. There has been some research on schemes for searching memory so that "remindings" and similarities can be quickly recognized [39, 30], but little in the way of quantitative analysis or results.

12.2.3. Other Macro-Operator Systems

In addition to STRIPS and MORRIS, both of which use the STRIPS EBL method, there are a variety of other macro-operator learning methods. While most of these are not particularly relevant to EBL, there are some that are worth examining with regard to the utility issue.

If a small set of macro-operators can be generated that "cover" the relevant problems in the domain, then macro-operator learning can be an extremely effective strategy. For example, Korf's Macro Problem Solver [41] is powerful enough to generate a set of macros (for solving puzzles such as Rubik's cube) that completely eliminates search. However his technique only works for domains that exhibit operator decomposability. Korf's work provides a good demonstration of the leverage that one can achieve by trading-off generality for power. Korf's macro-operator learning strategy is quite limited in scope, but when applicable it is more powerful than any of the strategies investigated in this thesis. Interestingly, Laird, Rosenbloom and Newell [43] have demonstrated that Korf's technique can be emulated by chunking in SOAR. However, in order for SOAR to do this, the problem space must be structured so that subgoals are solved in just the right order. I believe that Korf's technique could equally well be implemented or "programmed" in PRODIGY in terms of an appropriate target concept and set of proof schemas, although this has not been attempted.

Dawson and Siklossy's REFLECT [14], another macro-operator learning system, is one of the few that conducts a static analysis of the domain to improve performance. In a "preprocessing" stage, REFLECT analyzes the domain in order to isolate pairs of literals that are inconsistent with each other. This enables the problem solver to prune many branches of the search tree that have unachievable goal sets. During preprocessing, REFLECT also attempts to combine every pair of operators into a BIGOP (a macro-operator of length 2). By analyzing which pairs of operators are compatible, REFLECT selectively produces BIGOPS which are more likely to be useful. According to Dawson & Siklossy, these preprocessing steps can improve the problem solver's performance by an order of magnitude. However, their techniques are only practical with very short macro-operators due to the high combinatorics involved.

Finally, Iba has written a macro-operator learning system that selectively generates macro-operators using a "peak-to-peak" heuristic. According to this heuristic, the most promising macro-operators are those that traverse valleys in the state-space with respect to an evaluation function. This strategy is quite similar to one of MORRIS's strategies for selecting the most useful macro-operators. Obviously, while this strategy is fairly general, it is still limited to domains that have an appropriate evaluation function and in which operator sequences behave consistently with respect to their effect on the evaluation function. (I.e., a macro-operator must produce the same relative effect regardless of the state in which it is applied.)

12.3. Summary

There are a variety of dimensions along which I have compared the learning methods described in this chapter. Below I list several recurring themes that have surfaced along the way.

1. *Generalization algorithms:* The EBL systems described employ very similar generalization algorithms that (essentially) find the weakest premises of an explanation. There are some minor differences, for instance, EBS is a one-pass algorithm, whereas most of the others are two-pass algorithms. However, the more significant differences in the EBL programs lie not in their generalization algorithms but in the explanations that they produce and generalize.

2. *Types of theory:* There is a spectrum of approaches to providing a theory to drive the learning process. One end of the spectrum is best exemplified by STRIPS, whose theory is completely represented by its domain operators. The system's "proofs" are not proofs in the usual sense, but sequences of domain operators. The limited scope of the theory reflects the fact that STRIPS' target concepts are limited to the goals of the problem solver. At the other extreme, PRODIGY employs explicit, separable theories about both the domain and the problem solver itself. This is necessary because PRODIGY's target concepts are meta-level problem solving phenomena

(e.g., problem solving failures, goal interactions, etc.), rather than simply domain-level problem solving goals. PRODIGY's theory is external to, and distinct from, the problem solving subsystem; in contrast, STRIPS' theory consists solely of its problem solving operators. Because PRODIGY's theory is declarative and external to the problem solver, it can be modified easily if the set of target concepts change. The core of STRIPS itself would have to be changed to accommodate different optimization strategies.

Many of the other systems can also be classified as intermediate points within this spectrum. The EBG approach clearly accommodates a separate, fully declarative theory describing the performance system, as illustrated by the FAILSAFE implementation. In contrast, SOAR's theory consists completely of the set of productions that constitute the system, and there is no separate theory that lies outside of the problem solver. In DeJong and Mooney's scheme, as in STRIPS, explanations are constructed by observing operator sequences, but explanations may also include inference rules and related information describing relevant features of the task domain. Even so, as with STRIPS, their approach operates by analyzing why a plan achieved a goal, thus the theory does not describe the problem solver itself and does not allow learning based on other target concepts.

3. *Methods for mapping from examples to explanations:* One of the significant practical requirements for any EBL system is that it be able to efficiently construct explanations from examples. PRODIGY's EBS method uses discriminator functions which examine the search tree generated by the problem solver to control the explanation construction process. In contrast, the EBG method does not specify any particular mechanism for identifying or constructing explanations. As stated previously, recent implementations of EBG [34, 64], have relied on a theorem prover to construct explanations, which may be prohibitively costly. For STRIPS and SOAR, the cost of mapping an example to an explanation is small. This is because the explanation is directly built from the sequence of operators or productions used by the problem solver in a problem solving episode. Thus, the explanation is essentially formulated by observation, and all the search is done in the problem solver. Similarly, in DeJong and Mooney's EBL scheme, the explanation process starts with an observed operator sequence.[50] However, there is some additional flexibility in their scheme, because the system may augment the observed sequence with inferences to improve the explanation. Finally, in so far as the analogical methods are concerned, the process of identifying the analogical mapping (which corresponds to building an explanation in EBL) is currently an area of active research, and several very different methods have been proposed.

4. *Utility:* As we have seen, there has been little explicit consideration given to the utility problem in any of the work on knowledge-intensive learning

---

[50]In DeJong and Mooney's scheme the observed operator sequence is optional. If it is not available, an explanation will be built from scratch, as in EBG.

methods. Most of the explanation-based methods are general methods, in that they can be used for any problem domain, but no one has really attempted to characterize the domains for which their methods work well. The same can be said of the analogical and case-based methods (but perhaps this is less surprising, since most of these methods have not been implemented in running problem solvers). On the other hand, the macro-operator systems (other than STRIPS and MORRIS) are not as general, and so it is easier to see where they derive their power from. For example, the tradeoff between generality and power is quite easily seen in Korf's macro learning system.

13. Conclusion

Although the tradeoff between search and knowledge is a well known phenomenon in AI, this dissertation is perhaps the first to investigate how the tradeoff effects the utility of learning. The primary claim, or the "thesis of the thesis", is that a learning system must be sensitive to the knowledge/search tradeoff if it is to have a positive influence on performance. Figure 13-1, adapted from Ebeling [22], graphically illustrates the prototypical relationship between knowledge and search speed (e.g., time per node expansion). The curves represent a constant level of performance over a range in knowledge and search speed. The arrow labeled "positive utility" indicates the best case that a learning program can achieve; knowledge is added to the system without a corresponding decrease in search speed, resulting in improved performance. The arrow label "negative utility" represents the converse case where adding knowledge impairs performance, an all too likely possibility. The results of my research indicate that an EBL system can reliably improve performance by *searching* for effective control knowledge. The choice of target concept and training example, the representation of the resulting control knowledge, and the determination of whether the control knowledge is actually useful all play an important role in EBL.

The following sections review the primary contributions of this research and the principles underlying the PRODIGY/EBL system, and briefly discuss areas for future work.

13.1. Summary of Central Principles and Contributions

This dissertation has investigated EBL as a technique for optimizing problem solving performance. As discussed in chapter 1, in order for control knowledge to be useful, its benefits must outweigh its costs. However, EBL is essentially a form of rule composition, a heuristic technique that may produce useless control knowledge, as shown in chapter 2. This is because the cost of repeatedly matching learned control knowledge to see whether it is applicable can outweigh the savings produced when it is applicable. Unfortunately, rule composition simply trades off problem space search with memory search. And, because the matching problem is intractable in the worst case, faster hardware for matching is unlikely to eliminate the utility problem. I have argued that the best way to overcome this problem is to search for control knowledge that makes the most of the tradeoff. This approach

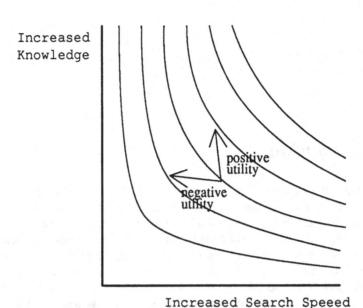

Figure 13-1:   The effect of knowledge and speed on search performance.
The curves represent constant performance.

was tested and implemented in the PRODIGY/EBL system.

Chapter 3 described the PRODIGY problem solver and its search control mechanism. A key idea introduced here was PRODIGY's *casual commitment* search strategy in which control knowledge is only used to guide decisions with important implications. If no control knowledge is present, the problem solver makes an arbitrary (and quick) choice. Thus, control knowledge is used only on a "need to know" basis.

PRODIGY's EBL component uses three new extensions that enable it to produce effective control knowledge. Together, these three techniques turn EBL into a search process; the system is searching for useful control rules. The first extension is to have a variety of meta-level target concepts available, so that for any particular example PRODIGY can select the target concept(s) that are most likely to be useful. Secondly, PRODIGY *compresses* the left-hand sides of each learned control rule in order to reduce its match cost. Finally, the system empirically tests the utility of the learned control rules so that it can reject any rules that are not useful.

Following a description of these extensions, a variety of examples were presented illustrating the different target concepts and the compression process. But, as discussed in chapter 10, the real test of an EBL problem solver is not whether learning produces improvement on individual examples, but how it performs over a "population" of problems. Thus, large-scale experiments were carried out in three different domains, providing a comprehensive test of the learning method. The experiments were performed by randomly selecting problems from well-specified populations of problems.

Finally, a rigorous model of EBL was described, enabling a correctness proof for the generalization algorithm used by PRODIGY to be carried out. The correctness issue itself is minor; the main point is to provide a clear definition of what is meant by an "explanation" and how it is used in EBL.

13.2. Where is the Knowledge?

One method for analyzing a complex AI system is to consider what knowledge is available to the system and how that knowledge is employed. The PRODIGY/EBL architecture consists of three separate modules, each of which has available its own knowledge sources.

The first module, the OBSERVER, scans the search tree to select target concept/training example pairs, and invokes the EBS algorithm. The observer makes use of the following knowledge:

- The target concept specifications, each of which includes an example recognizer function, a set of example selection heuristics and a template for constructing search control rules.

- The proof schemas, both architectural-level and domain-level.

- Discrimination functions, which map from a problem solving trace to a proof.

- A problem solving trace.

The architectural-level proof schemas, discrimination functions and target concept specifications, including the recognizer functions and selection heuristics, are all provided by the human "schema-writer". Although the target concept specification is declarative, the recognizer functions and selection heuristics named in the specification are procedurally encoded. Of all the knowledge sources in the system, the architectural-level proof schemas are the most complex, and took the most time to complete. (It took approximately one man-year to write and debug the proof schemas and their discriminator functions).

The domain-level proof schemas are automatically constructed from the domain specification (the operators and inference rules) provided by the domain expert. The domain expert, unlike the schema-writer, does not need to have any expertise regarding the learning system. He has only to write the domain specification, and provide a source of training problems. (These may be automatically generated as in the experiments reported in chapter 10, or constructed by hand.) As it solves a training problem, the problem solver automatically constructs a problem solving trace -- a record of the search tree. As explained in chapter 10, the learning process may be greatly influenced by the choice of training problems. Presumably, however, it is not necessary to have a deep understanding of the learning system in order to generate appropriate problems. (The PRODIGY user interface is designed to make it easy a human being to understand the system's behavior, enabling him to provide useful training examples.) In any event, the learning process is quite robust with respect the sequence of training examples; providing better examples simply means that the system learns more rapidly.

The second module, the COMPRESSOR, searches for a representation of the learned description (produced by the OBSERVER) that minimizes match cost. The knowledge sources employed by the COMPRESSOR are the following:

- For each static predicate that can be partially evaluated, a function that carries out the partial evaluation process. Only meta-level predicates are partially evaluated.

- A set of domain-independent, equivalence preserving transformations (procedurally encoded).

- A set of domain-specific simplification axioms (primarily used by the theorem prover.)

Except for the simplification axioms, these knowledge sources are domain-independent and unchanging. (There are no provisions made for partially evaluating domain-specific predicates, for example; this is a possible improvement that could be made to the system.) The simplification axioms are provided by the domain expert along with the domain specification.

The third and last module of the learning system is the MONITOR, which carries out utility evaluation. The MONITOR's primary knowledge source, if it can be called that, is the sequence of training problems that it uses to empirically decide if a learned rule is useful. The cost/benefit formula, and the MONITOR's methods for estimating and measuring utility, are built into the system.

13.3. Looking Ahead

There are a variety of incremental changes that can be made to the PRODIGY/EBL architecture to improve its performance and flexibility. For example, currently the compressor will find a semantically equivalent description that is less expensive to match; a potential improvement would be to allow the compressor to consider transformations that are not equivalence preserving. Another possible improvement to the system would be to change the utility evaluation process so that the time saved by a rule is sampled empirically, instead of relying solely on the savings estimate. In general, such modifications trade off learning time for improved flexibility and utility of the learned rules.

Further ahead, more significant changes are in store. In the preceding chapters I have argued that to learn useful control knowledge a system must be sensitive to the costs and benefits of using that knowledge. The PRODIGY/EBL system does in fact take these costs and benefits into account as it learns. But PRODIGY is only a first step towards a *reflective* learner, one that can reason about itself in order to learn. In PRODIGY, the explanation space in which it searches is *fixed* once the target concepts, theory, and selection heuristics have been determined by the implementor. The system can neither modify or reflect on it target concepts, theory, compression procedures, nor utility evaluation procedures. Perhaps the next step towards a truly reflective learning system is put these aspects under the system's own control, so that it can modify or adjust them to improve the effectiveness of the learning process. This would enable the system to "learn about learning", so to speak.

Reflective learning can not only improve the effectiveness of learning, but also take some of the responsibility and burden out of the schema writer's hands. Writing the proof schemas, selection heuristics, etc., is a time consuming and difficult process. Approximately one man-year was spent writing, rewriting, and debugging the schemas used by the PRODIGY/EBL system. If the system could take over some of this work, perhaps even write the schemas itself, it would be an important step towards making this type of learning more practical. However, to do so the learning system will have to reason about the problem solver's efficiency, the proof schemas' bias, and a variety of other complex issues. Initial steps towards reflective learning capabilities have been taken by Keller [36], Kedar-Cabelli [34], Mostow [63], and others [21], but practical applications are still many years away.

Appendix I
Domain Specifications

I.1. Scheduling World

The initial state for scheduling world problem consists of an empty schedule, a variety of objects and bolts. The goal statement is a conjunctive expression consisting of one or more ground atomic formulas describing attributes of the objects. Unsolvable problems are legal in the scheduling world (in contrast to the other test domains).[51]

I.1.1. Procedure for Generating Scheduling Problems

The procedure takes parameters LAST-TIME, NUM-OBJECTS, NUM-BOLTS, and MAX-GOALS. The initial state is generated as follows. The parameters NUM-OBJECTS and NUM-BOLTS determine the number of existing objects and bolts. Objects have, independently, a 1/3 chance of being either smooth or polished, a 1/3 chance of being painted with one of four types of paint, and a 1/3 chance of having a hole. Holes have one of 7 widths, and one of 4 orientations, both randomly assigned. Bolts also have one of these 7 widths randomly assigned. The number of available time slots in the schedule is determined by the value LAST-TIME. The objects are all initially LAST-SCHEDULED at time-0. Each object is initially COLD, and it has one of four types of shapes (cylindrical, rectangular, irregular, or undetermined).

A set of goal attributes is formulated as follows. A initial set of attributes is selected for each object. The object can have a hole (with one of 7 widths and one of 4 orientations), one of four types of paints, the shape CYLINDRICAL, the surface-condition SMOOTH or POLISHED, and be joined to another object (with a random orientation). This set of attributes is filtered to insure that no groups of three or more objects are joined together (for simplicity). Then a random number from 1 to MAX-GOALS of the remaining attributes are conjoined to form the goal expression.

---

[51]The goals never include creating new objects. Two trivial control rules (not shown here) were included as part of the scheduling domain to prevent WELD and BOLT being considered to create new objects. This was done primarily for technical purposes, since WELD and BOLT both expect the object to be joined to be bound by the effects-list.

I.1.2. Domain Specification

These are the operators used in the scheduling domain:

```
(POLISH (obj time prev-time)
  (PRECONDS (AND (IS-OBJECT obj)
                 (OR (CLAMPABLE obj POLISHER)
                     (SHAPE obj RECTANGULAR))
                 (LAST-SCHEDULED obj prev-time)
                 (LATER time prev-time)
                 (IDLE POLISHER time)))
  (EFFECTS ((DEL (SURFACE-CONDITION obj old-cond))
           (ADD (SURFACE-CONDITION obj POLISHED))
           (DEL (LAST-SCHEDULED obj prev-time))
           (ADD (LAST-SCHEDULED obj time))
           (ADD (SCHEDULED obj POLISHER time)))))


(ROLL (obj time prev-time)
  (PRECONDS (AND (IS-OBJECT obj)
                 (LAST-SCHEDULED obj prev-time)
                 (LATER time prev-time)
                 (IDLE ROLLER time)))
  (EFFECTS ((DEL (SHAPE obj old-shape))
           (DEL (TEMPERATURE obj old-temp))
           (DEL (LAST-SCHEDULED obj prev-time))
           (DEL (SURFACE-CONDITION obj old-cond))
           (DEL (PAINTED obj old-paint))
           (DEL (HAS-HOLE obj any1 orient>))
           (ADD (TEMPERATURE obj HOT))
           (ADD (SHAPE obj CYLINDRICAL))
           (ADD (LAST-SCHEDULED obj time))
           (ADD (SCHEDULED obj ROLLER time)))))


(LATHE (obj time shape prev-time)
  (PRECONDS (AND (IS-OBJECT obj)
                 (LAST-SCHEDULED obj prev-time)
                 (LATER time prev-time)
                 (IDLE LATHE time)
                 (SHAPE obj shape)))
  (EFFECTS ((DEL (SHAPE obj shape))
           (DEL (SURFACE-CONDITION obj old-cond))
           (ADD (SURFACE-CONDITION obj ROUGH))
           (DEL (PAINTED obj old-paint))
           (DEL (LAST-SCHEDULED obj prev-time))
           (ADD (SHAPE obj CYLINDRICAL))
           (ADD (LAST-SCHEDULED obj time))
           (ADD (SCHEDULED obj LATHE time)))))
```

```
(GRIND (obj time prev-time)
  (PRECONDS (AND (IS-OBJECT obj)
                 (LAST-SCHEDULED obj prev-time)
                 (LATER time prev-time)
                 (IDLE GRINDER time)))
  (EFFECTS ((DEL (SURFACE-CONDITION obj old-cond))
           (ADD (SURFACE-CONDITION obj SMOOTH))
           (DEL (PAINTED obj old-paint))
           (DEL (LAST-SCHEDULED obj prev-time))
           (ADD (LAST-SCHEDULED obj time))
           (ADD (SCHEDULED obj GRINDER time)))))

(PUNCH (obj time hole-width orientation prev-time)
  (PRECONDS (AND (IS-OBJECT obj)
                 (IS-PUNCHABLE obj hole-width orientation)
                 (CLAMPABLE obj PUNCH)
                 (LAST-SCHEDULED obj prev-time)
                 (LATER time prev-time)
                 (IDLE PUNCH time)))
  (EFFECTS ((ADD (HAS-HOLE obj hole-width orientation))
           (DEL (SURFACE-CONDITION obj old-cond))
           (ADD (SURFACE-CONDITION obj ROUGH))
           (DEL (LAST-SCHEDULED obj prev-time))
           (ADD (LAST-SCHEDULED obj time))
           (ADD (SCHEDULED obj PUNCH time)))))

(DRILL-PRESS (obj time hole-width orientation prev-time)
  (PRECONDS (AND (IS-OBJECT obj)
                 (IS-DRILLABLE obj orientation)
                 (NOT (SURFACE-CONDITION obj POLISHED))
                 (LAST-SCHEDULED obj prev-time)
                 (LATER time prev-time)
                 (IDLE DRILL-PRESS time)
                 (HAVE-BIT hole-width)))
  (EFFECTS ((ADD (HAS-HOLE obj hole-width orientation))
           (DEL (LAST-SCHEDULED obj prev-time))
           (ADD (LAST-SCHEDULED obj time))
           (ADD (SCHEDULED obj DRILL-PRESS time)))))


(SPRAY-PAINT (obj time paint)
  (PRECONDS (AND (SPRAYABLE paint)
                 (IS-OBJECT obj)
                 (SHAPE obj s)
                 (REGULAR-SHAPE s)
                 (CLAMPABLE obj SPRAY-PAINTER)
                 (LAST-SCHEDULED obj prev-time)
                 (LATER time prev-time)
                 (IDLE SPRAY-PAINTER time)))
  (EFFECTS ((ADD (PAINTED obj paint))
           (DEL (SURFACE-CONDITION obj old-cond))
           (DEL (LAST-SCHEDULED obj prev-time))
           (ADD (LAST-SCHEDULED obj time))
           (ADD (SCHEDULED obj SPRAY-PAINTER time)))))
```

```
(IMMERSION-PAINT (obj time paint)
  (PRECONDS (AND (IS-OBJECT obj)
                 (HAVE-PAINT-FOR-IMMERSION paint)
                 (LAST-SCHEDULED obj prev-time)
                 (LATER time prev-time)
                 (IDLE IMMERSION-PAINTER time)))
  (EFFECTS ((ADD (PAINTED obj paint))
            (DEL (LAST-SCHEDULED obj prev-time))
            (ADD (LAST-SCHEDULED obj time))
            (ADD (SCHEDULED obj IMMERSION-PAINTER time)))))


(BOLT (obj1 obj2 time orientation bolt)
  (PRECONDS (AND (IS-OBJECT obj1)
                 (IS-OBJECT obj2)
                 (CAN-BE-BOLTED obj1 obj2 orientation)
                 (IS-BOLT bolt)
                 (IS-WIDTH width bolt)
                 (HAS-HOLE obj1 width orientation)
                 (HAS-HOLE obj2 width orientation)
                 (LAST-SCHEDULED obj1 prev-time1)
                 (LAST-SCHEDULED obj2 prev-time2)
                 (LATER time prev-time1)
                 (LATER time prev-time2)
                 (IDLE BOLTING-MACHINE time)
                 (COMPOSITE-OBJECT new-obj orientation obj1 obj2)))
  (EFFECTS ((DEL (LAST-SCHEDULED obj1 prev-time1))
            (DEL (LAST-SCHEDULED obj2 prev-time2))
            (ADD (LAST-SCHEDULED new-obj time))
            (ADD (IS-OBJECT new-obj))
            (DEL (IS-OBJECT obj1))
            (DEL (IS-OBJECT obj2))
            (ADD (JOINED obj1 obj2 orientation))
            (ADD (SCHEDULED new-obj BOLTING-MACHINE time)))))


(WELD (obj1 obj2 time orientation)
  (PRECONDS (AND (IS-OBJECT obj1)
                 (IS-OBJECT obj2)
                 (CAN-BE-WELDED obj1 obj2 orientation)
                 (LAST-SCHEDULED obj1 prev-time1)
                 (LAST-SCHEDULED obj2 prev-time2)
                 (LATER time prev-time1)
                 (LATER time prev-time2)
                 (IDLE WELDER time)
                 (COMPOSITE-OBJECT new-obj orientation obj1 obj2)))
  (EFFECTS ((DEL (LAST-SCHEDULED obj1 prev-time1))
            (DEL (LAST-SCHEDULED obj2 prev-time2))
            (ADD (LAST-SCHEDULED new-obj time))
            (DEL (TEMPERATURE new-obj old-temp))
            (ADD (TEMPERATURE new-obj HOT))
            (ADD (IS-OBJECT new-obj))
            (DEL (IS-OBJECT obj1))
            (DEL (IS-OBJECT obj2))
            (ADD (JOINED obj1 obj2 orientation))
            (ADD (SCHEDULED new-obj WELDER time)))))
```

These are the inference rules used in the scheduling domain:

```
(IS-CLAMPABLE (obj1 machine)
  (PRECONDS (AND (HAS-CLAMP machine)
                 (TEMPERATURE obj1 COLD)))
  (EFFECTS ((ADD (CLAMPABLE obj1 machine))))))


(INFER-IDLE (mach  time-t)
  (PRECONDS (FORALL (obj2 m) SUCH-THAT
                    (SCHEDULED obj2 m time-t)
             (NOT-EQUAL m mach)))
  (EFFECTS ((ADD (IDLE mach time-t))))))
```

I.2. Gridworld

Gridworld is a three-dimensional robot problem solving domain. The space is divided into a 3-D grid of cubes (referred to as "squares"). The robot always is of size 1x1x1, so he always occupies only a single square. There can be blocks of different size, and the robot is supposed to be able to move itself and the blocks to achieve a particular configuration (specified in the final state). The robot (named RMG) can pick up blocks, move them, and climb on top of them.

The gridworld domain employs the operators PICK-UP, PUT-DOWN, and MOVE. The robot can pick up a block of any size if it is in a contiguous square and it is not holding anything else. When the robot is holding a block, the robot itself and the block occupy *one* square no matter the size of the block, just as if the block had disappeared. (This simplification was introduced so that the full 3-D path planning problem could be avoided.)

Blocks in the domain must be rectangular, but they can be of arbitrary size (e.g. 3x5x2). They maintain their initial spacial orientation in the world, since they cannot be rotated. The specification for locations (an arbitrary rectangle in space) is given by a vector of length six. The first three numbers indicate the square in the location that is closest to 0,0,0, (lower-left-corner) and the last three indicate the square that is farthest from 0,0,0 (upper-right-corner).

RMG can move around (even when it is carrying a block) using the operator MOVE. The robot is of course not allowed to move through squares occupied by blocks. RMG can put down a block that he is holding if there is room for the block in a contiguous location.

I.2.1. Domain Specification

These are the operators used in the Gridworld:

```
(PICK-UP  (ob ob-loc RMG-loc)
  (PRECONDS (AND (OBJECT ob size)
                 (AT ob ob-loc)
                 (NEXT-TO ob-loc RMG-loc)
                 (AT RMG RMG-loc)
                 (WITHIN-HEIGHT ob-loc RMG-loc RMG-reach)
                 (CLEAR ob)
                 (ARM-EMPTY)))
  (EFFECTS ((DEL (AT ob ob-loc))
            (ADD (HOLDING ob)))))


(PUT-DOWN  (ob new-loc RMG-loc)
  (PRECONDS (AND (VACANT-LOC new-loc)
                 (OBJECT ob ob-size)
                 (NEXT-TO new-loc RMG-loc)
                 (LOCATION-SIZE new-loc loc-size)
                 (IS-EQUAL loc-size ob-size)
                 (SUPPORTED-LOC new-loc)
                 (SUPPORTED-LOC rmg-loc)
                 (HOLDING ob)
                 (AT RMG RMG-loc)
                 (WITHIN-HEIGHT new-loc RMG-loc RMG-reach)))
  (EFFECTS ((DEL (HOLDING ob))
            (ADD (AT ob new-loc)))))


(MOVE  (adj-loc to-loc)
  (PRECONDS (AND (TYPE to-loc LOCATION)
                 (SUPPORTED-LOC to-loc)
                 (VACANT-LOC to-loc)
                 (ADJACENT-LOCS to-loc adj-loc)
                 (AT RMG adj-loc)))
  (EFFECTS ((DEL (AT RMG adj-loc))
            (ADD (AT RMG to-loc)))))
```

These are the inference rules used in Gridworld:

```
(INFER-VACANT-LOC  (loc)
  (PRECONDS (FORALL (obj obj-loc)
                    SUCH-THAT (AT obj obj-loc)
                    (DISJOINT loc obj-loc)))
  (EFFECTS ((ADD (VACANT-LOC loc)))))


(INFER-SUPPORTED-LOC  (loc)
  (PRECONDS (FORALL (sqloc)
               SUCH-THAT (SUPPORTING-SQLOCS loc sqloc)
               (OCCUPIED-SQLOC sqloc)))
  (EFFECTS ((ADD (supported-loc loc)))))


(INFER-OCCUPIED-SQLOC  (sqloc obj)
  (PRECONDS (AND (OBJECT obj obj-size)
                 (COVERS loc obj-size sqloc)
                 (AT obj loc)))
  (EFFECTS ((ADD (OCCUPIED-SQLOC sqloc)))))
```

```
(INFER-CLEAR (ob)
 (PRECONDS (FORALL (loc) SUCH-THAT (AT ob loc)
               (AND (ABOVE-LOC above-loc loc)
                    (VACANT-LOC above-loc))))
 (EFFECTS ((ADD (CLEAR ob)))))

(INFER-ARM-EMPTY
 (PRECONDS (NOT (EXISTS (ob) SUCH-THAT (HOLDING ob))))
 (EFFECTS ((ADD (ARM-EMPTY)))))
```

I.3. Blocksworld

In the initial state of a blocksworld problem, each block is either on another block, on the table, or being held. At most one block can be held at a time. The goal statement is a conjunctive expression consisting of one or more ground atomic formulas. Only goal expressions that can be solved in some linear order (i.e. by a linear problem solver) are considered legal[52].

I.3.1. Procedure for Generating Problems

This procedure takes parameters MAX-BLOCKS and MAX-GOALS. First, the number of blocks, from 2 to MAX-BLOCKS is generated randomly. To generate the initial state, the following subprocedure is used. For each block, with probability 1/3 it is put on the table, otherwise a previously generated pile is randomly selected and place the block is placed on top. After all blocks have been placed, with probability 1/3, the the last block placed is removed from whereever it was placed, and put in the robot hand.

To create the goal expression, a goal state is generated by following the same subprocedure used to generate the initial state. Then a set of goals is selected as follows. Each of the assertions in the goal state is filtered out with probability 2/3 if it is true in the initial state. Then a random number, from 1 to MAX-GOALS, of these assertions are conjoined to form the goal expression. If all the goals are already true in the initial state the procedure is repeated.

I.3.2. Domain Specification

These are the operators used in the blocksworld. (There are no inference rules.)

---

[52]In practice, very few problems were filtered out because of this constraint.

```
(PICK-UP (ob)                              (PUT-DOWN (ob)
  (PRECONDS (AND (OBJECT ob)                 (PRECONDS (AND (OBJECT ob)
                 (CLEAR ob)                                 (HOLDING ob)))
                 (ON-TABLE ob)              (EFFECTS ((DEL (HOLDING ob))
                 (ARM-EMPTY)))                        (ADD (CLEAR ob))
  (EFFECTS ((DEL (ON-TABLE ob))                       (ADD (ARM-EMPTY))
           (DEL (CLEAR ob))                           (ADD (ON-TABLE ob)))))
           (DEL (ARM-EMPTY))
           (ADD (HOLDING ob)))))


                                           (UNSTACK (ob underob)
(STACK (ob underob)                          (PRECONDS (AND (OBJECT ob)
  (PRECONDS (AND (OBJECT ob)                                (OBJECT underob)
                 (OBJECT underob)                           (ON ob underob)
                 (CLEAR underob)                            (CLEAR ob)
                 (HOLDING ob)))                             (ARM-EMPTY)))
  (EFFECTS ((DEL (HOLDING ob))               (EFFECTS ((DEL (ON ob underob))
           (DEL (CLEAR underob))                      (DEL (CLEAR ob))
           (ADD (ARM-EMPTY))                          (DEL (ARM-EMPTY))
           (ADD (CLEAR ob))                           (ADD (HOLDING ob))
           (ADD (ON ob underob)))))                   (ADD (CLEAR underob)))))
```

I.4. Extended STRIPS Robot Domain

A problem in this domain is defined by an initial state, in which there is a set of interconnected rooms containing a robot, boxes and keys, and a goal statement, which is a conjunctive expression consisting of one or more ground atomic formulas. As in the blocksworld, only goal expressions that can be solved in some linear order are considered legal. The following procedure was employed for generating problems.

The rooms have doors connecting them, and each door may have a key. Doors can be open or closed, and locked or unlocked. Open doors are always unlocked. Boxes may be pushable, carriable, or neither, whereas keys are always carriable. Objects may be next to each other. The robot can hold at most one object at a time, and only if it is carriable.

I.4.1. Procedure for Generating Problems

The procedure takes parameters MAX-BOXES, MAX-GOALS and ROOM-CONFIG. The room configuration lists the rooms and the doors that connect them, and whether each door has a key or not. Three standard room configurations, shown by figure I-1, were used (as opposed to being randomly generating), so that teacher could better understand the actions of the problem solver and debug the domain description when necessary. To generate the initial state, the procedure begins by generating the number of of boxes, from 2 to MAX-BOXES. Then all objects (the boxes, keys and the robot) are all put in random rooms. With probability .4 each object is put next to another object in the same room, assuming there such an object and it is not already next to a third object. (Thus no more than two objects can be next to each other in the initial state). Each door is locked with probability 1/3, but only if there exists a key for that door. If the door is not locked, it is open with probability 1/4. Otherwise it is closed. Boxes are declared pushable with probability 1/3. If they are not pushable, they are declared carriable with probability 3/4. In the initial state, the robot is not holding anything.

Room Configuration 1

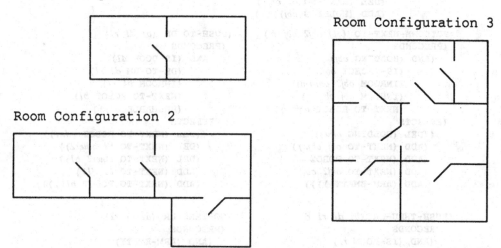

Room Configuration 3

Room Configuration 2

Figure I-1: Room Configurations for STRIPS Domain Experiments

The goal expression is generated in the following manner. First a goal state is generated by following the procedure described above (but without regenerating a new set of objects). Then each non-static assertion in the goal state is made a goal with probability 1/3 if the assertion is true in the initial state, or with probability 2/3 if the goal is not true in the initial state. With probability 1/6, the goal of holding a random object is added to the list of goals. If the list of goals is greater than MAX-GOALS, the system randomly selects a subset of size MAX-GOALS. The list of goals are the conjoined to form the goal expression.

If the resulting problem is not solvable (e.g. the goals include (INROOM ROBOT ROOM1), and the keys to ROOM1 are locked inside ROOM1), the entire procedure is repeated.

I.4.2. Domain Specification

These are the operators used in the extended STRIPS robot domain. (There are no
inference rules.)

```
(PICKUP-OBJ (obj))
  (PRECONDS
    (AND (ARM-EMPTY)
         (NEXT-TO ROBOT obj)
         (CARRIABLE obj)))
  (EFFECTS ((DEL (ARM-EMPTY))
            (DEL (NEXT-TO obj o2))
            (DEL (NEXT-TO o3 obj))
            (ADD (HOLDING obj)))))
```

```
(PUTDOWN (obj)
  (PRECONDS (HOLDING obj))
  (EFFECTS
    ((DEL (HOLDING other))
     (ADD (NEXT-TO ROBOT obj))
     (ADD (ARM-EMPTY)))))
```

```
(PUTDOWN-NEXT-TO (obj obj2 obj-rm)
  (PRECONDS
    (AND (HOLDING obj)
         (IS-OBJECT obj2)
         (INROOM obj2 obj-rm)
         (INROOM obj obj-rm)
         (NEXT-TO ROBOT obj2)))
  (EFFECTS
    ((DEL (HOLDING other))
     (ADD (NEXT-TO obj obj2))
     (ADD (NEXT-TO ROBOT obj))
     (ADD (NEXT-TO obj2 obj))
     (ADD (ARM-EMPTY)))))
```

```
(PUSH-TO-DR (bl dl rl)
  (PRECONDS
    (AND (IS-DOOR dl)
         (DR-TO-RM dl rl)
         (INROOM bl rl)
         (NEXT-TO ROBOT bl)
         (PUSHABLE bl)))
  (EFFECTS
    ((DEL (NEXT-TO ROBOT other))
     (DEL (NEXT-TO bl other2))
     (DEL (NEXT-TO other2 bl))
     (ADD (NEXT-TO bl dl))
     (ADD (NEXT-TO ROBOT bl)))))
```

```
(PUSH-THRU-DR (bl dl rl r2)
  (PRECONDS
    (AND (IS-ROOM rl)
         (DR-TO-RM dl rl)
         (IS-DOOR dl)
         (OPEN dl)
         (NEXT-TO bl dl)
         (NEXT-TO ROBOT bl)
         (PUSHABLE bl)
         (CONNECTS dl rl r2)
         (INROOM bl r2)))
  (EFFECTS
    ((DEL (NEXT-TO ROBOT other1))
     (DEL (NEXT-TO bl other2))
     (DEL (NEXT-TO other3 bl))
     (DEL (INROOM ROBOT other-rm))
     (DEL (INROOM bl other-rm))
     (ADD (INROOM ROBOT rl))
     (ADD (INROOM bl rl))
     (ADD (NEXT-TO ROBOT bl)))))
```

```
(GO-THRU-DR (dl rl r2)
  (PRECONDS
    (AND (ARM-EMPTY)
         (IS-ROOM rl)
         (DR-TO-RM dl rl)
         (IS-DOOR dl)
         (OPEN dl)
         (NEXT-TO ROBOT dl)
         (CONNECTS dl rl r2)
         (INROOM ROBOT r2)))
  (EFFECTS
    ((DEL (NEXT-TO ROBOT other))
     (DEL (INROOM ROBOT other-rm))
     (ADD (INROOM ROBOT rl)))))
```

```
(CARRY-THRU-DR (bl dl rl r2)              (GOTO-DR (dl rl)
  (PRECONDS                                 (PRECONDS
    (AND (IS-ROOM rl)                         (AND (IS-DOOR dl)
         (DR-TO-RM dl rl)                          (DR-TO-RM dl rl)
         (IS-DOOR dl)                      (INROOM ROBOT rl)))
         (OPEN dl)                           (EFFECTS
         (IS-OBJECT bl)                        ((DEL (NEXT-TO ROBOT other))
         (HOLDING bl)                           (ADD (NEXT-TO ROBOT dl)))))
         (CONNECTS dl rl r2)
         (INROOM bl r2)
         (INROOM ROBOT r2)
         (NEXT-TO ROBOT dl)))
  (EFFECTS
    ((DEL (NEXT-TO ROBOT other))
     (DEL (INROOM ROBOT other-rml))
     (DEL (INROOM bl other-rm2))
     (ADD (INROOM ROBOT rl))
     (ADD (INROOM bl rl)))))

(PUSH-BOX (bl b2 rl)                       (GOTO-OBJ (b rm)
  (PRECONDS                                  (PRECONDS
    (AND (IS-OBJECT bl)                        (AND (IS-OBJECT b)
         (IS-OBJECT b2)                             (INROOM b rm)
         (INROOM b2 rl)                             (INROOM ROBOT rm)))
         (INROOM bl rl)                      (EFFECTS
         (PUSHABLE bl)                         ((DEL (NEXT-TO ROBOT other)))))
         (NEXT-TO ROBOT bl)))                  (ADD (NEXT-TO ROBOT b))
  (EFFECTS
    ((DEL (NEXT-TO ROBOT other))
     (DEL (NEXT-TO bl other2))
     (DEL (NEXT-TO other3 bl))
     (ADD (NEXT-TO ROBOT bl))
     (ADD (NEXT-TO ROBOT b2))
     (ADD (NEXT-TO bl b2))
     (ADD (NEXT-TO b2 bl)))))

(OPEN (door)                               (CLOSE (door)
  (PRECONDS                                  (PRECONDS
    (AND (IS-DOOR door)                        (AND (IS-DOOR door)
         (UNLOCKED door)                            (NEXT-TO ROBOT door)
         (NEXT-TO ROBOT door)                       (OPEN door)))
         (CLOSED door)))                     (EFFECTS
  (EFFECTS                                     ((DEL (OPEN door))
    ((DEL (CLOSED door))                        (ADD (CLOSED door)))))
     (ADD (OPEN door)))))
```

```
(LOCK (door kl rml)                        (UNLOCK (door kl rml)
  (PRECONDS                                   (PRECONDS
    (AND (IS-DOOR door)                         (AND (IS-DOOR door)
         (IS-KEY door kl)                            (IS-KEY door kl)
         (HOLDING kl)                                (HOLDING kl)
         (DR-TO-RM door rml)                         (DR-TO-RM door rml)
         (INROOM kl rml)                             (INROOM kl rml)
         (NEXT-TO ROBOT door)                        (INROOM ROBOT rml)
         (CLOSED door)                               (NEXT-TO ROBOT door)
         (UNLOCKED door)))                           (LOCKED door)))
  (EFFECTS                                    (EFFECTS
    ((DEL (UNLOCKED door))                       ((DEL (LOCKED door))
     (ADD (LOCKED door)))))                       (ADD (UNLOCKED door)))))))
```

I.4.3. Initial Control Rules for STRIPS Domain

The learning project described in this book largely ignored issues concerning the quality of plans. However, without control rules, in the STRIPS domain PRODIGY will consider using operators such as CARRY to move the ROBOT to another room. It can do so successfully, because carrying an object to ROOMX also moves the ROBOT to ROOMX. The only problem is that the resulting plan is highly suboptimal. STRIPS got around this problem by allowing one to to indicate that only a certain subset of the effects of an operator should be backchained upon. In PRODIGY, we can achieve the same effect using control rules. Therefore, this domain specification included the control rules shown below so that the system would have approximately the same domain specification as STRIPS. The rules were also included in the hand-coded set of control rules for the experiments described in chapter 10.

```
(DONT-PUSH-BOX-TO-MOVE-ROBOT
    (LHS (AND (CURRENT-NODE node)
              (CURRENT-GOAL node (NEXT-TO ROBOT x))
              (CANDIDATE-OP node PUSH-BOX)))
    (RHS (REJECT OPERATOR PUSH-BOX)))

(DONT-CARRY-BOX-THRU-DOOR-TO-MOVE-ROBOT
    (LHS (AND (CURRENT-NODE node)
              (CURRENT-GOAL node (INROOM ROBOT x))
              (CANDIDATE-OP node CARRY-THRU-DR)))
    (RHS (REJECT OPERATOR CARRY-THRU-DR)))

(DONT-PUSH-BOX-THRU-DOOR-TO-MOVE-ROBOT-THROUGH-DOOR
    (LHS (AND (CURRENT-NODE node)
              (CURRENT-GOAL node (INROOM ROBOT x))
              (CANDIDATE-OP node PUSH-THRU-DR)))
    (RHS (REJECT OPERATOR PUSH-THRU-DR)))
```

```
(DONT-PUSH-BOX-THRU-DOOR-TO-MOVE-ROBOT
    (LHS (AND (CURRENT-NODE node)
              (CURRENT-GOAL node (NEXT-TO y x))
              (CANDIDATE-OP node PUSH-THRU-DR)))
    (RHS (REJECT OPERATOR PUSH-THRU-DR)))

(DONT-MOVE-OBJ-TO-FREE-ARM
    (LHS (AND (CURRENT-NODE node)
              (CURRENT-GOAL node (ARM-EMPTY))
              (CANDIDATE-OP node PUTDOWN-NEXT-TO)))
    (RHS (REJECT OPERATOR PUTDOWN-NEXT-TO)))

(DONT-MOVE-OBJ-NEXT-TO-ANOTHER-TO-GET-IT-IN-ROOM
    (LHS (AND (CURRENT-NODE node)
              (CURRENT-GOAL node (INROOM xx yy))
              (CANDIDATE-OP node PUTDOWN-NEXT-TO)))
    (RHS (REJECT OPERATOR PUTDOWN-NEXT-TO)))
```

References

1. Aho, A.V., Sethi, R. and Ullman, J.D. *Compilers: Principles, Techniques and Tools*. Addison Wesley, 1986.

2. Anderson, J.R. Knowledge Compilation: The General Learning Mechanism. Proceedings of the Second International Machine Learning Workshop, Montecello, Ill., 1983.

3. Banerji, R.B. *Artificial Intelligence: A Theoretical Approach*. Elsevier North-Holland, 1980.

4. Berliner, H. J. Search vs. Knowledge: An Analysis from the Domain of Games. In *Artificial and Human Intelligence*, Elithorn, A. and Banerji, R., Eds., Elsevier Science Publishers, 1984.

5. Brown, F.M. "An Experimental Logic Based on the Fundamental Deduction Principal". *Artificial Intelligence 30*, 2 (1986).

6. Burstein, M.H. Concept Formation by Incremental Analogical Reasoning and Debugging. In *Machine Learning, Volume II*, Michalski, R.S., Carbonell, J.G. and Mitchell, T.M., Eds., Morgan Kaufmann, 1986.

7. Campbell, M. and Berliner, H. Toward an Understanding of the Balance between Search and Knowledge. Unpublished Report, Carnegie-Mellon Univ.

8. Carbonell, J.G. and Gil, Y. Learning by Experimentation. Proceedings of the Fourth International Workshop on Machine Learning, Irvine, CA, 1987.

9. Carbonell, J. G. Derivational Analogy: A Theory of Reconstructive Problem Solving and Expertise Acquisition. In *Machine Learning, Volume II*, Michalski, R. S., Carbonell, J. G. and Mitchell, T. M., Eds., Morgan Kaufmann, 1986.

10. Carbonell, J. G. Derivational Analogy and its Role in Problem Solving. Proceedings of the National Conference on Artificial Intelligence, Washington, D.C., 1983.

11. Carbonell, J.G. Learning by Analogy: Formulating and Generalizing Plans From Past Experience. In *Machine learning: An Artificial Intelligence Approach*, R. S. Michalski, J. G. Carbonell and T. M. Mitchell, Eds., Tioga Press, Palo Alto, CA, 1983.

12. Carbonell, J.G. and Minton, S. Metaphor and Common Sense Reasoning. In *Formal Theories of the Common Sense World*, Hobbs, J. and Moore R., Eds., Ablex Publishing Co., 1984.

13. Chien, S. A. Extending Explanation-Based Learning: Failure-Driven Schema Refinement. Proceedings of the Third IEEE Conference on Artificial Intelligence Applications, Orlando, Florida, 1987.

14. Dawson, C. and Siklossy, L. On the Role of Pre-Processing in Problem Solving Systems. Proceedings of the 5th International Joint Conference on Artificial Intelligence, 1977.

15. DeJong,G.F. and Mooney, R. "Explanation-Based Learning: An Alternative View". *Machine Learning 1*, 2 (1986).

16. DeJong, G. F. Acquiring Schemata through Understanding and Generalizing Plans. Proceedings of the Eighth International Joint Conference on Artificial Intelligence, Karlsruhe, West Germany, 1983.

17. DeJong, G. F. An Approach to Learning from Observation. In *Machine Learning, Volume II*, Michalski, R. S., Carbonell, J. G. and Mitchell, T. M., Eds., Morgan Kaufmann, 1986.

18. Dietterich, T.G. "Learning at the knowledge level". *Machine Learning 1*, 2 (1986).

19. Dietterich, T. G. and Michalski, R.S. A Comparitive Review of Selected Methods for Learning from Examples. In *Machine learning: An Artificial Intelligence Approach*, R. S. Michalski, J. G. Carbonell and T. M. Mitchell, Eds., Tioga Press, Palo Alto, CA, 1983.

20. Doyle, J. "A Truth Maintenance System". *Artificial Intelligence 12*, 3 (1979).

21. Doyle, J. On Rationality and Learning. Submitted to AAAI-88.

22. Ebeling, C. *All the Right Moves: A VLSI Architecture for Chess*. Ph.D. Th., Carnegie-Mellon University, April 1986.

23. Ellman, T. Generalizing Logic Circuit Designs by Analyzing Proofs of Correctness. Proceedings of the Ninth International Joint Conference on Artificial Intelligence, Los Angeles, CA, 1985.

24. Fikes, R. *Monitored execution of Robot Plans produced by STRIPS*. Proceedings IFIP Congress, 1971.

25. Fikes, R., Hart, P. and Nilsson, N. "Learning and executing generalized robot plans". *Artificial Intelligence 3*, 4 (1972).

26. Flann, N.S. and Dietterich, T.G. Selecting Appropriate Representations for Learning from Examples. Proceedings of the National Conference on Artificial Intelligence, Philadelphia, PA, 1986.

27. Forgy, C. "Rete: A Fast Algorithm for the Many Pattern/Many Object Pattern Matching Problem". *Artificial Intelligence 19*, 1 (1982).

28. Garey, M.R. and Johnson, D.S.. *Computers and Intractability: A Guide to the Theory of NP-Completeness*. W.H. Freeman and Co., 1979.

29. Hammond, K. J. *Cased-based Planning: An Integrated Theory of Planning, Learning, and Memory*. Ph.D. Th., Yale University, October 1986.

30. Hammond, K.J. Learning and Reusing Explanations. Proceedings of the Fourth International Workshop on Machine Learning, Irvine, CA, 1987.

31. Hirsh, H. Explanation-based Generalization in a Logic-Programming Environment. Proceedings of the Tenth International Joint Conference on Artificial Intelligence, Milan, Italy, 1987.

32. Kahn, K. "Partial Evaluation as an Example of the Relationship between Programming Methodology and AI". *AI Magazine 5*, 1 (1984).

33. Kedar-Cabelli, S.T. and McCarty, L.T. Explanation-Based Generalization as Resolution Theorem Proving. Proceedings of the Fourth International Workshop on Machine Learning, Irvine, CA, 1987.

34. Kedar-Cabelli, S.T. Formulating Concepts According to Purpose. Proceedings of the National Conference on Artificial Intelligence, Seattle, Washington, 1987.

35. Keller, R.M. Learning by Re-expressing Concepts for Efficient Recognition. Proceedings of the National Conference on Artificial Intelligence, Washington, DC, 1983.

36. Keller, R.M. *The Role of Explicit Knowledge in Learning Concepts to Improve Performance*. Ph.D. Th., Dept. of Computer Science, Rutgers University, 1987.

37. Keller, R. M. Defining Operationality for Explanation-Based Learning. Proceedings of the Sixth National Conference on Artificial Intelligence, Seattle, Washington, 1987.

38. Kibler, D. and Morris, P. Don't be Stupid. Proceedings of the Seventh International Joint Conference on Artificial Intelligence, Vancouver, B.C., Canada, 1981.

39. Kolodner, J.L., Simpson, R.L. Jr. and Sycara-Cyranski, K.. A Process Model of Cased-Based Reasoning in Problem-Solving. Proceedings of the Ninth International Joint Conference on Artificial Intelligence, Los Angeles, CA, 1985.

40. Kolodner, J.L. Extending Problem Solver Capabilities Through Case-based Inference. Proceedings of the Fourth International Workshop on Machine Learning, Irvine, CA, 1987.

41. Korf, R. E. Operator Decomposability: A New Type of Problem Structure. Proceedings of the National Conference on Artificial Intelligence, Washington, D.C., 1983.

42. Laird, J., Rosenbloom, P. and Newell, A. Towards Chunking as a General Learning Mechanism. Proceedings of the National Conference on Artificial Intelligence, Austin, TX, 1984.

43. Laird, J.E., Rosenbloom, P.S., and Newell, A. "Chunking in SOAR: The Anatomy of a General Learning Mechanism". *Machine Learning 1*, 1 (1986).

44. Mahadevan, S. Verfication-Based Learning: A Generalization Strategy for Inferring Problem-Reduction Methods. Proceedings of the Ninth National Conference on Artificial Intelligence, 1985.

45. Mahadevan, S., Minton, S. and Tadepalli, P. Solving the Generalization-to-N Problem: The Use of Recursive Explanations in EBL. Unpublished Abstract.

46. McCarthy, J. Epistemological Problems of Artificial Intelligence. In *Readings in Knowledge Representation*, Brachman, R.J and Levesque, H.J., Eds., Morgan Kaufmann, Inc., 1985.

47. Minton, S. Constraint-Based Generalization. Proceedings of the National Conference on Artificial Intelligence, Austin, TX, 1984.

48. Minton, S. A Game-Playing Program that Learns by Analyzing Examples. Tech. Rept. CMU-CS-85-130, Computer Science Dept., Carnegie Mellon University, 1985.

49. Minton, S. Selectively Generalizing Plans for Problem Solving. Proceedings of the Ninth International Joint Conference on Artificial Intelligence, Los Angeles, CA, 1985.

50. Minton, S. and Carbonell, J.G. Strategies for Learning Search Control Rules: An Explanation-Based Approach. Proceedings of the Tenth International Joint Conference on Artificial Intelligence, Milan, Italy, 1987.

51. Minton, S., Carbonell, J.G., Etzioni, O, Knoblock, C.A., and Kuokka, D.R. Acquiring Effective Search Control Rules: Explanation-Based Learning in the PRODIGY System. Proceedings of the Fourth International Workshop on Machine Learning, Irvine, CA, 1987.

52. Minton, S., Knoblock, C.A., Kuokka, D.R., Gil, Y. and Carbonell, J.G. *PRODIGY 1.0: The Manual and Tutorial.* Computer Science Dept., Carnegie-Mellon Univ., 1988.

53. Minton, S. *Learning Effective Search Control Knowledge: An Explanation-Based Approach.* Ph.D. Th., Dept. of Computer Science, Carnegie-Mellon Univ., March 1988. (Available as Tech. Rept. CMU-CS-88-133).

54. Mitchell, T. "Generalization as Search". *Artificial Intelligence 18*, 2 (1982).

55. Mitchell, T. Toward Combining Empirical and Analytical Methods for Inferring Heuristics. Tech. Rept. LCSR-TR-27, Computer Science Dept., Rutgers University, 1982.

56. Mitchell, T., Mahadevan, S. and Steinberg, L. LEAP: A Learning Apprentice for VLSI Design. Proceedings of the Ninth International Conference on Artificial Intelligence, Los Angeles, CA, 1985.

57. Mitchell, T., Keller, R., and Kedar-Cabelli, S. "Explanation-Based Generalization: A Unifying View". *Machine Learning 1*, 1 (1986).

58. Mitchell, T., Utgoff, P. and Banerji, R. Learning By Experimentation: Acquiring and Refining Problem-Solving Heuristics. In *Machine Learning: An Artificial Intelligence Approach*, Carbonell, J., Michalski, R. and Mitchell, T., Eds., Tioga Publishing Co., 1983.

59. Mitchell, T. The Need for Biases in Learning Generalizations. Dept. of Computer Science, Rutgers Univ., 1980. Tech report CBM-TR-117.

60. Mitchell, T., Mason, M.T., and Christiansen A.D. Toward a Learning Robot. Submitted to 1988 Machine Learning Conference.

61. Mooney, R.J and Bennet, S. W. A Domain Independent Explanation-Based Generalizer. Proceedings of the National Conference on Artificial Intelligence, Philadelphia, PA, 1986.

62. Mooney, R. and Dejong, G. Learning Schemata for Natural Language Processing. Proceedings of the Ninth International Conference on Artificial Intelligence, Los Angeles, CA, 1985.

63. Mostow, J. Machine Transformation of Advice into a Heuristic Search Procedure. In *Machine Learning: An Artificial Intelligence Approach*, R. S. Michalski, J. G. Carbonell and T. M. Mitchell, Eds., Tioga Press, Palo Alto, CA, 1983.

64. Mostow, J. and Bhatnagar, N. Failsafe -- A Floor Planner that uses EBG to Learn from Its Failures. Proceedings of the Tenth International Joint Conference on Artificial Intelligence, Milan, Italy, 1987.

65. Nilsson, N.J.. *Principles of Artificial Intelligence*. Tioga Publishing Co., 1980.

66. O'Rorke, P. Generalization for Explanation-based Schema Acquisition. Proceedings of the National Conference on Artificial Intelligence, Austin, TX, 1984.

67. O'Rorke, P. LT Revisited: Experimental Results of Applying Explanation-Based Learning to the Logic of Principia Mathematica. Proceedings of the Fourth International Workshop on Machine Learning, Irvine, CA, 1987.

68. Paterson, M.S. and Wegman, M.N. Linear Unification. Tech. Rept. IBM Research Report 5304, IBM, 1976.

69. Porter, B. W. and Kibler, D. F. A Comparison of Analytic and Experimental Goal Regression for Machine Learning. Proceedings of the Ninth International Joint Conference on Artificial Intelligence, Los Angeles, CA, 1985.

70. Porter, B.W. and Kibler, D.F. "Experimental Goal Regression: A Method for Learning Problem-Solving". *Machine Learning 1*, 2 (1986).

71. Prieditis, A.E. Discovery of Algorithms from Weak Methods. Proceedings of the International Meeting on Advances in Learning, Les Arcs, Switzerland, 1986.

72. Prieditis, A.E. and Mostow, J. PROLEARN: Toward a Prolog Interpreter that Learns. Proceedings of the Sixth National Conference on Artificial Intelligence, Seattle, WA., 1987.

73. Rosenbloom, P.S. and Laird, J.E. Mapping Explanation-Based Generalization onto SOAR. Proceedings of the National Conference on Artificial Intelligence, Philadelphia, PA, 1986.

74. Russell, S.J. Analogy and Single-Instance Generalizations. Proceedings of the Fourth International Workshop on Machine Learning, Irvine, CA, 1987.

75. Sacerdoti, E. D.. *A Structure for Plans and Behavior*. Elsevier Publishing Co., 1977.

76. Schank, R.C. Looking at Learning. Proceedings of the Fifth European Conference on Artificial Intelligence, Paris, FRANCE, 1982.

77. Segre, A.M. On the Operationality/Generality Trade-Off in Explanation-Based Learning. Proceedings of the Tenth International Joint Conference on Artificial Intelligence, Milan, Italy, 1987.

78. Segre, A.M. *Explanation-based Learning of Generalized Assembly Plans*. Ph.D. Th., University of Illinios at Urbana-Champaign, 1987.

79. Shavlik, J.W. and DeJong, G.F. An Explanation-Based Approach to Generalizing Number. Proceedings of the Tenth International Joint Conference on Artificial Intelligence, Milan, Italy, 1987.

80. Silver, B. Precondition Analysis. In *Machine Learning, Volume II*, Michalski, R.S., Carbonell, J.G. and Mitchell, T.M., Eds., Morgan Kaufmann, 1986.

81. Silver, B. Learning Equation Solving Methods from Worked Examples. Proceedings of the International Machine Learning Workshop, Montecello, ILL., 1983.

82. Steier, D.M., Laird, J.E., Newell, A., Rosenbloom, P.S., Flynn, R.A., Golding, A., Polk, T.A., Shivers, O.G., Unruh, A. and Yost, G.R. Varieties of Learning in Soar: 1987. Proceedings of the Fourth International Workshop on Machine Learning, Irvine, CA, 1987.

83. Sussman, G. J.. *A Computer Model of Skill Acquisition*. Elsevier Publishing Co., 1975.

84. Tadepalli, P. Towards Learning Chess Combinations. Tech. Rept. ML-TR-5, Dept. of Computer Science, Rutgers University, 1986.

85. Tambe, M. and Newell, A. Why Some Chunks are Expensive. Tech. Rept. CMU-CS-88-103, Computer Science Dept., Carnegie-Mellon Univ., 1988.

86. Utgoff, P. Adjusting Bias in Concept Learning. Proceedings of the Eighth International Joint Conference on Artificial Intelligence, Karlsruhe, West Germany, 1983.

87. Utgoff, P.E. *Shift of Bias for Inductive Concept Learning*. Ph.D. Th., Rutgers University, May 1984.

88. Utgoff, P.E. Shift of Bias for Inductive Concept Learning. In *Machine Learning, Volume II*, Michalski, R. S., Carbonell, J. G. and Mitchell, T. M., Ed., Morgan Kaufmann, 1986.

89. Waterman, D. "Generalization Learning Techniques for Automating the Learning of Heuristics". *Artificial Intelligence 1* (1970).

90. Winston, P. Learning Structural Descriptions from Examples. In *The Psychology of Computer Vision*, Winston, P., Ed., McGraw Hill, 1975.

91. Winston, P. "Learning New Principles from Precedents and Examples". *Artificial Intelligence 19*, 3 (1982).

Index